SHEER
FICTION

SHEER FICTION

PAUL WEST

McPherson & Company

Library of Congress Cataloging-in-Publication Data

West, Paul, 1930–
   Sheer fiction.

   1. Fiction—20th century—History and criticism.
I. Title.

| PN3503.W44 | 1987 | 809.3'04 | 86-33252 |

ISBN 0-914232-82-7

Published by McPherson & Company, Publishers, Post Office Box 638, New Paltz, New York 12561. The first printing has been made possible in part by grants from the literature programs of the New York State Council on the Arts and the National Endowment for the Arts, a federal agency. Designed by Bruce R. McPherson. Typeset in Times Roman.

10 8 6 4 2 1 3 5 7 9   1987   1988   1989   1990

ACKNOWLEDGMENTS

The pieces collected in this book have appeared, usually in rather different form, in the following: *Book World (The Washington Post), The Nation, New Literary History, The New York Times Book Review, Parnassus, Quimera* (Barcelona), *Review, Saturday Review,* and *The Southern Review.*

For Art and Dava

C O N T E N T S

I

Note to the Essays

11

A Rocking Horse on Mars

15

The Shapelessness of Things to Come

21

The Fable's Manger

33

In Defense of Purple Prose

47

The Jazz of Consciousness

57

The Tiger in the Music Room,
the Mollusk in the Zoo

77

II

Note to the Reviews

87

Juan Goytisolo   Mario Vargas Llosa   Carlos Fuentes
Alejo Carpentier   Mario de Andrade   Osman Lins
Julio Cortázar   Gabriel García Márquez   José Donoso
Augusto Roa Bastos   Ariel Dorfman   Hermann Broch
Hermann Hesse   Günter Grass   Heinrich Böll
Uwe Johnson   Arno Schmidt   Christa Wolf
Peter Handke   Jakov Lind   Lautréamont
Blaise Cendrars   Louis Ferdinand Céline   Samuel Beckett
Michel Tournier   André Schwarz-Bart   Italo Calvino
Primo Levi   Witold Gombrowicz   Ludvik Vaculík
George Konrád   Vladimir Nabokov   William H. Gass
Walter Abish   Guy Davenport   Evan S. Connell
Ivy Compton-Burnett   Michael Ayrton   G. V. Desani

I

Note to the Essays

I did not plan it that way, but the essays here reprinted come from a ten-year period, 1976–86, whereas the pieces reprinted in the second part of the book come from a period extending from 1962 to 1986. I wonder if it is harder to write six good essays in ten years than some fifty reviews in twenty-five. Is it harder to dream than to talk? To dream the right dream it is. "A Rocking Horse on Mars" grew out of questions put to me by George Plimpton for an interview tucked into the back of my fifth novel, *Caliban's Filibuster* (1971) and from later questions also put to me for *The Paris Review* by Ronald Christ. The final stimulus came to me from *Town and Gown,* published in State College, Pennsylvania. The title comes from Trollope's *The Warden.* "The Shapelessness of Things To Come" I just wrote for myself originally, to get certain things straight. "The Fable's Manger" appeared under another title in *New Literary History* in response to a request from Ralph Cohen. "In Defense of Purple Prose" grew out of some conversations with Rebecca Pepper Sinkler of *The New York Times Book Review,* although the idea had been simmering in my head for fifteen years. Prompted, I delivered, and it became perhaps my best-known essay. "The Jazz of Consciousness" appeared in *The Southern Review* under another title, but before then had been the Virginia Woolf Lecture at the University of Tulsa; I think Woolf has finally come into her own, being at least read, although too little for her style. "The Tiger in the Music Room, the Mollusk in the Zoo" was commissioned by Indiana University for a symposium held in Bloomington under the title *"La Novela en Castellano, hoy,"* whence Juan Goytisolo flew with it, maybe uplifted by it, to Juan Riera, editor of *Quimera,* in Barcelona, to have it translated for that handsomest of literary periodicals. I think that symposium was the finest literary event I have been at, and I had there for the first time a sense that I belonged to a community of fiction writers, foreigners all but one, but so much the better. Having had so much fun in Bloomington, I decided to attend other symposia, but they were never quite up to the mark. I think we should repeat the first one.

Essays considered but finally decided against include one on Thomas Mann printed in *The Southern Review* and, in German, in *Sinn und Form;* a rather Aristotelian piece called "The Nature of Fiction," with which I no longer agreed; and an earlier version of "The

Fable's Manger," also published in *New Literary History,* back in 1970. Perhaps, one of these days, I will revise them, as well as my essays on Dylan Thomas and D.H. Lawrence, with which I am no longer satisfied. I mention them here only to goad myself publicly into tidying them up soon for second publication; they belong together, but not here.

Because in both parts of this book I explore and celebrate one kind of fictional prose, it is logical to mention the prose that is its complementary opposite: a prose with few discernible attributes, practiced mostly by writers whose names one does not remember except as having drowned in some poignant magma of anonymity. I do not recall the names of minimalists, if indeed there are *any* writers wholly intent upon reducing the wonder and the enigmatic abundance of life to glum sentences whose only virtue is to be grammatically correct and not draw attention to their maker. Minimalism is close to mediocrity and mindlessness, a way for the ungifted to have a literary career, and for readers who really hate literature to pretend to be reading something serious. I have always been impressed by the interchangeability of the prose done by different students in graduate workshops; their stories and chapters are as alike as bottles of liquid paper, and this is where minimalism must have begun—not with Swift, for his plain prose is drenched in *saeva indignatio,* which they do not have, or with Beckett, for his reductive rage has a brilliant analytical mind behind it (as well as such a flamboyant book as *Murphy*). No, it begins in self-righteous ordinariness and ends up posing as the zero degree of style, as imagination with teeth clenched and loins girded, when it is really the ponderous ho-hum of the gull who thinks fiction somehow photographs life instead of mimicking life's creative ways. Minimalism to me is what there cannot be too little of, with its implicit doctrine that everyman is a prose genius if he will only write like all the other plodders.

Indeed, there is a certain kind of prose—you find it everywhere—I find invisible. Someone shoves it under my nose and I read it, but I have no response to it because there is next to nothing to be aware of. The books discussed here, however, are books I couldn't get out of my mind, for year after year; I doubt if I ever will, and one of my main regrets, even if that of the happy concocter engrossed in his own novels, is that the most excellent, the most entrancing of them all, have had to compete with my own imagination even as I read. I once gave a talk on Alain Robbe-Grillet's *La Maison de Rendez-vous,* which I appreciate very much, and at one juncture referred to a certain incident. This incident, my students finally persuaded me, did not exist, was not in the novel; I had unwittingly invented it, out of vicarious zeal. "Sheer fiction," they said, providing me with my title, and I felt as preposterous, *de trop,* as Sterne's cow which, he writes, "broke in tomorrow morning." In what follows I have tried to keep intruders at bay.

P.W.

A Rocking Horse
on Mars

I WAS BORN in Lady Chatterley's village, a silver spoon's throw from Renishaw Hall, where the poet Edith Sitwell lived, an extraordinary and vivid woman who wanted literature to be like herself. Her hands were encrusted with rings. She slept in a coffin (or so the locals said). She was kind to budding writers, as I found out. She championed the work of Dylan Thomas, Alejo Carpentier the Cuban novelist, John Piper the painter, and William Walton the composer. Good, selective taste she had, and this belies the rumor that all you had to do at the Hall was mention the names of any living writers except those of Edith and her two literary brothers, Osbert and Sacheverell, and all hell would break loose. In the next street from mine lived a man called Robert Herring, a Sitwell satellite who edited, right there behind a drab green door, the literary periodical *Life and Letters* and strolled the village with a big German shepherd dog and a look of catastrophic abstractedness.

Among writers to begin with, I mention all this only to underline my sense, way back then, of being a changeling given to things French or, in the Sitwell sense, exotic. I yearned to go, like the Sitwells, to Italy, where I read the Italian poets—Montale, Ungaretti, even Satta the Sardinian, some of whose poems I translated. I was contributing poems to *Botteghe Oscure,* a book-sized periodical published in Rome in several languages, and remarkably generous with its checkbook. Even later, after I had left for Canada, and come to the United States to stay, old friends would say, with outraged incredulity, you've become an *American?* It was not the done thing. It was the best move I ever made. You see, when I was supposed to be a student of scansion, or of the so-called cruxes in *Beowulf,* I was really an existentialist suckled on Sartre, Camus, Heidegger, Marcel. My head had emigrated already, even if not to here. I never quite got over reading a lecture Sartre gave (and later withdrew, I think), called *Existentialism and Humanism.* I used to know it by heart, even the interview appended. *That* was what an intellectual life was like, I told myself. High-octane debate light-years from the likes of Sir Walter Scott. I adored Bunyan, though, as the great narrative innovator he was. I still have my copy of that lecture by Sartre, and I treasure it along with his brilliant essay on Tintoretto, and my much-thumbed edition of Rousseau's *Reveries of a Solitary Walker.*

Our village had a rather good public library, and one day I came upon a shelf of blue-bound books lettered in gold. It was the uniform format run of Faulkner, almost complete up to then. I read them all, marvelling at the many things he did in prose. What dithyrambic hesitation, what fierce long-winded guesses, what majestic disruptive contrasts. Sometimes there were four pages of narrative to one word of dialogue—an act of sublime defiance. I thought he was the most fluent writer I'd ever read. Some days I still think the same. I began to practice writing Faulknerian sentences, none of which have survived. I was sixteen.

Nowadays I try to write for five hours a day, but it most often works out at ten hours some days and none others. Until I switched on at school, aged about fifteen, the only thing I could handle was French. They said I was not bright enough to do Latin, and not gifted enough for Art, so I did Shop. Metals and Woods. All I need is a good bench and I can make a bookshelf. Looking back, through the veils of Latin at last acquired, I am proud and pleased to have come out of the academic process a fully qualified carpenter and metalsmith. English, having no rules, takes forever to learn, and doing it right is mainly a matter of sticking one thing next to another so as to stave off the main ambiguities. English is a language of collocation. English grammar is a collage. And it doesn't so much matter that the etymology is dubious as that the dubiology is etymous. It is that rich, vague, and permissive.

After my time at Oxford and Columbia, I served in the postwar R.A.F., and, although a ground officer training cadets, I was in the air much more than I was in my office. War heroes surrounded me, men with so many ribbons their chests blinded you on a sunny day. To earn their flying pay, they had to fly a minimum number of hours a month, and I went up with them whenever I could. It's amazing how soon you become accustomed to seeing terra firma vertical beside you out the side window. One day, the base adjutant showed me one of those wide group photographs and pointed out himself and one other pilot. All the others, he said, were dead. Maybe fifty of them. It was a photograph to ponder. Quite a few of our officer cadets were noncoms who'd distinguished themselves in the war. Lots of vivacious guys, easily bored, and they all killed themselves in silly flying accidents during the peace, including one who, during the war, had baled out of his Spitfire and had broken his back on the tail. Without being in the least heroic, I learned about the heroic at first hand. I had epics for breakfast. Then I came back to the States to stay.

On the Mall, once, at Penn State, I greeted the venerable professor of philosophy, Henry Finch, who was sitting on a bench and looking ruddier, even more plethoric than usual. Rashly—you should never ask a philosopher any such thing—I asked him what he was doing, and he answered that he'd been staring at the sun, but it had so far failed to recognize him. I admired the farcical implication that he would persist, however, until the sun gave in. Less amusing is what sometimes happens at 1 a.m. when one of my favorite classical music stations closes down. Actually, it comes in on the weather channel. Sometimes they leave the channel open and the transmitter seems to pick up the tick-tick of pulsars, especially one whose fairly slow rhythm goes ONE-two-THREE-four-five, ONE-two-THREE-four-five. There it is, over at the other side of the universe, the neutron core of a supernova, spinning like mad, with a pulse period of much less than a second. Superdense. Only a few kilometers wide, perhaps. Ten billion degrees Kelvin hot and sheathed in an outer lattice of iron atoms only centimeters thick. It comes into the silence of no-music, an indifferent intruder, and I think of what Hermann Broch in *The Death of Virgil* calls "the fateful, flat laughter of the pre-creation."

When I asked a long-suffering astronomer friend if there is anything mathematically inevitable about what scientists call the wobble or the degeneracy of the genetic code, he answered no. It is arbitrary, random, and final that some amino acids—leucine, for instance—can be made in six different ways, whereas trypotophane (the one you take to ensure a good night's sleep) can be made in only one. UGG, which is uracil plus two guanines. Six to one looks like favoritism in the code, but it's just a fluke. Like death, this stuff remains incurable, and we have to stay abreast of it. We are in its midst, in the thick of it. Not that long ago, when I was ill, I found I was being treated with drugs of various kinds: a rat poison; something made from foxgloves; and something else made from a Peruvian bark. Does Creation contain a cure for everything? Is that the grand plan behind the assorted phenomena of Nature? Perhaps not: the fourth drug was a synthetic thing, invented for one illness but found, unpredictably, good for others too, including migraine and stage fright. I wonder how many panaceas we daily trample into dust, and how much medicine there is in muck.

Accustoming ourselves to Broch's externalized, abstract laughter, which of course isn't laughter at all, is maybe the most durable burden of being alive. It never goes away, even when you do; it's behind everything. You can study quiddities all your life—the essential nature of this and that—and never learn anything more than how things work and interrelate. Yet that may be enough: a career of sensuous opportunism. What folly it would be to ignore things just because we couldn't figure out their reason for being, or for being that way.

I got a good dose of this the other day, if any dose of it is ever good enough. For once distracted by work until dawn, I found myself staring at a blaze behind pink-looking leaves. The fog was drifting ever so slowly westward. Hardly a bird was up, only the deep-throated ones with awkward, baritone voices as if trapped between pheasant and crow, and at a speed I found hard to believe, the spectrum shuffled its plates in front of me, purple to azure to rosy to an imminent blast of vermilion that made me hold my breath. The planet had faced the sun again, and, oh, the slate tracery of trees, the bleached green of the unwatered grass, the almost awkward mutation of the sky as it hovered and glowed, with violet shifting into pink, and that into salmon-tangerine! That was an awakening, or a non-sleeping, to marvel at, as if colors from elsewhere had poured over us, indifferent but awesome, and I wondered why I usually slept through all of it. It was the best light show on Earth. The thrill of being on a planet that spins comes to you only at the rise and the declension, at the tilt and the narrowing of light.

It is as if music that you have all along wanted somebody to compose had given up hope of coming into being and had deviated into color instead.

That big yellow star out there only spins about four times faster than the *Concorde* flies. There is something intimate and neighborly about our speeds, our local speeds. By human standards, the sun is slow, fairly slow, which makes it more buddy-like. Deciding whether to sleep instead of having coffee, I had a bit of breakfast instead, and I could not dismiss the image of just about the finest aerobatic pilot in the land, who also being a power in the aviation industry, wears a suit whenever he flies a *Shrike Commander* upside down without power from either engine. His necktie, he said, proves useful, and when he flies he tucks it behind his neck so that, when he finally lands, still without power and gliding in right to his point of departure in a hush of full-flapped wings, he can hide his vomit by putting the tie back in place again, down central where it belongs, and where a corporate executive should keep it, whether he's a sky maven or not. Ridiculous? No more than what happened when I went outside. A green seed alighted on my hand, and it was a small flying insect, nose higher than its rear, like a tail-dragger plane. When it flew away it covered at least a couple of yards in one swoop, up and off, no wind-up. It just hurled itself away, in rueful exultation.

A University of Florida gerontologist, Leonard Hayflick, has discovered that cells from human embryos, fed and incubated in a dish, will keep on multiplying only to a certain point. After fifty doublings or splittings, they die. And the older the donor, the sooner the cells do it. Cells have memories too, he found, and cells frozen in liquid nitrogen remember where they left off; thawed out, they resume doubling until the fifty limit. Working with fruit flies and mice, other researchers have established a link between near-starvation and longevity, especially if you begin in the early years. Swamping your specimen with Vitamin E helps too. Proportionately speaking, mice so treated have lived twenty human years longer. Maybe, at some mysterious point, when all the fruits (and flies) of these researches have coalesced, we should be able to correct body chemistry itself, prevent our DNA from making mistakes, and live on into a golden paradise founded on not merely the long but the infinite division of our cells. What troubles me about this is that certain literary dinosaurs will go on forever, stunting the future as they dote on a bigger and bigger past, spurning the brilliant as they laud the mediocre. But Leonard Hayflick's brave new world may be just round the corner. Ultraviolet light, of which we are likely to go on getting more rather than less, bombards our DNA all the time, sometimes beyond our enzymes' capacity to fix us up again. What appeals to me in all this is the arbitrariness, the flukiness, and, at root, the apparent malleability of what makes us what we are. What could be more creative than tampering with our cells, courtesy of several billion mice and fruit flies, to make us last until the sun burns us to a crisp?

Nothing is separate from anything else. Yet so much of what's written, in prose anyway, reflects so little of what makes us what we are. The provincialists, the minimalists, the suburbanists, the hacks of all persuasions, haven't the faintest idea of—or reverence for—the idea of humanity as a local fungus that has so far prospered, thanks to a whole train of biological flukes. Superstitious primitives have a sharper sense of life, of our place among other forms of being, other creatures. Sir Thomas Browne had it. Lewis Thomas has it. And D'Arcy Wentworth Thompson, whose classic *On Growth and Form* I just saw praised as "beyond comparison the finest work of literature in all the annals of science recorded in the English tongue." Something like that. Maybe one tires of trying to see the human antic in the round, as a chemism— Dreiser's word—relished holistically. But literature is about feeling too, and the range of feelings expressed in it today strikes me as short-sighted, dumbly selective, miserably minor.

Painful as it is, this world can regale us with costly splendors, even if, seen clinically, it's only Hayflick's lethal casino in which you gamble your cells for merely temporary wins. Neutrinos and monopoles flash through us and the prize pumpkins we raise while waiting. I rest my case on the imaginably available wholeness of the human experience. Be a busy witness, then say an intransitive thank you, and cease.

[1985]

The Shapelessness
of Things to Come

SOMETIMES THE GAME WE PLAY with literature interests us more than literature itself, especially if we are French and so assume from the outset that an idea about a book is always more interesting than the book. Not that long ago, there was a good deal of earnest, but glib talk about the dead or dying novel. Had the novel served its purpose? Had it revealed its all? Had it met its match, ousted by the culture of the cathode ray tube? Or was it in a slump, like lyric poetry before Wyatt and Surrey, like science before Einstein and Heisenberg? Was it a Lazarus or a Nero? Or, rather than picking up its bed and walking again, or fiddling while civilization flamed out, was it terminally discredited, like the idea of phlogiston?

It must have been fun to toy with these random hypotheses, to draft obituary while wondering, ever so faintly, why no one talks about the dead or dying *poem*. Fun, but foolish, inasmuch as no one had ever defined what the novel was or is. How could anything that various be dead? Like the corpse of Emiliano Zapata, it was everywhere and nowhere. Like the corpse of Eva Perón in an unpublished novel of Julio Cortázar, it was burgeoning mightily underneath all of Latin America, ready to surface in that ancient horror mode: the living dead. Its possible origin went back to Longus and Thomas Nashe, Lucian and Homer. It was, turn and turn about, romance, epic, fable, history, anthropology, sociology, a chart of manners, a graph of social climb, likely to beget as many hybrids as Polonius, in *Hamlet,* attempting permutations of the literary modes—"tragical-comical-historical-pastoral"—and then seeming to give up with his "scene individable, or poem unlimited." All or nothing. It was bound to provoke self-mocking definitions such as a prose fiction of a certain length having something wrong with it, which is as useful as a shoehorn made of sheep's liver. If you couldn't pin the pesky thing down, you could at least back away from it wittily, as if you had encountered a genie from outer space.

Since then we have had the rise and fall of the French New Novel, an ostensibly plotless, characterless, unpsychological mode based on doting, almost philatelical observation; the rise and slight fall of Latin American Magic predicated on only a sampler of that continent's modern fiction; and the so-called non-fiction novel, from Truman Capote's *In Cold Blood* to Beryl Bainbridge's *Young Adolf,* in which we meet young Adolf Hitler in darkest Liverpool. We have also seen the re-working of traditional texts, such as Frederick Busch's *The Mutual Friend,* told by Dolby, the factotum of Charles Dickens's last years, and Walter Abish's assemblages of sentences appropriated from works in print, named by Joseph Pestino "The Bartlett Appropriation School of Text Construction." We may be forgiven if, confronted with this on top of what the novel became in the eighteenth and nineteenth centuries, we conclude that the novel is as mutable and various as cancer, though mostly less deadly. There it is, in the heads of thousands upon thousands of readers and living practitioners, blundering or fidgeting forward, making you wonder if indeed the thing has a life of its own, a destiny to which it has been called by a force or forces unknown. (By *it* I intend a longish prose fiction substantial enough to be bound separately as a book.) Perhaps it even has a special drive within it, urging it on toward fulfillment: a goal we can only guess at as, maybe, a short text denuded of everything inessential, resembling crystals in a crucible, or a lethal prodigy of verbal fusion, bound for safety's sake in the lead of which pencils used to be made. Indeed, trying to envision the next phase or the terminus of the novel is a fictional enterprise in its own right, and the right use of the novel form over the next fifteen years may well be the fingering of the novel's future, a whole series of prophetic demonstrations predicated on almost three centuries of its entrails, a triumph of frenzied self-appraisal done by master craftsmen while the hacks, still twiddling around with plain novels about plain folks, in a style whose poverty masquerades as pregnant discipline, look only to write within the expectations of the reading public, who purchase novels with much the same arm-motion as they lift up pounds of margarine. For every discovery, every innovation, there will be a thousand banal returns to the fold.

I myself do not believe in such givens as the inevitable novel, decreed from on high by some Calvinistic trinity made up of E. M. Forster, Georg Lukács, and Alain Robbe-Grillet (bewitching as I find the last's little book of essays, *For A New Novel*). A genre, a form, lives only in the heads and at the mercy of those who use it. *For A New Novel* spawned no school, except perhaps a school of critics, and clashed with Robbe-Grillet's own novel-writing practices. And *Finnegans Wake,* sublimely imitable as it is, generated no school of imitators, but has remained a combination of Taj Mahal and dead-end. Not even the majestic exhortations of William Gass *(Fiction and the Figures of Life)* or the moralistic tootings of John Gardner have had that much effect, except as late vindications of what stylists or homilists have done already. The whole thing is more or less random, which is perhaps why critics try to tidy things up. My own version comes close to that of Sir James Jeans, the doyen of science popularizers, who many years ago in *The Mysterious Universe* talked of a room full of radium atoms, all of them identical, to just one of whom each year, for reasons unknown, came atomic death, regular as clockwork (as we used to say). Out of the cascade of potentials drops this norm, more predictable than what will come next into my own head, or into those at present blank pages of the history of the novel form.

Maybe, as some have suggested, texts write themselves, using authors as their vehicle, and breed among themselves, using the authorial imagination as a bedsheet, in a kind of backstairs promiscuity. Even as I write this, Mrs. Gaskell's *Cranford,* which I dipped into last week, is working on me subliminally, most of all some phrase about being possessed by Amazons. Let it. Reciprocal seepage is out of the question; we can't influence *Cranford* any more, but we can modify its image, and we do each time we read the book, each time we surrender to it and let it influence us in a thousand ways we could never pick apart.

Influence apart, though, the fascinating thing is how the novel evolves, much as astronomy or metallurgy has evolved. I ought to know better, perhaps but I dote on the idea that the form in which I have now made a dozen forays can be made to yield this or that result, with almost no holds barred, as if it were plasticine, or a geranium being made to make the vertical U-turn along a wire frame. Like the sonnet, the essay, the soliloquy, it is there for use: malleable, adaptable, open to experiment as the codified embodiments of music were open to Schoenberg, Cage, the young Copland. You do not hear this kind of thing from the mercantile novelists, or indeed the mercantile composers, but you do hear it, beginning maybe as a whine or a whimper of hubristic aspiration, and then you hear something more assured as the novelist-composer (call him Marcel Woolf-Mann) contemplates the shapeability and the rigors of the medium, open before him or her like the continents of Cathay or Ind. My own view is more that of a vacancy perceived, as when a lodger has moved out, say, and the room is mine or do over as I think fit. You can be haunted, and persuaded, by the ghosts of forerunners, but you have to remind yourself of how much you inherit that they did not have, in science, history, and the sheer simple accumulation of their own artifacts, to be ignored or built upon.

Expressed in greater detail, this means that we have the gorgeous images of Jupiter and Saturn from Voyager fly-bys, history-repeating-itself with new variations in Vietnam, the bizarre verbal and structural experiments of Raymond Roussel, the oneiric wasteland of self-abuse dreamed up by Jean Genet, the dense, mordant cameos in the fiction of Djuna Barnes. And, on a perhaps less illustrious plane, we know that Rimbaud could have added jet-lag to his recipe for garbling the mind, and that the man in Xenophon who rightly (if redundantly) cried out *"thalassa!"* when he saw the sea, might have been moved even more had he known that the chemical make-up of ocean saltwater matches that of our cardiac cells, where sodium and potassium are king. It is possible, of course, to ignore what goes on around us, but such an attitude ill-fits those who wish to create the future; they end up, like so many novelists in our time, re-creating the past, yet wanting huzzahs for doing so. My own view would be that, cognizantly immersed, we doggy-paddle forward to the next rough epiphany: nearer than ever to seeing the edge of the expanding universe, yet awfully far away, which means there is still room to imagine something without being corrected by the Jet Propulsion Laboratory in Pasadena, whose name itself comes from an earlier era.

Of course, trying to create the future of the novel is only a fancy way of saying trying to write our next few novels; but the fateful aura abides of experimenting until something already there in the matrix of life pops into view for the first time. In other words, penicillin, the quark, the monopole, were there all the time, or much of it. On the other hand, can we say that the interior monologue or stream of consciousness was built into the matrix, before Edouard Dujardin "discovered" it in 1887? I hasten to add that I mean the literary technique so called, since consciousness itself may be thought of not so much as streaming as of bouncing about. Where it was before we hit on it, it is hard to say, especially if you think that there would have been no *Ulysses,* and no Joycean prose, without James Joyce. One is entitled to wonder if esthetic experiment is more free than its scientific counterpart. Is there a true distinction between what was latent but unfound and what was unfound because no one had invented it? In Latin, *invent* means to *come upon* something that is in your way, but the something was there all the time, whereas the artist puts it there. Archimedes exclaiming his *Eureka!* (I have found it!) has not invented the twelve-tone scale or the clerihew. Or anything else.

In this sense, the imaginer experiments with himself, herself, and not with the givens of the physical life, imagining the imagination into being, whereas the scientist finds what he is going to find by imagining it. Notice too how the artist uses the word artifact to mean work of art, whereas to the scientist the word means an undesirable accidental flaw. Perhaps this is why scientists have no patience with complex metaphor, since their "coming-upon" things is different from that of artists. The scientist could no more devise a future for the novel than a novelist could produce the unified-field theory. We tend to think that, because artist and scientist overlap, they work in the same way, whereas the one deals with conjuring, the other with laws. When, some years back, I published my eighth novel, *Gala,* in which I used a framework based on the genetic alphabet, all but one of the scientists I knew were bemused. I was glad to have used a scientific finding as an esthetic discipline, and my schematic delighted the formalist in me because, for example, it was rooted in nature whereas the various rhyme schemes of the sonnet are not. It had a cosmic inevitability which added emotional weight to my narrative. Mostly, however, such abstruse patterns go unnoticed, or, if noticed, go unhailed; the scientist doesn't want the facts turned into a novel, and the novelist by

and large can't see the cosmic force of a recondite natural pattern. Hidden form, as Holst once said, is mere refrigeration; even so, as a hidden constraint, it constrains the artist, and that may be all he or she is looking for, like Raymond Roussel shaping a novel outward from one central pun which you may never detect. Not all hair shirts are visible.

Look now at the novel, with not so many years to go before the end of the century. In all its varieties, it hangs in still. Bruised, broken, stunted, it has evolved without being much seen to have done so, mainly because critics are poorly read. In fact, the good old-fashioned novel has died repeatedly through the century, from body blows struck by Joyce, Beckett, Queneau, Cortázar, and others. It has lived on in the hands of literary taxidermists, of course, but effectively it was blown up before 1950, to take a handy date. When Joyce exclaimed that the rampaging Nazis should leave Czechoslovakia alone and read *Finnegans Wake,* he meant, I think, that the *Blitzkrieg* that mattered, the one against orthodox novels, was already over; the novel was a blown-up city and wide open to reconstruction. Of course. Since then, we have been building with the wreckage as best we can, putting up newer houses of words from older ones, trying to find, as Beckett puts it, a form that will accommodate the mess. Not long ago, I came up with the phrase "The Lost Tribe," meaning, perhaps in some forlorn echo of a Conan Doyle adventure novel, those who were busy picking up the pieces, after Joyce, after the French New Novel, after the novel of black humor (which tried to find wrong only with society what is wrong with life), what was left? Beckett had given a lead in *Watt,* written while he was picking potatoes in hiding from the Gestapo in France. It was clear, at least to some of us, that the most-touted American novelists of the Sixties and Seventies had changed the novel little and had left America snoozing amid tame, palatable books while the rest of the world forged ahead.

The tribe were recognizable names—Abish, Arthur Cohen, Connell, Davenport, Richard Dillard, Federman, Gass, Hawkes, L'Heureux, Nemerov, Nova, Purdy, Sontag, West, Edmund White— heirs of Djuna Barnes, all; but they did not add up to a movement, each one doing a different thing for special reasons. What they had in common, at least in retrospect, was a desire to rehabilitate the novel form, perhaps to Europeanize it, to reveal it to American readers as not the final version of anything but a volatile entity capable of subtle construction and inventive deployment. Not a formulaic thing at all, and certainly light years away from mere sociology, but another form of *art*—a word that few American novelists care to use about what they do, as if art were a somehow retrograde thing, somewhere between lunacy and impetigo. I once told a scientist that the artist really wanted to make something perfect, and he scoffed, but not ironically: "Is that *all?*" Well, the First Cause did not accomplish it in the fateful seven days, so I don't see why humbler artists should not drive themselves mad with the vision of it. Another scientist, in fact Hans Bethe who figured out on a train how the sun works, said a more enlightening thing. I'd told him how, to help with the writing of *Gala*, which was a "walk" through the northern Milky Way, I'd built a model of the Galaxy in my basement. He paused, then said: "A *working* model?" At that moment he was entertaining a fiction, indulging the novelist, to be sure, but also letting himself hope a little. After all, so long as there's a reader, or a novelist willing to re-read, a novel itself is a working model of some world or other, and what is a particle accelerator if not that? Models minify gigantic dreams.

Anyone hunting a basis for a late-century fictional *Poetics* would do well to examine the essays of the novelists named above, especially those of Abish, Davenport, and Sontag, whose lengthy "Against Interpretation" tackles the raw material of many a deliberately manufactured literary enigma such as you find strewn through, say, Beckett's trilogy: *Molloy, Malone Dies, The Unnameable.* That would be the local basis, anyway. Farther afield, but available in translation, there are the so-called Morelliana, the aphorisms of a failed novelist Morelli which Julio Cortázar appended to *Hopscotch,* the novel with appended optional chapters too. Morelli cannot write the super-novel he has in mind, but he can theorize about it almost voluptuously, all the way from the crazy logic he calls "lo(co)gic" and his view of the novel as a *liber fulguralis* (a lightning bolt) to something he calls anthropophany—the showing forth of humanity in a novel that, appropriately enough, seems to abandon the dualisms and the deceits denounced by Alain Robbe-Grillet.

It contains not only the idea that the word *text* is perfectly adequate, since it means something woven, but also the bolder idea that the Western novelist is not necessarily obligated to any orthodoxy, any more than the Latin American novelist, poised between voodoo and tyranny, is obliged to the novel of Europe or North America. This means that the novel, far from being hidebound, as the bookstore chains would like it to be, qualifies for a term that André Gide came up with: *disponible,* meaning at its own disposal, to which you might add Paul Valéry's own bit of jargon: *implex,* for awareness made maximal. For those who need one, and they seem to be many, it would not be hard to assemble a little catechism for the novel-to-come, or for the future novel already dispersedly here. As always the jargon is arch, awkward, and inadequate, but it embodies close-ups that carry a whole climate with them, of divergent critical thinking about the novel by its current practitioners. *Erotics of reading. Involute. Lo(co)gic. Liber fulguralis. Anthropophany. Text. Disponibility. Implex.* Buzz words all, they have the charm of horseflies laid out on a window sill. Even so, if I had room and time, I would add Nathalie Sarraute's "suspicion," for the disabused frame of mind in which the modern reader regards the all-knowingness of the old novel, and "sub-conversation," her version of Valéry Larbaud's "the very first spurting of thought." Then I would bring in the notion, for which there is no readymade word, of composition: the novelist *composes* the novel as if it were a symphony, shifting large masses around like tectonic plates, in the fashion of Mario Vargas Llosa, and grooming stylistic detail as if each word were a tiny drama, each phrase a potential *Lohengrin.* I suppose that is part of the (to play the game a moment) disponible implex, or the available max. As I say, these terms come from practitioners whose immediate aim was never the creation of suave technical argot, and you have to take them as impatient gestures, impromptu asides, semi-rational sparks from within the psychoanalysis of fire.

Other things to think about, whether you are writing or trying to fathom those who do, include the increasing problem: Where is the narrative voice coming from? Whose is it? Is it the author's? If not, is the narrator anonymous and impersonal, without a life to go with the voice? Is the narrator that entity with no more than a voice in things? Or, as in, say, Gabriel García Márquez's *The Autumn of the Patriarch* or Samuel Beckett's *Texts for Nothing,* does the narration amount more to something like polyphonic recitative, staged by a presence "off" who chooses the words only, but has no more overt presence

than that of an impresario? Often, too, as in Woolf, a first-person text
has given way to a third-person one, but eccentric verbal shadings
have remained, to give the oddest double flavor of unabashed
intimacy and savvy remoteness. For example, you first write: "I think,
daily, of my silky little bladder," then switch it to "She thought, daily,
of her silky little bladder," which puts your third-person narrator in a
curious bladder-fancying stance. There are some words that a
character will use about him- or herself which a narrator cannot use
without seeming tendentious. *Erlebte Rede* ("thought felt"), the
Germans still call it, which sounds awfully vague, but it amounts to
delineative precision of a subjective kind. You might make a whole
novel of it, in this day and age anyway, and thus dispense with
watching. Just listen. Make the voice the personage, in both its
utterances and its thoughts. That, in a sense, is what Arno Schmidt
created in his *Evening Edged In Gold,* a massive split-screen tome with
big pages like sails on which you see-hear all the different tellers of the
same "Fairytale," having your ear rove with your eye as the page
breaks up vertically or horizontally. The complementary opposite of
this, I suppose, is what Woolf does here and there in *To the
Lighthouse,* scooping up a long conversational exchange, in all its
twists and turns, its runs and stutters, and then with an almost
censorious ear compressing it into an oral contingency sample of only
one third of a page's length, setting it off to show that she has done her
duty *(they were talking, thus)* without being slavish about it.

You might go further, taking Nabokov's dictum that character is
merely a compositional resource and extending it to dialogue as well.
No people, as such, and no talk; but lots of minds at work in the
silence. It may be said that characters are the meat the burglar feeds
the housedog while he gets to work on the house's mind, while
dialogue in fiction is for the eye only—it need not replicate actual talk,
as, I think, among others, Woolf and Ivy Compton-Burnett proved. If
you're willing to give up some things you're used to, you'll get other
things you've rarely had. That goes for the old-fashioned omniscient
narrator, too, a term too Platonic to be useful inasmuch as there is no
all, no total, so no narrator can know it. The thing's a hedge, a front,
fostering, as Sarraute has said, a false attitude to the knowability of
both people and characters. There is no narrator in everyday life, so
why rehearse for it in novels that take you inside strangers' heads? I

can see her point, but all the same would point out that readers don't always read to fit themselves for everyday living: they read to escape, to break free, to take the impossible on trust and imagine what it would really be like to take the lid off someone's head and know everything that is going on in there. By the same token, they might go to the anti-novels of Robbe-Grillet, Sarraute, and Claude Simon, for the sheer novelty—after so much quasi-omniscience—of seeing people from the outside only, none of whom they get to know half as well as they know their daily friends. In old Spanish novels a little lame devil used to lift off the roofs of people's houses, in an extremer version of the mood that sent Virginia Woolf around London at night, peering in at windows. People are curious about people, but not always; and, sometimes, we are curious about their very incuriosity about us. The novel has made this its stock in trade for years, but novelists are entitled to work the market both ways, revealing *and* denying, opening *and* closing up shop. And to ring the changes is not to aim at a sharper realism, but to make the various movements in the prose symphony contrast with one another. The gesture is esthetic, not informative.

Other issues that need to be thought about include the selection of narrative tense: the past looks firmer and more final, the present more immediate and less congealed, the future altogether the most open of all, whereas in fact it is the most fate-ridden (they *will* go here, they *will* go there, and their napkin rings *will* gather a faint patina of mold). In fact, the whole thing is illusion: the past seems to confer on what's in it a certain security, but the words holding that illusion in place are just as arbitrary as those supporting an illusion in the present. At best, the past is a tone-retainer, like the present. All time in fiction is made of words, and the true, ecumenical time of fiction is the order in which the words reach the reader's eye, whether or not that is the order in which the novelist thought of them.

Speaking of illusion, there is such a novel as *Gulliver's Travels* which, especially at the outset, wants you to believe it isn't fiction, and then there is Howard Nemerov's *Journal of the Fictive Life,* which flaunts its very fictionality. Surely both ways are artful. It isn't an either/or problem. In a sense, a novel corresponds exactly to nothing but itself, and yet it cannot be made out of nothing, so the novel is derivatively nonmimetic and, like any other text, a verbal area to focus on so as to have it in common with others, more or less. But it is almost inappropriate to refer to a certain novel by Flaubert as *Madame Bovary;* the only accurate, unskimping mode of allusion to it is to read aloud the whole novel each time you want to refer to it. To do so would surely end all generalization and install in its place something good: a devout, patient, endless act of reading. That, maybe, is the only way of making permanent contact with the mind, Flaubert's, which his novel evinces: the fable's manger, so to speak. And that, of course, you could not do with prose that has no personality; prose—of a kind only too common—whose most blatant virtue is that, in aiming low, it makes no grammatical errors, and is intended to be read only once and then junked, certainly not to be pored over. The exceptions, Bunyan and Swift, but surely not Orwell or Dreiser, have an interesting mind behind them, and the plain prose gets you to it sooner; with most, all you get to sooner is the vacancy.

Well, it might be said at this point, as things fall away, if you have no personages, no talk, and possibly no plot, all you have left are the vicissitudes of a voiceless nobody, whereas these things rather than ruling the roost have come to rest as components of style—a color, noise, vigor, as faces, gabble, shove, accommodated into a sentence or two, serving the novel instead of the other way around. Everything, even a news item, is a "story" these days, so the novelist may be forgiven for not always telling one, as perhaps for no longer feeling obligated to a certain national or local tradition when all the planet heaves into view. Call it the holistic novel; it comes into being on the heels of the Museum without Walls of André Malraux, with all the world's art becoming available through postcards and reproductions. And now the planet as a whole has swum across our screens with entire oceans affixed to its hide, held down by the spin: an epiphany, I suggest, not just for SF writers, to whom it was far from new, but for all novelists, all poets, even if all it does to Our Town is install it in a wider and more baffling context.

Daily the presses churn out routine novels, noticed with routine politeness by reviewers who will never know better. Such is the last behavioral waltz of the nineteenth century. Fiction and the novel have moved on, never mind in how awkward and befuddled a disarray, reductive or bloated. Literary art may never offer a beginning, a middle, and an end, in that order again, except out of nostalgia, and maybe not even those three in any causal relationship whatever. The plural novel will have middles, ends, beginnings, held together in the auteur's mind, and the novel will have finally begun to catch up, technically speaking, with Pollock and Rothko, Debussy and Messiaen. Sheer consumerism has always kept the novel back, making it into a commodity rather than an art form whose calling is to say what it is like to be alive in a certain time, to remind us of our intimate selves by being there, on the paper, in the ink, as brand-new, warm, and tweakable as we are. And just as apt to be forgotten, overlooked, or left for dead.

[1986]

The Fable's Manger

L IFE OBLIGES US to talk to people we would otherwise ignore. But that paradoxical "otherwise" is a poor alternative, and I invoke it only to put in context my suspicion that, if others over the years had not advanced the idea that "thinking" is incompatible with art, I might not have hit on such twaddle myself, especially in regard to fiction.

First, there is the familiar slur, less argument than holy conviction, that discursive thinking isn't artistic. In other words, it isn't enough in its own right; it has to be deployed, invested in personable and ingratiating images, somehow transposed into action, made seductively three-dimensional. Not to make it so (according to this line) is to waste our mimetic, manipulative skills. Hence the fable and the parable, allegory, symbolism, and what we like to call characters.

Against such a view, one need only say that thinking can be beautiful in its own right and doesn't necessarily *precede* some embodiment into texture: the embodiment in words is not different from the embodiment in larger units of recognition. Indeed, some of the finest works provide matrices in which thinking can go on, from *Under the Volcano* to *Remembrance of Things Past,* from *Doctor Faustus* to Cortázar's *Hopscotch.* Such novels are organs and conduits of thought, and they have little impact if stripped of the assorted meditations they present. Only a primitive reader attempts such works for their "art" alone, for not only is the art inseparable from the onrush of the characters' ruminations: the ruminations lead the art by the nose.

And these novels' ideas, even rawly spelled out, would fascinate, whereas the modulations of strategy and style, if separable at all, would seem a kit of merely appetizing apparatus. The meal is the mind on show.

Second, there is the equally familiar line, stock-in-trade of literary reactionaries everywhere, that thinking isn't dramatic. According to this, thought must lead to salient behavior, which can then leave thought behind. Hence a craving for percussive anodyne, for sharks and shark-bitten folk over the agenbite of inwit or the protracted dying of a Malone. On principle, the editor at a publishing house does not envision the intelligent reader whom ideas excite, and indeed for commercial reasons cannot. This tribal weakness has seriously affected the kind of fiction published in the United States and has now driven serious fiction more or less underground. It remains to be seen, however, if the public has a stronger stomach for ideas than many editors suppose.

Third, characters who keep on thinking—not so much reasoning things out as mentally freewheeling and savoring mental activity from within as one of their vital signs—remind the reader of the author's presence. Indeed, the author is probably doing what the characters are doing. So goes the prejudice, its root the pipe dream that a fiction ought not to know about itself, or that an author should be present at his/her own absence, absent from his/her own presence. And the more thought there is in a novel, the more chance there is of the book's being an author's mirror.

A fourth objection (I confess to as little patience with it as with the other three, but offer all four here as dead albatrosses by way of preliminary) says that thought should stay within its own bailiwick: the essay, the tract, the monograph, and so forth. This lets out, along with other things, Ivan Karamazov's dossier against God's world, chapter 44 of *The Confidence-Man* ("In which the last three words of the last chapter are made the text of the discourse"), and Gide's "Journal of *The Counterfeiters*." Such compartments exist only in the minds of purist fanatics, of course, and the history of fiction from Rabelais to Nabokov exemplifies the plural-mindedness of fiction writers. Yet the objection persists, like astrology, in the teeth of all the evidence, and might be related on the level of anthropology to suppositions about mystery, virgin birth, and literature as the unexplained counterpart to the unexplained universe.

A fifth objection is that the thinking reader doesn't like to have his/her thinking done by someone else, but likes to generalize from vivid instances. What a fragile breed this reader must be, forever noetically preempted by the novel of ideas and deterred from thought by thought.

Lest it be thought that these are straw dogmas I have fudged up for easy demolition, I should add that their proponents can be found in Manhattan, or on campuses: Polonius-Canutes of the artifact, ill-read non-adventurers with Vatican pretensions. I meet them all the time, but I still don't know how to address dinosaurs, especially the American kind who, with a flick of the powerful tail made of the same substance as Hemingway's arm, dismiss thinking fiction—along with the noetic provenance of all fiction—as just so much quasi-European folderol. Myself, I see nothing effete, still less jejune, in a mind's being aware of itself as the birthplace of the artifact, indeed the fable's manger. And, while I can see that someone interested in mind might not care about fiction, I can't see how someone interested in fiction can fail to care about the mind behind it. Only someone, I presume, of monumental mindlessness to begin with, whom no work of art or of mind can shift. So much for the fool's gold of others; I turn now to fool's gold of my own.

II

As a novelist who has also written nonfiction, and indeed has been accused from time to time of writing fictional nonfiction, I become exercised about the business of thinking and fiction, not because I care about categories, but because it's virtually impossible not to wonder what exactly is the process in which I engage and what are its implications. I wonder especially what I would feel about one of my own fictions if I could read it without knowing I'd written it. Beyond that impossible dispossession of my self, I wonder why, so often, I find myself more interested in the mind behind than in the artifact itself, as if the latter were merely a sample, a clue, an almost arbitrary index or gunsight to the idiosyncratic whole of the author's mind.

I see the writing of fiction, my writing of it, as a compulsive activity, so therefore don't know all about it, and no doubt never will. Whole areas, where explanations might otherwise be, are full of

images. I try to speak of fiction writers, or fictioneers, rather than
anthropomorphically of Fiction, though I recognize that one's fictions
develop a life of their own, an almost irresistible entelechy which, in
fact, saves one a lot of work. It's not a matter of the fictions' writing
themselves, but rather of the mind's tossing out a host of images,
combinations, and incomplete syntheses, from among which—if one is
quick enough—one is free to pick and choose. They come and they go.
Unwanted, they come. Wanted, they go. Unwanted, they sometimes
go. And, wanted, they sometimes come, can even on occasion be
tickled or prodded into being. What follows is an attempt at self-
decipherment, whose conclusions may shed light on the doings of
others.

Although the fiction writer has enormous freedom to modify and
recombine items he find ready-made, he cannot invent *ex nihilo* and is
therefore always in some degree, no matter how slight, dependent on—
and truthful to—life as most people know it: to what one might call, if
in the mood for a monstrous coinage, the ecumenical hypostasis, that
which stands under and supports the whole world, including the world
of fiction. I mean the housing of mankind.

If this is true, all fiction is ultimately derivative in that, whether or
not the writer sets out to mimic or replicate phenomena, he or she
inevitably evinces them in some shape or form. In other words, even in
such a rarefied set of texts as Beckett's thirteen "For Nothing," the big
buzzing blooming confusion comes through. Indeed, one can only
write about Nothing as if it were something, as Beckett says, and even a
tiny something implies willy-nilly a bigger something. It is impossible to
use words without implying something, even if you carefully devise
centrifugal gibberish. So all fiction—whether so-called fantasy or so-
called realism, is, *ipso facto* referential, which means that realism is
only a matter of degree, of ostentatious profession.

Take Proust's taking a napkin in the dust as a pencil of light, or his
likening a wife and her son to a pair of flowering ranunculi. Whether
the comparison is congruous or not, it never quite denatures the
component items. And no matter how far you go in breaking down the
napkin, or the wife-and-son, you still end up with something—
molecule, atom, nucleus—which you can't dismiss. The same holds
true for Wallace Stevens' derisory image of a shrimp playing an
accordion; it sounds fantastic, gross, implausible, but you can't, I think,
reduce that preposterous pair to nothing.

The fiction writer, whether addressing himself to the world as we know it or pointedly seeking to lose it (or distort it), cannot break the umbilical that ties him to it. All fiction evinces some fact or other, and the only problem for the reader is exactly how much concern, care, and reverence he can bring to, say, the molecular or the cytological, compared with, say, the domestic or the societal. Most readers are more at ease pondering Madame Bovary the character than Madame Bovary's ovaries. There aren't many novels about ovaries, molecules, or cells, but there are going to be; it's just a matter of readers' being schooled to see things, people, in the maximum context, which includes atoms and stars, pores and black holes, little velleities and giant dreams.

Of course, a Mary Shelley or an H. G. Wells has much more permutational freedom than a Frankenstein or a Dr. Moreau would have outside the fantasy he inhabits, but only to a point, up to which one can be highly arbitrary in transmogrifying givens. Such arbitrariness terrifies Beckett, on the one hand, who seems to wish the deity had written his prose for him, but it delights Nabokov, the relativistic dandy who is content to pass for a god in his own right and finds the view from up there ravishing. Either way, arbitrary or not, glad or not, everyone ends up transcribing the same basic core of what it is to be alive. Different styles are simply different delusions about liberty, indices to the ingenuity, the lexical and manipulative skills of minds at play. One can be forgiven, perhaps, for saying that, whereas Chateaubriand and Céline are alike in being unable to force the imagination past its limit, they are dissimilar minds within that limit: one reads *René* and *Nord,* for instance, less as self-sufficient fictions than as exercises in energetic mental play. Their problem is less to say what they mean than to mean what they say. It is easy to say (or to babble), whereas it is almost impossible to mean, that is, to make verifiable statements about our place in the universe. In one sense, literature is only a catalogue of stuffs, complaints, and counter-patterns, very much the doodling of minds that have to find something to do, minds in a bind. And what a novel is provisionally about is not necessarily what it is basically about: on the one hand, there are characters accommodated into, and causing, certain concordant imaginary situations; on the other, there is the mind which just has a lot of energy which it burns by inventing minds to play with, just as much to expend as to reproduce.

Character is a special problem in itself. Among French fiction writers. Robbe-Grillet and Sarraute have said a good deal about it, contending (he) that omniscient narrators are frauds who foster in us the appetite for wholly comprehensible people, not one of whom exists, and (she) that there is always more to character than meets the eye, or the ear, and that the educated reader requires not a charade about the accessible aspects of human beings but some indications of the vast amount inside them that never sees the light of day. Both argue against received notions of fictional character, he in favor of outsides, she in favor of just-plumbable depths. He says: let us not fool ourselves. She says: let us be suspicious. Both say: make fiction more like life. I say: there is no need to try. Fiction is only what life and mind have made it. There is no part of fiction that isn't a part of life. The Cretan who says all Cretans are liars is at least evincing his own presence and the privilege of the mind to formulate paradoxes that, whatever else they do, draw attention to the act of thought itself. Why, then, bother about explicable characters' incapacitating you for everyday living, or explicable ones' capacitating you for it? A wider view of the housing of mankind includes all versions, including those we haven't yet devised. In other words, a fiction is an ontological token, and one can legitimately concern oneself with only how interesting is the mind it reveals and how well written it is.

By such criteria as these, character *is* merely a compositional resource, akin to metaphor, event, dialogue, and not a special thing in a class of its own. Thus, when Raymond Queneau in *The Sunday of Life* mutates the family name from Bulocra to Brélugat, from Brédéga to Botigat, and so on, he is reminding us of his own presence, making the device of character generic, and leaving thumbprints, verbal spoor.

So far, then. I have said that one evinces, whatever one professes to do. The so-called realist comes up with so much that is fantastic that he/she overlaps with the fantast who, in fact, can only make fantasy out of pieces that already exist. Life—the unfinished experiment as one biologist calls it—is so extraordinary that, rather than go on opposing one mode to another, we should concentrate on which writing is shallow and which is not. The realism of a Galsworthy never goes deep enough and would be very different if it did. The fantasy of a Tolkien does not go deep enough and would be very different if it did. But the realism of certain stories by Virginia Woolf goes just as deep as the fantasy of Italo Calvino. Perhaps the most astonishing juxtaposition we shall ever see is that of the mind and the world. As Isaac Asimov says in *Eyes on the Universe: A History of the Telescope.* "Mind is, indeed, a magnificent object, far greater than the mere physical matter of the stars, and we have no cause to be abashed by the mere size of all the nonmind about us." Nor should we join the nonmind. It is one thing helplessly to evince our having many billions of brain cells: it is quite another to go beyond the evincing and inspect the cells themselves or use them to eye the bloodstream, the seashell, the Milky Way. If we are indeed the Sun's way of thinking about itself, then we shouldn't let it down. We should do as well by the Sun as we can. And that includes making our novels as thoughtful as we can, even at the expense of story, a word which after all comes from the Greek *histōr,* meaning "wisdom."

III

On the other hand, the novel is just one type of tree in the forest of fiction. It had a rise, and it may have a fall of sorts, whereas fiction—whether you call it feigning or fabricating or confecting or conjuring or optical illusion—is a primary drive, not so much revealing our social selves to us as transporting us beyond the bounds of common sense, possibility, and humanity itself. In this sense, fiction, the atavistic and even irresponsible thing, is always experimental. Its context is vast. Its license has never been printed, although it is imprinted in our brains. Its origin is dark as the day of the first daydream. It does not obey. It is often so gratuitous as to have no overt meaning. It dunks. It fools. It almost escapes. And, in a fashion that the novel can emulate, but rarely does, it deals with the total housing of mankind, confident that it will never find that *nihil* from which it is impossible to invent. I do not mean Chekhov, Maupassant, or Schnitzler, say, whose short stories display a societal emphasis akin to that of the novel, but rather—for certain stories at least—D. H. Lawrence, Virginia Woolf, E. M. Forster, Kafka, Calvino, Cortázar, whose range is wider, who see the fiction installed in the universe, who instead of comforting us with a blinkered look at limits, unnerve us with an almost scientific look at the basis of life itself. Of course, I'm not saying that this atavism, this cosmic-mindedness, doesn't get into novels; it does. I'm suggesting emphases

rather than dichotomies, finding myself prompted not by categories
but by vibrations in the text, by under-tows and, of course, by
deliberate nudging, as when Lawrence has Paul Morel look at the stars
after his mother's death and thus embark on a meditation about
nothingness. If, as I suspect it is, society is one way of distracting
ourselves from the ontological, then the novel, which is essentially
societal in emphasis, offers the authorial mind less scope than does
fiction which, like Mercury equipping Perseus, takes us out and
abroad.

Not that excellent work has not been done that probes nothing
wider than the price of butter, the purchase of a ring, or some minor
non-promotion. It has. Simply, the Bigger-All won't go away; it both
magnifies and minifies. I don't always see the cells beneath, or the
constellations beyond, but I do more often than I don't. Haunted by the
mystery of being here, and not as a doorknob, a hummingbird, a
peppermint starfish, an amu, a thistle, or quartz, I fancy we all might be
construed as what Carl Sagan calls tributes to the subtlety of matter. As
for the mind up close: if you're trapped in a maze with a rat for seventy
years, you might as well get to know the rat. This takes me to another
point.

IV

Fiction is not only truthful to the housing of mankind, it is also
truthful to its host mind, and indeed one of its main roles may be to
evince that mind—its scope, its stock, its motion, its ingenuity, its
texture—at the expense of such categories as fiction/nonfiction,
narrative/essay, biography/autobiography, and so on. The final
artifact cannot but bear the stamp of its creator's sensibility: selection,
phasing, build, and style all manifest it, and one would certainly be able
to tell a piece of Hemingway's prose from a piece of Henry James's (to
take an obvious example), or *The Sound and the Fury* from *Barbary
Shore*. I can see that a fiction writer would want to appear in the artifact
only through some kind of idiosyncratic impersonality, but I can't see
how, at bottom, that evinces the producing mind less than a work
offered candidly in the first person. Indeed, the purist's notion that,
once the fiction is finished, there is no one behind it, or that there was

no one anterior to it, or that it wrote itself like a toboggan going over the crest of a hill and down, seems to me just another fiction: of alibi or nonentity. I may be succumbing to the latest depravity in the fall of Man: I may be flirting with an absolute of innocence lost: but I cannot help seeing the mind behind the images: which may just be another way of saying that I don't read, or compose, fiction as myth. As Frank Kermode says in *The Sense of an Ending,* fictions can degenerate into myths whenever they are not consciously held to be fictive. Myth operates within the diagrams of ritual. Fiction is for finding things out. Myth is the agent of stability, fiction the agent of change. Myth calls for absolute, fiction for conditional, assent. Or, as Vaihinger puts it in *Als Ob,* the fictional "as if" has to be distinguished from what we call hypothesis because, at the end of the finding-out process, the "as-if" goes by the board. After the fiction is over, you have a reunion with reality. After the myth, you find reality rearranged. And both are different from hypothesis, after the testing of which you know something new.

This is to see fiction as a mode of tethered autobiography, or *autofiction,* in which the thing of paramount importance is the presiding mind itself, which endures after the fiction collapses. Confronted with such a mode, the reader has a wider variety of criteria to choose from, and doesn't need to be categorically imperious. The question of "plausibility," for example, doesn't arise when the fiction is visibly an instrument of the author's mind. Indeed, certain writers have made sure that it doesn't, from Cortázar, who appends Expendable Chapters to *Hopscotch,* to Marc Saporta, whose first shuffle-novel *Number One* hands the question over to the reader. For every counterfeiting there is a Journal of the Counterfeiter; it's just a matter of its being made public or not. To go even farther, the willing suspension of disbelief implies something dumb and slavelike, whereas about the notion, advanced by Cortázar and others, of the reader as an accomplice, there is something alert and dignified. I mean mind conspiring with mind in order to think the more richly, instead of one mind's agreeing to let the other gag it with a big prose lollipop: not an objective correlative, but an abject relative.

Yet surely it is just as naive to insist on the author's presence as to disguise it: beyond both resorts, there is a subtler mode of response which allows a symbiotic traffic of enormous variety to flow back and forth between author and book, between book and reader, and indirectly between the two minds present. Perhaps "mind reading" will become a respectable term and complicity a privilege once the initial phase, now going on, is over, and we no longer read a text while seeking, or preferring, to forget the mind in charge of it.

V

But not only does fiction evince both the housing of mankind and the host mind: it goes farther, is *made* to go a stage farther, by fiction writers who allow the process to oust the product, so that the ostensible product becomes a pretext for creating a total pre-text. The story becomes the story's own story. Such fiction as this is an object lesson in the arbitrary, at best mental adventure, at worst self-nullifying prankishness. It all depends on how interesting the mind at work is. When you read Genet's *The Miracle of the Rose,* for instance, a book written for no reader save Genet himself, you witness the author in the act of confirming to himself the omnipotence of the masturbator, shuffling his fiction this way and that, having his cake and eating it too, in the hot oven of the jail, and actually free to choose whatever kind of cake he'll have. Or when you read Robbe-Grillet's *Project for a Revolution in New York,* you are reading an intensely self-conscious book about a book that couldn't *get* written, or that (according to some) wouldn't have been worth writing anyway. Claude Simon's novel, *Conducting Bodies,* is an exercise in the same kind, generated as it is by a Rauschenberg collage (or so Simon claims) and dedicated to the idea that literature isn't expressed *through* language, but *is* language.

If I evoke the specter of decadence, the tinkle of a Silver Age, I can only say that we are better employed in looking at what intelligence can do, and how it does it, than in assembling semi-myths that celebrate some macho epic of seven or seventy years before the mast, or of killing animals merely because a rifle or a sword equips one with the gift of death. I am not even sure that decadence, so-called, which is a lapse from a condition judged preferable, isn't itself a coercive myth evolved by scoutmasters and Jaycees, by crypto-victims of Maule's curse and hebephrenic flagwavers who denounce Darwin in the boondocks.

Speaking on "The Creative Process" at the Nobel Conference on Creativity in 1970, Jacob Bronowski said, "it is not the thing done or made which is beautiful, but the doing. If we appreciate the thing, it is because we relive the heady freedom of making it." Yes, and no. Why should this be a dilemma? Surely it is more rewarding to savor both process and product. So far we have favored product over process, no doubt out of some consumerish innocence; but process is catching up, and we are less superstitious about the artifact, its provenance and its autonomy. The next stage could be one in which authors publish their minds, in whatever medley of forms and modes they fancy. Michel Leiris, that exponent of self-lacerating confessions, has already passed through this stage, while Maurice Blanchot remains at it, obligated to mind and hardly able to make it into anything else (a predicament which *Thomas the Obscure*, for example, presents with a candor both winning and tiresome). Evan Connell, in *Points for a Compass Rose*, has written a lovely specimen characteristic of this stage. Kerouac would have reached it had he had more of a mind. Others who have come near it have been St.-Exupéry *(Citadelle)*, Lautréamont *(Les Chants de Maldoror)*, the Austrian, Jakov Lind *(Counting My Steps)*, and Frederick Ted Castle in his copiously discursive novel, *Anticipation*. Films by Bergman and Buñuel enact it. Marcel Duchamp and Magritte depict it. The spiral-galactic score of George Crumb's *Makrokosmos 12* embodies it. It might be called the reinvasion of art by mind, or a new high fidelity to mental process. Caviar to the general, it might become a staple diet for some.

Such fiction can be less deliberate than other kinds. It can be unthematic, several-minded, sumptuous, open, and a-tomic: indivis-' ible, not fraught with old dichotomies such as teller and tale, figure and ground. It might even not "make sense," but only reveal a mind that can't, and in that way generalize itself back through self-consciousness into impersonality, becoming, say, emblematic, a focus for dubiety, a homemade chunk of the impossible; something that baffles, yet engrosses, like the particle's being a wave, and vice versa; like the radio galaxy, 3C 236, eighteen million light years across, the largest known object in the universe.

Maybe we suffer because we don't understand such things: how they began, or what their teleology is, if any. Maybe we are also rather glad they do exist, glad to be part of such an amazing whole. Maybe this attitude of *gaudens patior*—jubilant Angst—is what the autofiction at its highest reach will school us in, as when it stages the impossible, as when Beckett stages in *Watt* Mr. Knott the deity, in *Texts for Nothing* the next-to-nothing that sometimes feels like nothing itself, and, in his trilogy, death, the dying of one already dead, and a man giving birth to himself. Such a fiction of the impossible, obligated only to mind and to writing excellence, might help itself to natural structures such as the spectrum, the genetic code, the spiral of a shell, the division of cells, the expansion of the universe, and so forth. It might even duplicate these things in its design. Concoct enigmas of its own, such as Duchamp's Green Box (which contains an alternate physics), Ives's never-written "Universe Symphony," and Mallarmé's never-finished Book.

VII

With so much emphasis on the processes of the creative mind, even on the seismic anxiety of doing what one is doing, it should come as no surprise that some writers turn to nature, or number, for some kind of determinism, and in so doing approach what has been going on in music for some time. I am not thinking of such a celebratory pattern as Holst's *The Planets* (although Holst made some sharp remarks about certain kinds of form as being mere refrigeration) or even George Crumb's curtsy to the zodiac in *Makrokosmos.* I am thinking more of such works as Crumb's *Black Angels,* which is constructed according to numerology, and of music made by connecting an analog computer to oscillators and a tape recorder; the computer is then made to add or multiply sine-wave voltages which actuate the oscillators. Less human-sounding, and closer to John Cage, is Charles Dodge's *Earth's Magnetic Field,* which consists of one year's measurements adapted into music by relating graph levels to pitch. The result is music that represents the sun's playing on the magnetic field of the earth, music that has the eerie gravity of certain compositions for pipe organ. In fiction, so far, we have had such comparable efforts as the numerological novel from Queneau, the geometrical novel from Philippe Sollers, the alphabetical novel from Walter Abish. Thanks to the pertinacity of Rayner Heppenstall, we are looking again at the novels of Raymond Roussel, who liked to develop a fiction out of one central pun.

But, even if we muster every bit of evidence, arguing Beckett's *Molloy* as an example of cell division, and calling up at least one junked novel in the shape of a shell, and leaning over into poetry to snap up Louis Zukofsky's Bach-like recourse to conic sections, it's clear that writing hasn't gone as far in this dimension as music (or, for that, painting). Talk to thoughtful fiction writers, though, and you will find them shifting away from a merely reportorial role towards poetry and its disciplines, towards an attitude in which one *composes* a fiction as one composes music.

At this point, it might be helpful if I outline some of my own doings in this area. In the novel called *Caliban's Filibuster* I moved the narrative across the spectrum and headed the first chapter ".9," the second ".99," and so on, augmenting the novel chapter by chapter toward an unattainable unity. Since then, I've experimented with the systemics—the composed wholes—to be found in accounts of such things as spiral galaxies, irregular galaxies, black holes, and the architecture of molecules.

In *Gala,* I have the first-person narrator arrange his paragraphs according to the 64 three-groups of the *messenger* RNA chain, a ruse to which he confesses at the halfway mark. The interesting thing is that no one who has read the book so far has been aware of anything unusual in the structure, except some indefinable straining, until the halfway point, at which what the straining was after became clear. So the reader tackles the second part only too well attuned to the visible presence of what had been invisible in the first. The only difference between the two parts is that, in the first, the narrator uses the sixty-four groups at random, whereas, in the second, he uses them in the order tabulated in most textbooks of genetics. I found this system useful for other reasons, not least that the narrator is writing about someone with genetic abnormalities, with whom he happens to be building a large scale model of the Milky Way.

If such a deliberately sought-out constraint sounds like an unnecessary hindrance, all I can say is that I don't find it so. It is no more paralyzing, or merely cerebral, than a stanza form, and it leads the imagination to unlooked-for chances. It also enforces a certain variety of sentence structure at the beginning of each paragraph: after all, when you can begin paragraphs only with words whose initial letter is A, C, G, or U, you need to be ingenious, especially with the U-words. Sticking to the rules, while trying to create natural-sounding sentences

on the narrator's behalf, is an attractive challenge, and the compensa-
tions are several. For example, three of the triplets in the genetic code
(UAA, UAG, UGA) are labeled "nonsense" or "stop," according to
which version of the table you use. One can exploit those three in
various ways, of course, and my narrator does, performing all
through—another compensation—as a specimen of someone doing
this particular harebrained-sounding thing. The sense of using a
universal given, in a not altogether spurious way, intensifies and
disciplines the writing experience as well as, I trust, the reading one. A
reader on the right wavelength may feel enlivened, enlarged, through
experiencing such systemic devices in the narrative. I would hope
he/she might respond as D'Arcy Wentworth Thompson does in his
book *On Growth and Form* when, in a footnote to the chapter on "The
Forms of Cells," he juxtaposes the catenary curves to be found in a
vertical section of a topsoil bellied out by wind with those to be found in
Dürer's drawings of the wrinkles under an old man's eyes.

[1976]

In Defense
of Purple Prose

A WORD IS ITS USES, as William H. Gass shows in his rollicking conspectus, *On Being Blue,* although he might have ogled purple as well. Purple does seep into his blue-book, however, here tinting some "spent body like a bruise," there leaving a "lavender thumb"-print of "broken veins." In fact, as well as being a book of blue's uses—in talk, literature, and the dictionary—*On Being Blue* is a prime, up-to-date example of purple prose, not so much a patch as it is a pyramid, a pandemonium, a seething nuclear pile of words. Infatuated with blue, its optical resonance and its metaphorical range, Gass picks up samples from far and near, revelling in the word's every appearance, teasing and inciting and delving until the little tome glides off on its own like emancipated lava, announcing I Am Words, I Am Language, I Am Style. The book is elaborate without being ornate, ambulatory without ever being pedestrian, and, for those whose tastes run to purple, a definitive joy. It reminds us that the almost lost art of phrase-making attracts the scorn of only those who have never made up a stylish phrase in their lives, as if style, somehow, had become taboo, a menace to people, gods, and cars.

Of course, purple is not only uses of the word. It is the world written *up,* intensified and made pleasurably palpable, not only to suggest the impetuous abundance of Creation, but also to add to it by showing—showing off—the expansive power of the mind itself, its unique knack for making itself at home among trees, dawns, viruses, and then turning them into something else: a word, a daub, a sonata.

The impulse here is to make everything larger than life, almost to over-respond, maybe because, habituated to life "written down," in both senses, we become inured and have to be woken up with something almost intolerably vivid. When the deep purple blooms, you are looking at a dimension, not a posy.

Consider Paul Cézanne's famous doubt, eloquently pondered in an essay by Maurice Merleau-Ponty. Was what Cézanne saw, and painted, in his head or "out there"? Or was it, as an attuned spectator may well ask, in the paint itself, in the fine-ground lumps of geology he painted with? Plump for all three, in a mood of feckless empathy. You can see what nagged at him, as I think it must have nagged at such masters of purple as Browne, Macaulay, Joyce, Faulkner, Dylan Thomas, Wallace Stevens, Dahlberg and Nabokov. Is it something lacking in you that makes you want, in your visionary versions of the world, to load every rift with ore? The phrase is Keats's. Notice how he emphasizes the contributive, creative end of things, implying that the ore in the ordinary isn't enough. He wants ore-dinary. Maybe it's not a lack, though, but a lack's complementary opposite: that powerful early-warning-system of the sensibility we call imagination, the system that Coleridge called "esemplastic" because it fuses the many into one. Maybe some creative heads, in order to see the world at all, and to find it worth representing, need to begin by putting it in gaudy colors. More sternly, in a mood of utmost reverence, they recognize that what you bring to the act of perception is often just as important as what you perceive. "We receive," wrote the same Coleridge, "but what we give." He understood these things, maybe a bit too well for his productivity as a poet. I think the Romantic poets as a whole understood that the mind and the world interact, a fact which it has taken twentieth-century physics to remind us of. The gist of the whole thing is that a mind fully deployed, and here mind includes imagination, will find the merest thing an inexhaustible object of wonderment, itself included (in a fit of modesty, of course). A carrot. A wart biopsied. The way in which, in a recent Italian movie, *The Night of the Shooting Stars,* an old man caught in the rain shoves his head and shoulders into the crowd already occupying what space there is beneath a tarpaulin covering the back of a pick-up truck. They are holding the tarp over them with their hands. As he butts forward, his shirt rides up from his pants and an elliptical slice of his back gets wet. The camera does not linger on him, but my mind's eye did, making me wonder about our passion to keep our heads dry. Can it be because the brain is more like a chemical soup than it is like an abacus or a computer? Do we dread dilution?

Or take a horse moving about all night in its stall. Would it be worthless to write a whole novel about it? You never know. What you'd bring to the feat is what matters, and it might not be an advantage to know much about horses. All you need is a mind.

Or take the bald, blank end of a stem from which a hibiscus bloom has dropped, and you can feel the rough ends of the dried-up tiny tubes that fed it: micro-straws bound together by nature's clamp, like fascii, along which streamed the fuel of display. That's how a purple paragraph itself might start to bloom. The urge is more than the yen to make a well-upholstered paragraph that connoisseurs will clip and paste into albums of such things. It's a homage to nature and to what human ingenuity can do with nature's givens.

Certain producers of plain prose, however, have conned the reading public into believing that only in prose plain, humdrum, or flat, can you articulate the mind of inarticulate ordinary Joe. Even to begin to do that, you need to be more articulate than Joe, or you might as well tape-record him and leave it at that. This essentially minimalist vogue depends on the premise that only an almost invisible style can be sincere, honest, moving, sensitive, and so forth, whereas prose that draws attention to itself by being revved up, ample, intense, incandescent or flamboyant, turns its back on something almost holy, and that is the human bond with ordinariness. I doubt if much unmitigated ordinariness can exist. As Harold Nicolson once observed, only one man in a thousand is boring, and he's interesting because he's a man in a thousand. Surely the passion for the plain, the homespun, the banal, is itself a form of betrayal, a refusal to look honestly at a complex universe, a get-poor-quick attitude that wraps up everything in simplistic formulas never to be inspected for veracity or point. Got up as a cry from the heart, it's really an excuse for dull and mindless writing, larded over with the speciously democratic myth that says this is how most folks are. Well, most folks are lazy, especially when confronted with a book, and some writers are lazy too, writing in the same anonymous style as everyone else. How many prose writers can you identify from their style? Not many have that singular emanation from the temperament or those combinations of words all of them characteristic for a certain gait, a certain tone, a certain idiosyncratic consecutiveness of thought and image. Stone the crows by all means, but let the birds of paradise get on with the business of being gorgeous. Even Hemingway, who has much to do with this vogue for the flat, breaks his own habit in certain rapturous, long sentences in which he seems to recognize that, although being alive is just one damn thing after another, there is no ultimate sum, no total; you just go on adding as long as you live, which is perhaps why a medieval monk, illuminating one capital letter for months, say, was living as full a life as Brother Busymitts, who rushes through a dozen in an hour.

It is not an either/or thing anyway. Human beings need pageantry every bit as much as they need austerity. The apocryphal tale of Samuel Beckett's living in a totally bare room because he felt that furniture insulted the purity of space has its counterpart in certain over-furnished *salons* in Balzac. We are the richer for the tale and those *salons*. We hear it all the time for minimal prose, though, the complimentary epithets for which never vary: taut, clean, crisp, tight, terse, lean, as if all we ever wanted were the skeletal. Is it because humans dread obesity, or fullness, or the relentless tug of gravity, that the righteous cult of the vacant has done so well? It takes a certain amount of sass to speak up for prose that's rich, succulent, and full of novelty. Disgust, allied with some anti-pleasure principle, rules the roost and fixes taste. Out of these narrow and uninspected notions, the self-righteous have wrung moralistic criteria for esthetic deeds, which is understandable in a basically puritan country that is profoundly corrupt but hates to admit it. Purple is immoral, undemocratic, and insincere; at best artsy, at worst the exterminating angel of depravity. The truth would seem to be that, so long as originality and lexical precision prevail, the sentient writer has a right to immerse himself or herself in phenomena and come up with as personal a version as can be. A writer who can't do purple is missing a trick. A writer who does purple all the time ought to have more tricks. A writer who is afraid of mind, which English-speaking writers tend to be, unlike their European counterparts, is a lion afraid of meat.

After all, it is the mind that stages such apparently incongruous and impossible things as making a stone talk, speaking up for posthumous narrators and dead characters, and, as in Gabriel García Márquez's *The Autumn of the Patriarch,* tuning in to the collective imagination of a country's people as they begin to confect the myth of its dead dictator. The reader listens in to an unwieldy, ramshackle process that nevertheless is going to get where it is going. The people want an image: potent, nasty, and attractively damnable, and they are willing to lie, to fudge, to get it. It was the mind, surely, that led me to invent my story, "Those Pearls, His Eyes,"[1] in which a Rare Books Librarian finds himself afflicted with the grievous gift of seeing, not through a glass darkly, but as if through a scanning electron microscope: "The staples he tried to fit into his stapler were a vermilion ribcage. Outsqueezed toothpaste was a violet quicksand above which he floated weightlessly. Being nylon, his pajamas revealed themselves as an endlessly interlocking grid of repeated capital omegas." Indeed, there may be hope that, in purple, scientific writing (i.e. writing informed by science) may come into its own as a special genre of art as remote from science fiction, and its dipstick prose, as satellites are from bacon rinds. You solve mind's impasse with mind's instrument, not with your foot. One is always a godfather, never a god, although creative people through the ages have wanted it otherwise.

What can be done by way of being a demiurge is to fashion a material world out of the one already on hand, not allusively but close-up, so much so that the things the words denote seem right on top of the words, on top of the reader too. The ideal is to create a verbal world that has as much presence, as much apparent physical bulk, as the world around it. So you get it both ways: the words evoke the world that isn't made of words, and they as far as possible enact it too. The prose, especially when it's purple, seems almost to be made of the same material as what it's about.

This is an illusion, to be sure, but art *is* illusion, and what's needed is an art that temporarily blots out the real. In theory, a reader should not be able, at least while in the reading trance, to tell art from its matrix. So, reading Thomas Mann's description in *Confessions of Felix Krull Confidence Man* of a delicatessen window should, for a while, be nearly the same as staring into a comparable deli window in Manhattan. It's when the words blot out the real, and displace it, that prose comes into its own, conjuring, fooling, aping, yet never quite

---

[1] *New Directions International Anthology: 44.*

achieving the impression that, in dealing with an elephant, it is actually working in elephant hide. There lingers always, just out of view, on the conjectural fringe of vision, the fact that what's going on is verbal. It will not turn to the sun, like a plant, or wither without actually falling off its stem, or spawn tapeworms in its interior. It will not oxidize except through the material body of its vehicle: ink and paper. Yet it has mass, texture, and shape. It calls into play all the senses and it can interact at the speed of ionization with the reader's mind.

What an extraordinary thing: our minds loll in two states, ably transposing words into things, things into words, and also words-almost-things back into plain and simple words, and things-almost-words back into plain and simple things. As if there were any words or things as plain and simple as that. What goes on in this hybrid mental shuttling to and fro is something passive but active, a compromise in affairs of scale, dimensionality, and abstraction. The phrase "Teddy-bear" is smaller than the toy animal, which in turn is smaller (usually) than the big bear from the wilds; is almost entirely flat (a printed phrase stands up a little from the surface it is printed on); and lacks physical attributes conspicuous in any bear. The words represent, but they also re-present, and when the wordsmith turns to purple various things happen. The presence of the supervising wordsmith becomes more blatant, but the things being presented in words have a more unruly presence. They bristle, they buzz, they come out at you. It is predictable, I suppose, that writers pushing toward extremes will reveal themselves more at the same time as they re-energize what might otherwise have remained a sedate still-life.

Purple isn't quite *onomatopoeia,* whose modern meaning is different from what it meant in Greek. Now it means making a word sound like its referent (*hiss, crack, cuckoo*), but it used to mean *word-coining,* which is wider. Purple, I suggest, when it isn't just showing off, is phrase-coining; an attempt to build longish units of language that more or less replicate sizeable chunks of Being in much the same way as the hiss-crack-cuckoo words mimic a sound. There is language that plunges in, not too proud to steal a noise from Mother Nature, and there is language that prides itself on the distance it keeps itself at. Then there is purple which, from quite a distance away, plunges back into phenomena all over again, only to emerge with a bigger verbal ostentation. It is rather moving, this shift from parroting to abstraction, and then back from abstraction into what might be called symphonic hyperbole. It is almost like revisiting our ancestors, whose imaginations and throats our words evince. After all, words began as acts of abstract approximation, a simultaneous closeness and removedness that nabbed the essence of a thing in a shout, a grunt, a hiss, but partly in order to refer to it in general. Take the word muscle, for instance, which comes from some Roman's impression that, when a muscle flexes, a small mouse—a *musculus*—seems to be running underneath the skin. We have all but lost that mouse, and I am not saying that purple will retrieve it; it might, it might not, depending on how much etymology the purplist has. But purple will perhaps restore the shielded, abstracted modern reader to that more atavistic state of mind in which the observer can imagine a subcutaneous mouse. It is not a matter of coming up with new words, but, fiercer, of coming up with new and more imposing combinations of words, and of re-addressing the metaphorical state of mind to the old goings-on. It is certainly a long way from the clinical, almost philatelic doting on particulars we find in the French New Novel, but is quite near to the habits of Latin American magical realism, which is both a literary and a sociological thing. What might seem a literary flight of fancy exists already in parts of Brazil, where freshwater dolphins appear on birth certificates as the fathers of certain children. Purple relishes that sort of thing, zeroing in on it or concocting it as part of the thing it loves to make: a paste as thick as life itself; a stream of phenomena delighted in for their own sake. And it is not a matter of inventing something out of nothing, for that cannot be done; everything is derivative, so there is no getting away from what might be thought the bases of life, of art. The far-fetched always takes you home again, never mind how forced its colors, how strained its combinations, how almost unthinkable its novelties. The color we have never seen, the smell we have never smelled, the mind we have never known, can only be made from the colors, the smells, the minds, we already know. You can go very far away, but the umbilical never snaps, and home base can always reel you in. Purple, however, makes the most of the ride.

I am suggesting that purple prose, ornate and elaborate as it sometimes is, reminds us of things we do ill to forget: the arbitrary, derivative, and fictional nature of language; its unreliable relationship with phenomena; its kinship with paint and voodoo and gesture and wordless song; its sheer mystery; its enormous distance from mathematics, photography, and the mouths of its pioneers; its affinities with pleasure and luxury, its capacity for hitting the mind's eye—the mind's ear, the mind's very membranes—with what isn't there, with what is impossible and (until the very moment of its investiture in words) unthinkable. Purple, after phrases coined by Horace and Macaulay, it may always have to be called, but I would call it the style of extreme awareness.

I have heard it said that writing which ponders things in detail, takes its time, and habitually masticates things until a wonder leaps forth, is "Victorian," no doubt because the word evokes portly self-satisfaction or finicky dawdling. It makes more sense, though, to think of purple in both its deep and its shallow incarnations as Elizabethan or Jacobean: fine language, all the way from articulate frenzy to garish excess. Purple, it seems to me, is when the microcosm fights back against the always victorious and uncaring macrocosm, whose relative immortality we cannot forgive.

A wide net will bring in such treasures as the Gass book I began with, and the same author's *Omensetter's Luck;* Faulkner's purple masterpiece of spectacular and speculative dithyramb, *Absalom, Absalom!;* Lawrence Durrell's witty, crafted velvet; the poignant narcissisms of Juan Goytisolo, whose prose has a cutting edge whereas his fellow Spaniard, Juan Benet, sometimes turns a sentence into a closet oratorio, as in his novel, *A Meditation.* There is Dylan Thomas's prose, both letters and broadcasts and stories; the erotic skywriting of Guy Davenport; the quiet verbal accumulations of Walter Abish, intent upon quelling histrionics with an avalanche of ironic snowflakes; the rapturous, almost mystical fiction of the Brazilian Osman Lins, whose exquisite formal, visionary novel, *Avalovara,* deserves a wider audience; and, among autobiographies, Michel Leiris's honorable abjectness in *Manhood* and the rapt, exalted tenderness amid terror in Diane Ackerman's *On Extended Wings,* in which a metaphysical poet learns how to fly a plane. Cortázar, Tournier. Purdy, Richard Howard, Evan S. Connell, Jean Genet, Arno Schmidt, William Gaddis, the Hawkes of *The Passion Artist,* the Gombrowicz of *Ferdydurke,* the Thomas Bernhard of *Correction,* the Maurice Blanchot of *Thomas the Obscure:* they all partake of this favor, this pageantry of the mind, this candid *flambée.*

They tell us, these authors, that it is headily terrifying to be alive, that nonetheless living consists not of refusals, eschewals, or denials; no, we are besieged itinerants who do not belong to ourselves. We are more like Lucky in *Waiting For Godot,* when that bewitching mish-mash of data and names, echoes and useful things to remember, pours from him like expedited ectoplasm. We write in appalled fascination, wondering what chemical underwriters prompt the spasm into style. In order to be reverential of life, we do not have to work overtime to pin down the world-outlook of the nasturtium, but we may try to; nor do we have to linger too long on the curious aroma of mulled disappoint-ment that hovers in the hallways of university literature departments, although we may. We simply have to heed the presence of all our words and the chance, during life, of combining them deliberately in unprecedented and luminous ways. Prose is malleable, not ordained. Phrase-making is often a humble, almost involuntary virtuosity. And purple, whatever it may seem to cat-calling wallflowers as it flaunts by with eloquence raised to its highest power, is bound, because of what it does so well, to cause exhilaration. It is also bound, however, because of what it cannot ever do, to deepen the sense of metaphysical fear. And what it cannot ever do is start from scratch.

[1985]

The Jazz of
Consciousness

S TRANGE AS IT MAY SOUND, if Virginia Woolf were alive today
she would almost certainly feel obliged to resume the aesthetic
war which, in *Mr. Bennett and Mrs. Brown,* published fifty years
ago, she declared on the circumstantial and unreal realism of Arnold
Bennett, John Galsworthy and H. G. Wells; against the belief that, if
imagination has to exist, it had best behave itself like any half-decent
foreign camera; against what I might call Babbiturates, which sedate
sensibility to the point of philistine funk. (In retrospect, both Bennett
and Galsworthy merited the C– she gave them, whereas Wells perhaps
deserved better, especially on the strength of his romances and
fantasias, much admired, one gathers, by Vladimir Nabokov.) Her
indictment still holds good, anyway, against all literary greengrocers,
furniture dealers, and quantity surveyors, perhaps even against those
obsessive literary philatelists who conjured into being the novel of
chosisme. And yet, through some perverse ambiguity of favor,
attributable no doubt to forces of reaction that endure in the literary
world like colonial marine coelenterates—calcarious skeletons massed
in a wide variety of shapes, and often forming reefs or islands in New
York or London—she has been grudgingly admitted into literature
without, however, being taken seriously. Dubbed precious by the
ignorant, and obscure by some who ought to know better, her novels
remain on the library shelves, taken out only under the influence of a
movement that intends to change the status of women. As for her ideas,
these impress too many—among those who have even heard of them—

as hyper-exquisite aberrations to be looked away from, as if a genteel butterfly had vomited. The plain fact is that, as a creative artist, she has been tolerated (in other words, she is not George Eliot or Sylvia Plath), while, as a thinker, she has been popped into the same oubliette as Bergson and William James; those fervently creative ideas of hers, having to do with character and spirit, with the mercuriality of consciousness and the open-endedness of the universe, have by and large failed to register in the heads of publishers, editors, critics, and reviewers, not to mention the reading public. The unappetizing answer to Edward Albee's meretriciously lupine question is that far too many *are* afraid of her, as of her predecessor Laurence Sterne. They both consternate, just as Samuel Beckett's fiction does, just as each month's issue of *Scientific American* does, as does one's first (and maybe one's fiftieth) sight of a star-nosed mole.

Let me come at this another way. According to another distinguished practitioner of complex prose, John Hawkes (although less flow-conscious than Woolf), a fiction writer composes in order to create the future. I share that feeling, and I see Virginia Woolf as a literary counterpart of Max Planck, whose 1900 quantum theory recast nature as a flux and virtually junked the noetic truss that held together cause and effect, and of Einstein, who five years later merged space with time, and energy with mass and velocity. In her scientifically uninitiated way, she was thinking herself into the future—the not-yet-known—intuiting just as finely in her nimble words as, say, Eddington, Jeans, and Whitehead in the more sibylline of their formulas of the twenties. It is worth pointing out, however, that inasmuch as Woolf made herself a neighbor of their disciplines, they came pretty close to hers. For example, here is Sir Arthur Eddington, in *Stars and Atoms* (1927): "I am afraid the knockabout comedy of modern atomic physics is not very tender to our aesthetic ideals. The stately drama of stellar evolution turns out to be more like the hair-breadth escapades on the films. The music of the spheres has almost a suggestion of—jazz?" Another of his observations, just as winning, seems almost to imply an episode from a novel: "When an atom is excited, we may picture its electron as a guest in an upper story of an old-fashioned hotel with many alternative and interlacing staircases; he has to make his way down to the lounge—the normal unexcited condition." Sir James Jeans, in *The Mysterious Universe* (1933), is just as vivid, and if anything even pithier in his analogies: "The shadows which reality throws onto the wall of our cave might *a priori* have been of many kinds. They might conceivably have been perfectly meaningless to us, as meaningless as a cinematograph film showing the growth of microscopic tissues would be to a dog who had strayed into a lecture-room by mistake." He follows up with an image more dignified and more decorous: "The motions of electrons and atoms do not resemble those of the parts of a locomotive so much as those of the dancers in a cotillion." If we do not like either dismay through Terpsichore or alienation through the image of a canine intruder, we might settle for the more delicate relegation of our unconquerable mind to this: "our consciousness is like that of a fly caught in a dusting-mop which is being drawn over the surface of the picture...." Alfred North Whitehead is dourer than Eddington and Jeans, but he too has his moments. He can be slyly obvious, as in his Page-Barbour Lecture entitled *Symbolism* (1927): "mankind had gained a richness of experiential content denied to electrons." And, in the same lecture, prudently seditious: "language and algebra seem to exemplify more fundamental types of symbolism than do the Cathedrals of Medieval Europe." Or, in *Science and the Modern World* (1925), iconoclastic in a quite unfussy way: "my theory involves the entire abandonment of the notion that simple location is the primary way in which things are involved in space-time. In a certain sense, everything is everywhere at all times. For every location involves an aspect of itself in every other location. Thus every spatio-temporal standpoint mirrors the world." I find that very Woolfian indeed; but my purpose in assembling a few jewels from these salient thinkers is not so much to suggest, as I well might, that they and Woolf coincide in many things, as it is to liken their assault on an obsolete world view to hers.

Not only was Virginia Woolf on nodding terms with the *Zeitgeist;* she had opened herself up to it, as to the whole of Jeans's mysterious universe; and her effort seems almost comparable to that of Einstein who, in devoting himself after 1920 to the hunt for a unified field theory, risked looking just as deluded as did she—to some folk at any rate—in asking her contemporaries, in her famous essay, "Modern Fiction," (written in 1919) to "record the atoms as they fall upon the mind in the order in which they fall...trace the pattern, however disconnected and incoherent in appearance, which each sight or incident scores upon the consciousness. Let us not take it for granted," she went on, "that life exists more fully in what is commonly thought big than in what is commonly thought small." From stars to atoms indeed! Hers was very much a voyage out, an experimental foray, a piece of high phenomenological honesty. Where Einstein was hoping for a theory, a teleological cornerstone, and persisted in that hope right up to his death, she was being undogmatically receptive, on the *qui vive* for cosmic surprise. Had she, through some happy recombination of her atoms, been able to sample the astronomical theology of Professor John Wheeler, she might have responded without the prejudice of some scientists to his notion of the black hole, past whose so-called absolute event horizon there begins a condition called "singularity," in which all conventional physics goes by the board and the cosmic joker runs wild. I do not think it would even bother her, any more than it does Wheeler, that thus far no one has actually found a black hole (unless it is the invisible half of the binary star called Cygnus X–1); rather than dismiss the theory as noetic snakes-and-ladders, she might extol its quality as a phenomenon, its role as a challenge to imaginative agility. Whenever I think of certain characteristic images of hers, among the orchestrated copiousness of her manner at its most affable—fish and snail, river and sea, lighthouse and Kew Gardens, flamingo sunsets and Big Ben, Jacob's Ladder and a piece of glass, the steel blue feather of an airplane, an Orlando who is thirty-six or 336 years old—I sense a longing for mosaic, an apprehension of the One although she can convey it only through being an eclectic of the Many. For her, the universe keeps on adding to itself, but it does not add up; the sign for "equals" is only for someone who does not relish catalogues or lists.

   In the long run, she sees that nothing can fall out of the universe, although no one's notion of that universe is likely to be complete or accurate. Not only is Mrs. Brown, passenger in the train from Richmond to Waterloo, incapable of being known outright; by the same token, and coincidentally by the same name, there is Brownian Motion, the quantitative explanation of which came in 1905 from Einstein when he suggested that a body surrounded by a gas or liquid would acquire an energy of agitation equal to the average kinetic energy of a molecule of what surrounded it; for example. Mrs. Brown's body in the air of her compartment or Mrs. Woolf's in the water of the River Ouse. These analogies evince, I hope, the motions of her mind, which was more a piece of the main than even she knew. One need not invoke Indeterminacy or Complementarity in order to establish her almost innate modernity; one need only collect samples of her preferred idiom. Anyone who thought so naturally of flow and immersion, of duration and concentricity, of above all "this varying, this unknown and uncircumscribed spirit, whatever aberration or complexity it may display," meant not just the stream of—but an *extreme* of—consciousness, and, rather than being an over-fastidious Bloomsbury brahmin, was relativity's M. Jourdain, who had been talking scientific incertitudes all along without knowing it. Literary cousin of James Joyce[1] she may have been, and certainly in his debt, she in fact had fewer affinities with him than with those open-minded and untimid scientists of her own day, whose disabused attentiveness to the universe—not asking it to be anything that it was not and amazedly finding it stranger than they could even imagine—provides a model for creative artists for all time. In the words of Plotinus: "If a man were to inquire of Nature the reason for her creative activity, and if she were willing to give ear and answer, she would say: 'Ask me not, but understand in silence, even as I am silent and am not wont to speak.'" Indeed, Woolf's books, like those scientists' findings, are reservoirs of mental silence, silent mentality: thought-crowded, impression-crammed, rich with the kinesis of agitated pensiveness, yes; but more intended to evince than to argue, more acts of attentiveness than of initiative, and given over more to the joys of being disabused than to those of (as André Malraux would say) carving a scar on the universe. I offer her as a superb example of negative capability. Sufficient to say that, in trapping her in a moving railway carriage with Eddington, Jeans, Whitehead, Einstein and Company—quanta surveyors all—I am also trying to dramatize my hunch that an itinerant from another galaxy, slumming around a bit in our solar suburb, would be amazed to notice how little fiction has changed between 1905 and now, as if twentieth-century innovations in thought had never taken place. I mean the fiction of the English-speaking world in particular, and I am not ignoring science fiction, so-called; what I have in mind, and even more so after re-reading Woolf, is the extraordinary omission from serious, articulate, mainstream fiction

---

[1]See her diary for her response to *Ulysses:* "The book is diffuse. It is brackish. It is pretentious. It is underbred...." And so on.

of the almost unthinkably mysterious auspices under which we lead our societal lives, of the human spectrum in which our technological society is merely one gray flannel shade. The novel still has its head buried in the kitty-litter of Arnold Enoch Bennett, even though, behind the ostrich's behind, so to speak, there has come into view, as any merely casual reader will know, the identifiable edge of the universe. I cannot think that Woolf would not have responded to such a juxtaposition, built it into her prose and made her prose move toward it. After all, what concerned her most was not how the weather was (that animal-shooter's red badge of lyricism), or a Building Society Secretary's dream of a mortgaged paradise—nurseries, fountains, libraries, dining rooms, drawing rooms, marriages, or even miraculous barges that "bring tropical fruit to Camberwell by eight o'clock in the morning." What mattered most was the amazingness of being alive in the total context; and that is something one never gets over in the same way as one can get over being rich, say, or neurotic, or bad at arithmetic. In this, she comes close to another novelist who, expert with surfaces, images, and words themselves, has often been thought unfeeling or suavely aloof: Nabokov, who as a matter of fact writes this in *Speak, Memory:*

> Whenever I start thinking of my love for a person, I am in the habit of immediately drawing radii from my love—from my heart, from the tender nucleus of a personal matter—to monstrously remote points of the universe. Something impels me to measure the consciousness of my love against such unimaginable and incalculable things as the behavior of nebulae (whose very remoteness seems a form of insanity), the dreadful pitfalls of eternity, the unknowledgeable beyond the unknown, the helplessness, the cold, the sickening interpenetrations of space and time. It is a pernicious habit, but I can do nothing about it. It can be compared to the incontrollable flick of an insomniac's tongue checking a jagged tooth in the night of his mouth and bruising itself in doing so but still persevering.

He goes on:

> I have to have all space and all time participate in my
> emotion, in my mortal love, so that the edge of its mortality
> is taken off, thus helping me to fight the utter degradation,
> ridicule, and horror of having developed an infinity of
> sensation and thought within a finite existence.

Virginia Woolf's version of that superhuman tenderness (in all its senses) can be found in what she says just after coming up with the phrase "the inconclusiveness of the Russian mind," which she compares with the English bent for energetic euphoria. Her main point is this: "It is the sense that there is no answer, that if honestly examined life presents question after question which must be left to sound on and on after the story is over in hopeless interrogation that fills us with a deep, and finally it may be with a resentful, despair." One has only to halt at that comma ("fills us with a deep,") to receive the full vastation before she spells it out. Yet, there is nothing else—the novelist can only, in his quick inventory of the universe he's in, "convey this varying, this unknown and uncircumscribed spirit, whatever aberration it may display, with as little mixture of the alien and external as possible." No frills. No teddy bears. No distractions (such as, say, cricket, the weather, the stock market) from the underlying existential surd. And none of those "sleek, smooth novels, those portentous and ridiculous biographies," as she calls them, "that milk and watery criticism, those poems melodiously celebrating the innocence of roses and sheep which pass so plausibly for literature at the present time." Ultimately she hits on that nightmare of the ecumenical thinker: the apparent redundancy of the mind itself; and all that can be done is to report on minds to minds, tolerating "the spasmodic, the obscure, the fragmentary, the failure," because these are part of everyone's whole. It is a mature, harsh, and seemingly unhappy conclusion to have to come to, and upon which to base an invitation to the novelists of her own day. In the main, she accepted it herself, better than almost anyone; but she did so, not in the miser's verbal pellets of those who like their English plain, but in a complex, rippling prose that reproduces the mind's own motion amid a universe in which it feels beside the non-point. Her words, indeed, are the outpatients of a mind always, as minds are, in isolation.

II

Not only, then, is it not enough to recognize that she was attuned to the spirit of the age, as to a universe whose mathematics has something incalculable about it; we should be glad that at least one of the writers ordinarily dubbed genteel or whimsical had a mind subtle and unprejudiced enough to envision life as a total process inseparable from a radiant universe whose very fabric, as Orlando says, "is magic," whether in the red and hairy bulbs thrust into the humus of Kew Gardens in October or in light now reaching us that left Berenice's Hair before even the Sun and the Earth had formed. It is indeed possible, for us as well as Orlando, to observe how the mind becomes "a fluid that flow[s] round things and enclose[s] them completely," so much so that what she called "the narrow plank of the present" gives way to the Max Planck of timeless quanta. Connoisseur of social surfaces that Virginia Woolf was, she never lost sight of, or sense of, the mysteries that Creation—with its big-league capital C—and creation, with its lower-berth small c, irrefragably are.

That is what is so modern about her, as about Lucretius, say, whereas the ostentatiously modish stuff of so many science fiction writers has a vapidly obsolescent air; its prose is as dull as its cult. A quality of Woolf's, a rare and hardly imitable one, transcends even the significance of her writings on financial and intellectual freedom for women; I mean her uncategorical sense of wonder, her perpetual sense of the imminence of new forms, her being perpetually at her own disposal—what André Gide called disponibility. Let me exemplify. Looking the other day at an extraordinary composite photograph of the Milky Way, made by all-sky cameras, I saw a long, corrugated, transparent sausage crammed with planetary nebulae, dust clouds, and diffraction haloes: the peristalsis of a cosmic gut, both awesome and oddly homely. Yet it was Woolf, and not Beckett or Borges or even Joyce, of modern authors, that came to mind: not because she was overtly scientific, or professedly exobiological, in avocation; indeed, she insists less on nothingness than Beckett does, less on runic pattern than Borges, less on relativistic fission-fusion than Joyce. In fact, what brought her to mind was, to borrow Coleridge's word, her casually esemplastic power which transforms the many into the one, partly by discovering that everything is partly something else anyway: a particle a wave, a door a tree, a bush a bear, a sheep even in part a tall Mayfair house; partly by submitting herself to a process neatly expressed by Husserl when he writes in *Cartesian Meditations* that "Daily practical living is naïve. It is immersion in the already-given world, whether it be experiencing, or thinking, or valuing, or acting." I mean, and I think he means, something anonymous, almost impersonal: one is invaded; one achieves a naïvety of a higher level. Put shortly, this special gift of hers is a unifying innocence which, far from being uneducated or uncivil, both educates and civilizes: puts us on nodding terms with the infinite, on ecumenical terms with the finite, and gives us a *pied à terre* in the hinterland of harmony: the condition in which everything belongs.

An exhaustive devotee, with mind's eye perfectly adjusted for her deliberate and inadvertent tokens, would track her all the way from the Forsterian *The Voyage Out* (1915) to death by water in 1941: from the poignant figure-ground recognitions of Rachel the ewe-lamb, against a busy fresco of those *sui generis* misfits known as British tourists, to the noumenal quadrille done by four young Londoners, overlapping and withdrawing, in the Dostoyevskian *Night and Day* (1919); from the empty-centered ring nebula of minds in *Jacob's Room* (1922) to the organic complementarity of Septimus and Mrs. Dalloway of three years later; from the split and multiplied awareness of Mr. Ramsey in that diachronic Fingal's Cave of the Hebrides, *To the Lighthouse* (1927), the finesse of whose sea-music eludes Mr. Ramsay's inductive *geometrie,* to the three-century-long Moebius strip of reciprocal identities that is festively twisted together in *Orlando* (1928); from the magistrally intuitive brain chorus of *The Waves* (1931) to the generational overlaps of *The Years* (1937) and the visionary pageant that succeeds, by including within itself a visionary pageant that flops, in *Between the Acts* (1941). What a consistent yet minimally repetitious invigilation of consciousness it is, this *oeuvre,* a tide of long fictions coming in again and again upon the one hundred billion brain cells of each and every one of us, a prose corpus in which, and in response to which, metaphors no longer can be said to be mixed, whereas the mix is certainly metaphorical for *rizomata panton:* the all of created things, in which in a cosmic sense, just as amid the characteral permutations in an accomplice sense, we see ourselves (our *selves*) and perhaps en-lightenedly fail to recognize *who* we are while discovering *what.*

III

I would like now to restrict myself, and my view of Woolf's vision, to what many think her most extravagant, most exuberant novel, *Orlando,* published at the midpoint of her career. Born male in the Elizabethan age to wealth and status, as the benign paraphrast of one blurb puts it, Orlando through fingersnap androgyny and a well-tempered time machine turns into a Victorian woman of thirty at the bottom of page 137 of the Harvest paperback edition: a transsexual without benefit of surgery. Reading her twentieth-century adventures, one wonders why Woolf didn't adjust her character into Orland*a*, or even neuter her into a mutant of the twenty-first century, Orland*on*, as well. Beyond that dysgenic hypothesis the mind spins dizzily under Woolf's impetus, reminting Orlando(a)(on) as the first and subsequent person forms of the verb for not just changing sex, but for Ovidian metamorphoses of all kinds: *orlando, orlandeis, orlandei, orlandoume, orlandete, orlandoun.* Very irregular, of course, because the results include, I don't doubt, one Elizabethan Gregor Samsa, a Victorian griffin or manticore, and a twentieth-century nymphet who, an apparent mermaid, ingests relativity while living in sin in a Hampstead motel with H. G. Wells. The possibilities, as Woolf's limited permutation reveals, are endless, and it is an invincibly solemn reader of this novel who does not respond to its ebullient playfulness with gratuitous pantomine of his, her, own, and does not recognize how close Woolf came to the Borges who is the impresario of imaginary beings, the Calvino who in *Cosmicomics* upsets the laws of physics for intergalactic jollifications, the Beckett whose Watt miscellaneously talks backward and walks in the same way, whose Mahood is an aged fetus, whose Belacqua is a Dublin fugitive from the *Purgatorio.* If by now we have not accustomed our minds to doubleness, anachronism, sea-changes, and compound ghosts, we should not be reading twentieth-century literature, or even literature at all. For Woolf, what is imagined exists, has been irrevocably added to the sum of created things, reaffirming and proving the notion of an open-ended universe.

But her scope was wider than imaginative play for the sake of exercise. I think she saw too the element of play in the universe at large: the sheer foison, if I may use an old word, of the supposed, uncatalogable All; the web, the variety, the chancy interrelatedness of things, including the accident that human life possibly is. Unlike some writers who inspect the edifice of convention and find it intact, she inspected the flux of the universe and found it tactless. Especially in *Orlando,* that sample of available options, a novel whose mindscape is worth, just briefly, reducing to just the kind of scheme which it exists to dissipate.

Quite early on, Orlando metaphorically ties his heart to an oak tree and lies there by it, so still that the deer step nearer, the rooks wheel around him, and the swallows dip and circle, and the dragonflies shoot past, "as if," runs Woolf's simile, "all the fertility and amorous activity of a summer's evening were woven web-like about his body." An Orlando may indeed thus link himself to the universe, feeling both enclosed and supported by it. That is the close, hemmed-in version, but there is another as unlike it as web is unlike pod, and this is open, incalculably contingent coincidence: "Thus, the most ordinary movement in the world, such as sitting down at a table and pulling the inkstand towards one, may agitate a thousand odd, disconnected fragments, now bright, now dim, hanging and bobbing and dipping and flaunting, like the underlinen of a family of fourteen on a line in a gale of wind." Visibly, no body, no sensibility, can be out of touch with the field it is in, whether the operant forces, or stimuli, be visible or not. There is an ineluctable ground for each figure, and each figure helps to compose the ground for something else. Thus, one is just as ultimately related to the inkstand manufacturer as to the oak tree, the deer, the birds, the dragonflies, and by implication to, say, silversmiths, miners, convulsions of earth's mantle, and so by causality to whichever cosmogony one happens to favor. All that, for needing to ink a pen's nib; or for, however, shortly, fancying one has a heart of oak. Implicit in both purlieus, of course, there is the rheumatism that afflicts the English bucolic lounger as much as the penman. You ache when you stand up; your arm aches as you reach for the inkstand. These are, however remotely initiated, effects of the universe, complexer than any neurology; earnests of involuntary membership that can be indefinitely extrapolated to link us up with quasars receding at 82 percent of the speed of light, the musculature of the flea, the suicide of Virginia Woolf. Call it repercussive identity, or first-cause resonance, this vision of hers, quite abolishing compartments and categories, takes its impetus from her quite uncasuistically accepting the *uni*-ness of the universe. She has enough of the unknown to go on: what she knows she knows affects her; what she knows she doesn't know affects her too. It all ends up in the mind, in which no mosaic is arbitrary, in which no random juxtaposition of items cannot be cogently interrelated, all the way from Mary Queen of Scots's prayerbook, which she held on the scaffold, in which Orlando finds a bloodstain, a lock of hair, and a crumb of pastry, contributing a flake of tobacco of her own—all the way from that "humane jumble" to her irritated recognition that a sight of her ankles may cause a sailor to fall from a masthead.

Of course, too sensitive an attunement to this connectedness of things can paralyze. Contemplative excess misses trains, pays no taxes, never quite gets down the first word, "He———," of the novel *Orlando.* In Woolf's work and life, of course, the vision became almost competitive, combative even. Confronted by the enigma of Creation, she nodded, and invented enigmas of her own: not symbols, or allegorical emblems, but combinations just as odd and as beguiling as the universe itself, full of conflicts and dissonance. In the opening pages of *Orlando* we find "such a welter of opposites—of the night and the blazing candles, of the shabby poet and the great Queen, of silent fields and the clatter of serving men—that he could see nothing; or only a hand." A mild version, to be sure, it anticipates the much later and much more imposing welter that appears as a pyramid, or hecatomb, or trophy, "a conglomeration at any rate of the most heterogeneous and ill-assorted objects, piled higgledy-piggledy in a vast mound where the statue of Queen Victoria now stands!" Brought into being by a sunbeam, this bizarre miscellany deserves to be itemized in full, in the very words that imbricate it, and then I can wheel something, or several things, up to it, as to something as commanding as a ziggurat of skulls, or the crucifixion, or the pyramid into which the dying in the gas chambers of the extermination camps involuntarily arranged themselves. The passage follows:

> Draped about a vast cross of fretted and floriated gold were widow's weeds and bridal veils; hooked on to other excrescences were crystal palaces, bassinettes, military helmets, memorial wreaths, trousers, whiskers, wedding cakes, cannon, Christmas trees, telescopes, extinct monsters, globes, maps, elephants and mathematical-instru-

ments—the whole supported like a gigantic coat of arms on the right side by a female figure clothed in flowing white; on the left, by a portly gentleman wearing a frock-coat and sponge-bag trousers. The incongruity of the objects, the association of the fully clothed and the partly draped, the garishness of the different colors and their plaid-like juxtapositions afflicted Orlando with the most profound dismay. She had never, in all her life, seen anything at once so indecent, so hideous, and so monumental. It might, and indeed it must be, the effect of the sun on the water-logged air; it would vanish with the first breeze that blew; but for all that, it looked, as she drove past, as if it were destined to endure for ever. Nothing, she felt, sinking back into the corner of her coach, no wind, rain, sun, or thunder, could ever demolish that garish erection. Only those noses would mottle and the trumpets would rust; but there they would remain, pointing east, west, south, and north, eternally. She looked back as her coach swept up Constitution Hill. Yes, there it was, still beaming placidly in a light which—she pulled her watch out of her fob—was, of course, the light of twelve o'clock midday. None other could be so prosaic, so matter of fact, so impervious to any hint of dawn or sunset, so seemingly calculated to last for ever. She was determined not to look again.

Reading that passage, and re-reading it with the contributive complicity of one who salutes a kindred spirit, I am reminded of nothing so much as Antonin Artaud's appeal for "a fabricated Being... entirely invented, corresponding to nothing yet disquieting by nature, capable of reintroducing on the stage a little breath of... metaphysical fear." Woolf's passage does all of that and more, being the concocted version of what De Quincey called an "involute" and spelled out, in *Suspiria de Profundis* as follows: "Far more of our deepest thoughts and feelings pass to us through perplexed combinations of *concrete* objects, pass to us as *involutes* (if I may coin that word) in compound experiences incapable of being disentangled, than ever reach us *directly*, and in their own abstract shapes." How awkwardly constructed that sentence of De Quincey's is: yet I think he hits on something profound: a surdic or irrational element in experience, an element which resists—indeed prohibits—the half-clarifications of symbolism and can best be exemplified through the kind of "fabricated Being," on page as on stage, that Artaud described.

In this dimension, of surdic improvisation, Woolf excels, and her capacity for creating something unforgettable yet not altogether meaningful is expressionism raised to its highest power. Of course, there are other examples in *Orlando:* I think of the park-size space that suddenly opens in the flank of a sunbaked hill near Constantinople and reveals an English summer's day that turns to snow, and of Eusebius Chubb, in whose disordered imagination cucumbers accost him, cauliflowers grow higher than the trees, and hens incessantly lay "eggs of no special tint." Mindful of the thirty-five folio pages he has written only that morning, "all about nothing," and of his wife in the throes of her fifteenth confinement, he notes the sky above the British Isles, a "vast feather bed" reproducing the "undistinguished fecundity of the garden, the bedroom, and the henroost," goes indoors, writes "the passage quoted above," and lays his head in a gas oven. Predictably, too, Woolf's eminent lighthouse flashes into mind, plain as a pikestaff to the heirs of Freud, yet puzzling to several, including my onetime mentor William York Tindall, who in the chapter entitled "The Forest of Symbols" in his *Forces in Modern British Literature 1885–1956* observes, not without leprechaun malice, that: "What this stark erection embodies, as we might expect by now, is far from simple. Suggesting God, death, eternity, any absolute, and the goal of all endeavors, this solitary tower amid the flux provokes, without altogether satisfying, our curiosity as it informs us."

The more it seems to inform us, the more curiosity it arouses, as if epistemology were merely the fur on a forked tongue. One thinks of Jeans, in *The Mysterious Universe,* spelling out that magnetism depends on the peculiar properties of the twenty-six, twenty-seven, and twenty-eight-electron atoms, or that radioactivity is confined almost entirely to atoms having from eighty-three to ninety-two electrons, yet having to add in each case "we do not know why." Can it be that his mathematical universe is the graffito of a hare-brained numerologist? The fact is, Woolf knew in her heart, and knew by heart, that explicability is always at least one step away from definitive contact with Being. Twenty-six, twenty-seven, twenty-eight atoms make a magnet; Orlando's thirty-six and three hundred at 12:00 midnight on

October 11, 1928, make a wild goose chase, much as 365 bedrooms in her ancestral home, or the sixty-eight or seventy-two years allotted on tombstones, or the "seventy-six different times all ticking in the mind at once" and the "say two thousand and fifty-two" optional selves "all having lodgement at one time or another in the human spirit." Neither statistician, nor numerologist, Woolf shares Kandinsky's question of 1910: "To discuss mysteries by means of the mysterious—is not that the meaning?" In short, she counters God's enigmas with enigmas of her own making: reifications that echo deification without the faintest touch of dogma.

IV

Having said this much; having credited Virginia Woolf with an antihermeneutic poieisis in which negative capability partners a deep relish of creative evolution; having installed at least a couple of her conglomerative edifices alongside such other invented enigmas as Kafka's Great Wall of China, Jarry's Ubu Roi, Mallarmé's Faun, Breton's Nadja, Genet's Miracle of the Rose, the piano tuners in Beckett's *Watt,* the rhinoceros of Ionesco, the *Schmurz* of Boris Vian's play *The Empire-Builders* (a big inflatable-looking whipping boy), I must, almost redundantly, but not quite, draw attention to an entire idiom of the arbitrary. *Orlando* teems with it. When there is nothing left to do, for example, send to Norway for elkhounds. Why? Why not? The gypsies think Orlando's four- or five-hundred years of descent "the meanest possible," going back themselves two or three thousand. Mistaken for coal, a black cat gets shovelled on the fire. The phrase "the biscuits ran out" comes to represent "kissing a negress in the dark when one has just read Bishop Berkeley's philosophy for the tenth time." "Life literature Greene toady," runs Orlando's wire to Shel, ending, "Rattigan Glumphoboo," which was her own cipher language for "a very complicated spiritual state—which if the reader puts all his intelligence at our service he may discover for himself." In every human being, we learn from this novel, "a vacillation from one sex to the other takes place," which fact may or may not fortify us for the catadioptric moment when Orlando cries, "You're a woman, Shel!" and Shel cries back, "You're a man, Orlando!" Since the gypsies have no word for beautiful, Woolf cunningly obliges Orlando to exclaim "How good to eat!" when praising the sunset.

If these textural insinuations will not convert the reader to relativism, perhaps Orlando's winged and whiskered ink blot will, "something between a bat and a wombat," a modifiable trouvaille like the piece of glass in the story "Solid Objects" or the mark on the wall which turns out to be a real snail amid the Bayeux tropistry of moorhens, water beetles, and fish "balanced against the stream like flags blown out." It was at just such marks that Leonardo da Vinci counselled his students to peer in the hope of "arousing the mind to various inventions." Such was hopeful phenomenology in the late fifteenth and early sixteenth centuries. Enticed by that creative perceivership, Orlando thinks: "What a phantasmagoria the mind is and meeting-place of dissemblables," only to be kibitzed by her novelist-proprietor, who adds "and so bewildered as usual by the multitude of things which call for explanation and imprint their message without leaving any hint as to their meaning upon the mind, she threw her cheroot out of the window and went to bed."

If the reader cannot "understand" this protean novel—this "biography," this auto-fiction, this concentric textural opera, this chaosmos—he or she can hardly pretend he or she has not been warned. Remember, Woolf instructs us (though late in Orlando's rainbow career), "we are dealing with the most obscure manifestations of the human spirit." The entire thing is miasma, mirage, illusion, but then, as she insists, "illusions are the most valuable and necessary of all things"; the illusionist is among the supreme benefactors, whichever day he chooses to sleep or wake upon (Orlando *wakes* on the seventh); and "he who robs us of our dreams robs us of our life." Anyone who believes that has an abidingly profound respect for the mind in its own right. And Woolf had.

Addressing herself to the often disparaged activity of "sitting in a chair and thinking," or imagining, Woolf leaves us to recite the calendar for ourselves, initiating us into a special semicreative uneasiness through devices or tricks that look backward to Sterne, and forward to the various practitioners of the so-called *nouveau roman*. The copious roll call of the preface is a cheek in which she can lodge her native tongue. A time-travelling vaudeville, the eight illustrations have a surreptitious blatancy, as if to pun through visual obbligato: *ars longa, Vita* Sackville-West *brevis?* (Never!) Our index, all the way from Lord A. to Christopher Wren, happens to be something we truly need when re-reconnoitering the book, yet it seems a pert travesty of both the scholarly apparatus and of the fictional mode; it is a concordance to a plot which is actually a plot against the reader, who must cope inventively with the antic brio of the whole: most of all when, for example, Woolf suggests we can probably "imagine the passage which should follow"; or when, like some bellettristic coastguard, she enforces the six-line limit on Orlando's conclusions about Victorian literature; or when she draws the "said nothing" curtain over a three-hour conversation and, for the talk of Alexander Pope, refers us to sources outside the text. Needless to say, in such a context, it is no breach of any imagined civility to have expendable material included but "properly enclosed in square brackets" (indeed, one thinks of the optional chapters at the back of *Hopscotch* and the Addenda to *Watt:* "precious and illuminating material. . . . Only fatigue and disgust prevented its incorporation."): Arguably, such methods, for those who can abide them, send the mind on a chase and provide a sprightliness that readers must match with one of their own.

There are those, of course, who insist upon the purity of fiction, upon some ostensible underivedness, who do not relish invitations to suspend belief, who find such alienation effects not endearing but boorishly cute. I have never been among them, which is why I prefer the performative affair entitled *Orlando* to any product of those anti-quarians who keep on trying to invent the nineteenth-century novel in the age of quasars. Woolf's sideshows, bagatelles, optical illusions and elasticated mosaics assist, rather than disrupt, the words ("the thinnest integument for our thoughts"). What keeps on coming through the prose of *Orlando* is the paramountcy of thought as it assimilates,, and alters, the spirit of the age—a transaction, as Woolf says, of infinite delicacy, neither combative nor submissive. Orlando him-her-self makes a series of rapid adjustments in the presence of that abiding, fixed entity, the poem entitled "The Oak Tree," while Woolf herself, moving to and from, and through and past Orlando, entertains the relativism of all that can be thought, whether or not the sum of it can be interpreted. As she warns us early in chapter 2, concerning Orlando's week-long sleep, "there is no explaining it. Volumes might be written in interpretation of it; whole religious systems founded upon the signification of it. Our simple duty is to state the facts as far as they are known, and so let the reader make of them what he may." And, embarrassed or confused or (I would hope) intolerably stimulated by the book, we will do just that, with a frown, or with a vengeance, or with complicitous relish.

V

That there is such a thing as the spirit of the age, I do not doubt: or that it forces itself upon us, as Heisenberg says in *Steps Across the Frontiers,* while we are "proceeding as conservatively a possible." Picasso's cubism and Einstein's special theory of relativity appeared in the same year, 1905, not because the two of them were involved in some telepathic symbiosis, but because a certain phase in the European imagination was over: some old shibboleths were done for; some new recognitions were in. Almost a quarter of a century later, *Orlando* epitomized the new indeterminateness of things, not through psychological analysis but through re-creating the almost anonymous sensations that precede, accompany, and often smudge thought: the jazz of consciousness, not so very different from Eddington's jazz of the spheres. Woolf had put it well in a Cambridge lecture of 1928, mentioning reality as "something very erratic, very undependable— now to be found in a dusty road, now in a scrap of newspaper in the street, now in a daffodil in the sun." (Note how she says where each thing is, as if the figure's ground might come as a surprise.) It was to this undependability of things that she addressed herself, willing to seem subjective and diffuse, untidy and incoherent, rather than remain in thrall to the tyranny of an old epistemics or of a defunct societal realism. Sneered at by Nathalie Sarraute, whose imagination came from the Jardin des Plantes—whereas Woolf's seems to have come from Harrod's—Woolf nonetheless invented subconversation long before the era of suspiciousness; in fact, if *Orlando* doesn't make the reader suspicious, it hasn't worked at all. To Rilke's "It submerges us. We organize it. It falls to pieces. We organize it again and fall to pieces ourselves," she adds the transcendent punch line: We are meant to. Whatever one fails to learn from Woolf, one does learn gratitude for the senses five, for innumerable felicities of combination from within the permeable bubble of Woolfian rudiments: the red, thick stream of life; the unreliable kingfisher; the joyful treadmilling of "She wrote. She wrote. She wrote"; and the imperative repetition, " 'Ecstasy, ecstasy,' as she stood waiting to cross." As Woolf says so well at her most daedalian-Promethean, "the nerve which controls the pen winds itself about every fibre of our being, threads the heart, pierces the liver." Through the pen, as Orlando drives fast along the Old Kent Road and out of London, it all falls to pieces, anticipating unconsciousness and death, and then it comes together again as the "green screen"(s) of the countryside show up on both sides of her trajectory. It's all in the mind, as coercive optimists tell us, whereas the All never is; but, in Woolf's case, enough of the All, mentally skirmished with, does conjure up the total, the symbol of whose teleology is one wild goose. Chase it or not.

It is instructive to note that, in *Neutre* (1972), by Hélène Cixous, a French spiritual descendant of Woolf, the title noun signifies *ne* plus *uter,* meaning *not either:* neither this sex nor that, neither sex nor non-sex, neither singular nor plural, neither now nor then, not even either categorizable or not, but a phoenix-like multiplicity of recognitions through which the personal one becomes an impersonal many. Or just a blur.

Among all the permutations of creative guesswork, it is such autofictions as these, brain-orphans of Lewis Carroll, that overtly remind us of an ancient principle which, since relativity became a byword, we have rehonored, the hunt for teleology, across the ages, is the history of the mind's adventures in a looking glass. In a word, reflexive: the invitation to paradise is written by ourselves while *Logos* is just a word in the dictionary, a label denoting the best mathematician out of sight; and ultimately all human experience reduces itself to what Woolf called the "silent land," a zone of ineffable yet not unpleasurable bafflement, where "songs without words" (Woolf's phrase) prove as irresistible as indecipherable while, perhaps, answering a child's plea for reassurance.

At forty-five, in her diary, after an admiring note on her sister Vanessa's children, Woolf reiterated her own preference for art over maternity in face of "this ravaging sense of the shortness and feverishness of life." She saw each individual human life as a complex sentence, short even when at its lengthiest, meaningful only in evolutionary terms, but therefore a sample of a process she found "everlasting and perpetual." In such an agnostic, nonratiocinative dimension, one can only sympathize (or not) with her intuitings, her earth-ecstasy, her knowledge of the mind's exhilaration with itself, just for being available: something, at its least, to play with; something, at its most, with which to mimic the "microscopic eye" of aborigines. It is not often that we find so intricate a sense of wonder depressed to the level of diagnosis, or so granitic a vision made manifest in such radiant and, sometimes, bravura, sentences.

[1977]

The Tiger
in the Music Room,
the Mollusk in the Zoo

(An Address)[1]

ONCE UPON A DAREDEVIL TIME, before the trivialization of taste and the vulgarization of publishing, I cooked up a little essay for the old *Kenyon Review,* whose title I intended to be "Eloquentia Standing Still: The Novel in Modern Spain." When the essay appeared in print, its title had resentfully backfired into being "*Leo*quentia Standing Still"—which, I guess, is the Eloquence of Lions at the Halt. Whichever flukey deity oversaw that printer's lionization was right, I think. Lions, tigers (sad, trapped, or crouched on the belly of Mexico), jaguars, and a whole miscellany of other gorgeous enigmatic beasts, figured little in the fiction I was reared upon, I having been born in foreign parts of foreign parts. They—the lions et cetera, not the foreign parts—figured rather more in the fiction of the North America I fled to, and they abound in the fiction of that other America to the south, which I now believe was the imagined America I needed to find, like some disenfranchised addict looking for his drug, as if South America—primitive, bizarre, and lumped together just like that, were the land of heart's desire. Was it really that outlandish? Or were its scribes bizarre beyond belief? Down there (you could just hear it in the Sixties), kings of infinite space were playing bowls, and the cannonade got through to Pennsylvania, making a din in my creative sleep. That was where the Leoquentia was: the energy, the zest, the esemplastic

---

[1]Delivered at Indiana University, Bloomington, on September 20, 1980, in the presence of Juan Goytisolo, Carlos Fuentes, Mario Vargas Llosa, and William Gass.

77

license taken to the full, whereas where I had come to, the land of Rip
van Winkle and whales and timberwolves, was more like the Valhalla
of chimney sweeps, where people knew what fiction was for without
knowing what it was.

Had I come to the wrong place, then? Was my literary compass
that far off? My head was in Patagonia, or four hundred miles off the
Chilean coast, on the island of Más a Tierra, where the German master-
spy Admiral Canaris had played at being Robinson Crusoe nearly two
hundred years after the real (or the fabricated) Robinson had been
marooned. I am afraid my imagination has never quite grown up,
although it can still relish the incongruity of what Admiral Canaris
found in 1915 on Más a Tierra: a canning factory for crayfish. What
had happened in my head was clear, although it may not be clear to
you: the rebellious young student, who won the continual rebukes of
his tutors, had surfaced again, called out into the open by the
neighborly thunder of Latin America—a region of the mind so
ravishing in prospect, and propinquity, that I ought never to go near it.
That young student was always being told he should be studying the
lions of English Literature—Sir Walter Lion, Lion of Hawthornden,
Percy Bysshe Lion, Lord Alfred Lion, George Lion (a woman), and of
course Geoffrey Lion and Beowulf the Lion too. Don't waste your
time, I was told, with all that "foreign stuff," which included Gide,
Mann, and Pavese, and lots of Faulkner. Beware the foreign pox, and
above all steer clear of Walter Pater, that drawing-room atavist who
kissed cats on the mouth.

Well, compulsive exotophile that I was, I didn't cotton to English
puritans any more than I do to those who maul North America even
now, and I came to see my avocational truancy under the auspices of an
altogether more likeable lion, who turns tail and lies down when Don
Quixote tries to provoke him out of his cage. I too got an affidavit from
the keeper, proving I had tried: an imaginary non-event had become an
imaginary real one; and, when in my first novel I tried to entice a lion of
my own out of its cage, all I heard was a squeak from *The Times
Literary Supplement,* calling me the English Truman Capote. I moved
on, fast, coming to North America, my new-found-land, only to find
over almost twenty years yet another regime of deadheads: not a Gulf
Stream of the imagination, but a stale canal patrolled by the fanatics of
merely expository prose, and—what's worse—a sort of grassroots

humdrummery practiced by *under*-writers who pride themselves on writing within the expectations of the reading public. To put it very plainly: I had imagined North America as more exuberant. You could get by, of course. There were always enclaves of geniality in which imagination wasn't thought a blight; but they were few. They still are. South of the border, however, as I began to realize with a sense of envy verging on paranoia, things were happening of which, spiritually, I felt a part. (I don't mean politics, of course.) I thought of the fabled statue of Pallas Athene which guaranteed the safety of Troy as long as it remained within the city, and, in my inflationary war, I said to myself: The conversations and explosions in the cathedrals, the obscene birds trapped in the green houses and the music rooms, all those marks of identity scratched out of the Spanish calendar by requiem-singers doomed to count centenaries of silence in caustic exile, these in their tormented way ensure the safety of imagination in the old world, the new world, and the next world. They keep an available paradiso warm. And the statue goes into exile but from a distance sponsors a bad-luck reading room of the mind, making terra nostra firmer by contributing to literature without first passing through the sluices of this or that national catchment area. No doubt people more erudite and more painstaking than I have examined the role of exile as catalyst; all I can do, speaking from the tip of the plank I have walked from Oxford to Morningside Heights to what feels like nowhere at all, is to point to these three gentlemen, from Mexico, from Peru, from Spain, and realize that *from* designates not so much origin as the fact that they are *away from* those places. I see them, and some half dozen others who make the heart go Boom, as Magi in reverse: the wise men from the south (at least, below the Barcelona-Boston line, or, if you will, the line from El Paso to Casablanca), getting the hell out of Bethlehem to set up the statue of Pallas Athene in the international manger of the fable. Of course they write about the ethos their brain cells were born into: that's a tic you never lose; but, in so doing, they create, they have already created, the fictional counterpart to André Malraux's museum without walls, in which the voices of silence are loud and burly through sheer exercise, and I mean exercise of fiction's ancient privilege: to *transport* the reader or the listener from this place to one completely other. I'm reminded that, on one of his return trips to London, Sir Richard Burton's landlady asked him if in the course of his travels he'd ever met

Captain Gulliver. Now that, for better or for worse, is the world my mind moves about in—where the distinction (a dys, a stink, and a shone) between fact and falsity goes out the window. Or between what's Mexican, what's Peruvian, what's Spanish. Categories are so pervasive we need not suck up to them. Instead, we agree that fiction adds to the sum of created things; that the novel is only one of the trees in the forest of fiction; that the national or the regional is the plasticine which Promethean fiction-writers use to transcend themselves. Only, perhaps, in the work of some writers from behind the Iron Curtain— 'Abram Tertz,' Bruno Schulz, Uwe Johnson, Christa Wolf, say—does the scrupulous delineation of the at-hand exceed itself in the same way, as if the pressure of enormous energy or bison-sized emotion made every image curl and buckle. It's what happens, I suppose, when impulsive self-mythologizers light out for the territory of the word, where the dictionary is king, full of the voices of the dead, and of the way their throats, their mouths, were built.

Who indeed hasn't wondered at the instant ecumenicality of writers who deal copiously with the postrevolutionary bourgeoisie of Mexico, the seamy weathercock politics of Peru, the ritualistically quarantined decadence of Spain (and Spain's language). It sounds like rather specialized material, of enormous national interest but hardly likely to make the rest of the world hold its breath, and yet it comes through as shiny as fresh-cut sodium, as potent as some newly minted myth, and as important to know as one's own address. Wondering why, I've pondered various answers, among them the following. These nation portraits come to us from citizens of the world. Latin America was the Eden that Spain grabbed and then ignored, thus making it ripe for North American influence—so perhaps what lures us, Europeans and North Americans both, is the vision of yet another Rip van Winkle waking up. Something sequestered and retarded has broken loose, stirring up the dirty water of dreams we never knew we'd had, and paddling about in the cognate guilt of twin imperialisms. Something almost pre-literate comes to life again. The oldest surviving schizophrenia stalks among us, innocently answering its own questions. And it is all done with dionysian intensity, offered in the context of world history, and, in the least of its manifestations, coming home to roost, like a noetic hangover, between Andy Griffith and Abbott and Costello, at six-thirty in the morning, in Summer Semester, on the darkling plain of channels whose numbers no one knows. Mr. Fuentes talks on The Novel at dawn.

If I were in a hurry, I'd settle for that, I'd leave it at that; but there are two other elements, or factors, that matter a great deal. One is these writers' sense that so-called actuality is a mental thing, subjective and malleable and open to speculation, which means that the matter of Mexico, Peru, Spain—much like what used to be called the matter of Greece and Rome—can be narrated inventively, expressionistically; and what's lost as fact returns in a diagnostic dream. *Homo ludens* can tell the story of this history, then, without giving up a shred of literary artifice. I hear Hermann Broch's *The Death of Virgil* behind *The Death of Artemio Cruz,* and some hear Orson Welles. Flaubert stands behind Mario Vargas Llosa and Joyce behind Juan Goytisolo. Not only that: imagination *playing*—in other words weaving its text, because a text is *what's woven*—fuses Aztec sacrifice with Nazi extermination camp in Carlos Fuentes's *A Change of Skin.* Vargas Llosa, for all his voluminous documentary, has evolved a whole strategy, of secrecy, denying a character vital information, or turning time into a vertical layercake, or, when time is horizontal like a line of prose, changing tempo through short ellipsis or long hiatus. And Goytisolo's Count Julian, in that overflowing life-sentence of a novel he inhabits, has his tongue in his colon from the very first word.

Now all this, some would say, is trickery, optical illusion, narcissistic window-dressing, whereas to me it's the characteristic behavior of an agile, fertile mind, such a mind as you don't find behind the scenes of the class-conscious English fiction published over the last thirty years. To the English, class is as sovereign as Mother Nature herself; it's as if they wrote about umbrellas while ignoring the nature of the rain. . . .

In a way, that brings me to my second element or factor, which is that these writers have an acute sense of trauma, not just historical, but ontological too; so we get not only the viciousness of historical regimes, but also, infiltrating the social fabric like a beneficent plague, the trauma of being alive. I say trauma overall because there are the joys too, and the juxtaposition is shocking. You listen to your blood. You watch your lymph, your spit, your tears. Your pupils are made of the same pulp as your brain. Your nails grow. Your peristalsis loops the loop. And, just over the horizon, lurks the Hayflick Limit, past which no human cell can go; bungling proteins bump us off. I find that trauma in these writers, not denudedly as in the fiction of Beckett, and not peeping out through the gaps in between veils of mortified saving suavity, as in Nabokov, and not just technically either, as in Richard Selzer's *Mortal Lessons:* that fragrant sty of medical curiosa. I find it diffused, though not in any sense blurred, in their frescoes of what it's like to be alive, subject to almost incalculable forces best evinced in what Charles Darwin called panmixis—when chronology's garbled, places are fused, and what wasn't there before imposes on you to the point of hypnosis. Protocol sinks back into anthropology and formula back into the swill of phenomena. A thing is itself only a bit more than it isn't and its legitimate context is no less than all the things it's not. Call it the metaphysical mind, perhaps, as we find it in the poetry of Wallace Stevens and Dylan Thomas. It's a seeing into and beyond; it's a raising to exponential maximum of the drive to see things atomically, which is to say undividably from the molecular, mythic, magical matrix seen as a continuum. On this mental Rialto we find metamorphoses Ovid never dreamed of; and if fiction still deals in what happens next, then— at the hands of these novelists present, and of their congeners (not all of whom I can pronounce!)—we find out what's right next door to what happens next. I doubt if anyone of rather fixed literary taste would go away unchanged by a banquet of Cortázar, Carpentier, García Márquez, Puig; those engrossing Brazilians (Osman Lins, Lispector, and Piñon), the sonorous gourd of Lezama Lima, and the sprightly, antic other Cubans, Cabrera Infante, Severo Sarduy, and Reinaldo Arenas. And, if nothing is what happens next (when the lion really halts), then we find out what's next to that as well.

Did I imagine all this? Is this version of these writers' work as imaginary as my old image of America was? Hearing the natives of Madagascar shout *"indry!"* whenever a certain lemur showed up, the French naturalist Pierre Sonnerat concluded *indry* was its name; but *indry!* was the imperative of the verb "to look." Nonetheless, to this day, an *indry*'s called an *indry*, stuck with a name as I am stuck with a view. If I've sympathized for the wrong reasons, I still have sympathized. A recent book puts me in this company anyway, for my notion of the artist as a cosmic gangster who usurps the divine role and creates possibilities unrecognized in real creation. The same book mentions Mr. Gass, who long ago, it seems to me, emigrated from downhome

North America to his own private Sheikdom of sheer Style, taking along with him the special metallurgical radiance that is his own. I can see why he's here.

To be on the safe side, though—at least if you believe in graven images—you unfold a paperclip and, scoring until the blood comes, lengthen your life-line a couple of inches or so, right down past the so-called bracelet of your wrist. The tiger got away. The lion died. The mollusk has exceeded his time.

[1980]

II

Note to the Reviews

In 1962 I began to write about books for *The Washington Post*'s *Book World,* usually novels or story collections I would have bought and read anyway. Not long after that, I was asked if I would review some of the foreign fiction translated that kept showing up at the *Post.* This began what I sometimes think of (*pace* Oxford and Columbia) as the best education I ever had: over a quarter of a century some two hundred books, all of them teaching me, in the most intimately surreptitious manner possible, comparative literature of the twentieth century. Here began my fascination with Latin American fiction. Here continued my love of French literature, last indulged at Columbia in Wilbur M. Frohock's seminar on Georges Bernanos, and my amateurish interest in things German. Books from Italy, Poland, and Czechoslovakia also came my way, and some real stunners from the United States, tossed into the stream aimed toward me maybe to trick me into wondering what celestial language they had been translated from.

With one or two exceptions I culled *Post* pieces in which I was enthusiastic, or which I thought better written than others. The reviewer is at the mercy of all kinds of forces, most of all luck; I never got to write about books by certain authors I admire, such as Juan Benet, Marie-Claire Blais, Christine Brooke-Rose, Colette, Eva Figes, Jean Genet, John Hawkes, Nathalie Sarraute and Susan Sontag, some of whom figure in the essays preceding this part of the book, in a more discursive context. I plead guilty to chronic (but selective) exoticism and to finding congenial in North American authors qualities mainly Latin American or European. My gratitude to the authors mentioned in both parts of this book is explicit, I trust; they delighted me, fed me, regaled me, widened my horizons, and encouraged me while I was making my own creative way. My thanks go also to the successive literary editors I dealt with at *The Post,* most of all Eve Auchincloss, Brigitte Weeks, Michael Dirda, and Francis Tanabe, and to those at *Review,* published by the Center for Inter-American Relations (Ronald Christ and Gregory Kolovakos ran a tight, august ship, like Herbert Leibowitz at *Parnassus).* These paragons never changed a comma without asking me beforehand, and with exquisite marksmanship sent to my mailbox fiction which, in gathering bulk over the years, persuaded me I had creative siblings out there after all, some of them far away: a lost tribe found, or, rather a diaspora of excellence at last linked up, by complex lines, into the constellation Fictor Totus.

P.W.

Juan Goytisolo
Makbara

W HEN JUAN GOYTISOLO was a boy, his mother was killed in one of Franco's air raids, and when he grew up he left Spain for almost 20 years, in the course of which self-imposed defiant and caustic exile he brought out nine books, all banned at home. Now, however, he is persona grata, sees his books on the Spanish best-seller list, and aligns himself with the Latin American novelists who troop around the world like a flock of vivid, fondled birds of paradise. Spain's verbal scourge has transcended his homeland in the very act of returning to it, but his material remains just as Spanish as theirs remains Peruvian, Colombian, or Chilean. His models are Beckett, Genet and Céline, and he has become the virtuoso of accusation, the one who endears himself to Spain by reviling its recent past and the maladies that linger on.

Sex, Spain and language are his themes, as those who read his work know. Sex is freedom, never mind how undignified and repetitious. Spain is the vapid sequel to an old and violent nightmare, as seen from France, North Africa, or the U.S.A., but updated with ironic fervor by a novelist who remains an alien, an outsider, a deserter not so much gone sour as spikily aloof, a man who works just as hard to elude the country that wants him back as he worked to defy it when it shut him out. Language, without which he cannot think, is what he continually remakes, fashioning a style that lets him use Spanish without being obliged to those who deadened it for almost half a century. Among his more recent books, *Count Julian* was a sustained hymn of hatred, razing the ground of the language behind it, while *Juan the Landless* took him to a new, almost incandescent poise, as if the positive and negative qualities of his prose had fused for the most time.

In *Makbara* the style loosens up again while Goytisolo shoots at some of his favorite targets: propaganda and publicity jargon, prudes and priests and politicos, tourists and executives and roving reporters. The people he feels at home with—whether literally or not—are the drop-outs and the ne'er do wells, the outcasts and the misfits, in this instance writ eloquently large as the lovers who frequent "Makbara"— North African cemeteries used for trysts and rendez-vous. What a poignant central image it is: not only as an emblem of life in death, a fruitful and surreptitious paradox, but also as a vantage point from which to review the human antic in general.

As before, the colon and comma are just about the only marks of punctuation, so that everything feels in apposition to everything that's gone before, and all statements seem parallel and as simultaneous as they can be in a linear text. For Goytisolo, this is the perfect vocal-paginal device, enabling him to speak in a series of not quite joined asides, some of which work as variations on a theme while others leap away from the initial stimulus and generate new starts, reproducing the current of life's fecundity in a sentence that never ends. From the opening phrase "in the beginning was the cry" to the finish that has no period ("blackness, emptiness, the nocturnal silence of the page that is still blank"), an earthy pageant of lovers and fornicators swarms through the muser's mind, superimposed upon one another as in a palimpsest, yet just as specific as the pictures to some old edition of *The Thousand and One Nights.*

In a book of this lyrical kind, although you get many glimpses of a great deal going on, what you receive most of all is the cadence of the writer's mind, his constant trimming of his mental sails, his inability or refusal to make causative connections. So, while flamboyant beggars, North African porno shows, and tender inspections of extraordinary private parts loom large, what lingers in the mind is the texture of daydreaming insinuation. Little licking mice voluptuously come and go in an addict's dream. There are Beckettian echoes so finely tuned by Helen Lane they might be quotes: "good heavens, it's him, he's here, he's come back, where?" and "no, that's not how it is." The love story of a French Foreign Legionnaire and a camp follower goes awry, half-evoking a Dietrich movie. Pittsburgh, evoked from a travel brochure, is as real an Unreal City as Tangier itself. An ovum seachanges into "a blonde fairytale princess."

Such things combine as the various signatures of the same writer, who does different lovers in different voices, and like the blacksheep dervish of his own devising, emerges at night from the catacombs to move among those prowling and cruising, his heart set on "a story that, quite simply is never-ending: a weightless edifice of sound in perpetual de(con)struction: a length of fabric woven by Penelope and unwoven night and day: a sand castle mechanically swept away by the sea." There are other signatures too, such as the frequent use of French and the mention of the rue Poissonnière, where Goytisolo lives when in Paris: reminders, even if only to himself, that this isn't a novel but a prose image of his presence at the clandestine feast of love staged in the even bigger Makbara of the world at large.

It becomes harder to tell Goytisolo's books apart. They have more in common than they don't, and they make style an act of fresco in which prose as fierce as lush, as sinuous as telegraphic, returns you always to a "peddler of dreams" humbly prefigured as "a simpleminded soul [who] strokes the strings of his rebec, lovingly cradling it like a wet nurse: the crowd censors out his humble, wretched presence, hurries on past him ... allowing him to enjoy a diaphanous transparency, abandoning him to his monotonous, obsessive strumming: lips set in a perpetual smile, a strabismic gaze, a life projected toward an impossible horizon."

The same teller or player dedicates *Makbara* "To those who inspired and will not read it." It reminded this reader of *The Triumph of Life,* for an onrush just like that of Shelley's "waking dream."

Mario Vargas Llosa
Aunt Julia and the Scriptwriter

A CRESCENDO EPIGRAPH from Salvador Elizondo's *The Graphographer* guards this novel with a boobytrap: "I write. I write that I am writing. Mentally I see myself writing that I am writing and I can also see myself seeing that I am writing. I remember writing and also seeing myself writing. And I see myself remembering that I see myself writing and I remember seeing myself remembering that I was writing and...." On it dizzily goes, as if to warn us against, prime us for, a tome of voyeuristic narcissism, diminuendo in infinite regress, until we swoon.

In fact *Aunt Julia and the Scriptwriter* is deceptively straightforward, cast as an adroit exercise in good old-fashioned storytelling, with beginning, middle, and end in that order, reminding us that the

novel at its best is, among other things, one of the noblest forms of
gossip, gabble, and guesswork. The characters never shut up and rarely
stand still. Rather than think about talking, or talk about talking
(infected by that epigraph), they just talk some more, pounding one
another into submission. The whole book has this jubilant, racy feel of
an oral pageant going slightly wrong, akin to the bizarre soccer game in
chapter 16 between Peru and Bolivia, refereed by a Peruvian.

If you have read any of Mario Vargas Llosa's other novels, say
The Green House or *Conversation in the Cathedral* (the first title
evokes a brothel, the other a bar), you know that he is one of the least
self-conscious novelists around: a Peruvian Balzac. Yet Vargas Llosa, a
highly educated cosmopolitan who did his doctoral dissertation on
Gabriel García Márquez, is no stranger to the ploys of post-modern
fiction, from Raymond Queneau to Juan Goytisolo, and he uses them,
but in a way so discreet as to seem invisible. Ellipses, time shifts,
mingling and merging points of view, breaches of convention, sly
erosions of what the reader thinks is firm and final—all these, and post-
Proustian divagations into magical anthropology, recur in his mature
work. The result is a solid swift mirage that reads like Balzac, maybe,
but lingers on like an hallucination, with the reader belatedly watching
the novel melt and vanish, call itself into question and mutate into
something rich and strange which you think you have also read. He
makes you wonder about the artificiality of fiction only after the fiction
is over, and you feed richly on the illusion while the illusion lasts.

Most of this fits *Aunt Julia,* which alternates chapters told by
Varguitas, who falls in love with his 32-year-old divorced aunt and
marries her, and chapters impersonally narrated about the melodramas
to be found in everyday life in Lima. The twist, or rather the generative
structural device that turns the book into an implicit romp through the
theory of knowledge, is the fact that 18-year-old Varguitas writes news
bulletins for Radio Panamericana, where he gets to know scriptwriter
Pedro Camacho, to whose soap operas the whole of Lima listens daily.
While Varguitas tells his own story in first-person chapters, he
paraphrases the soaps in the other, third-person, chapters without
saying who he is. So he is both overt and subdued, both on and off
stage. Not only that: with one hand he turns Camacho's soap into
narrative prose far better than Camacho's dialogue, and with the other
writes short stories of his own, rapidly emerging as both a prodigal

apprenticed to a hack and a literary time bomb indistinguishable, much of the time, from the young Vargas Llosa himself. Perhaps the most poignant parallel, though, in these alternations is the way Varguitas, having nothing to learn from the senior scriptwriter, learns about love from his aunt, only in the end to leave them behind, both the worse for wear.

The full cumulative effect of this wholesomely profound comic novel evokes plate tectonics: massive chunks of narrative float and slide about, collide and overlap, bewitching the truth-seeker into accepting almost anything because it is so vividly, so abundantly, expressed, and you no longer care about appearance versus reality so long as you keep on getting more of Vargas Llosa's pungent, steady prose. Asked about experimentalism, the composer Varèse said he experimented *before* composing, and the same is true of Vargas Llosa. *Aunt Julia* works on you through hundreds of delicate repercussions built into a symphony of dualism, beyond which there is only the silence of what can never be said but can be inferred from Varguitas, who has almost more to say than he can manage, repeatedly cramming afterthoughts into parentheses like a chipmunk with nut-stuffed cheeks.

Whereas Aunt Julia takes time to grow on Varguitas, and the reader, like an outline filling in, Pedro Camacho is a garish, extraordinary presence from the outset: a long-haired runt in bow tie and black suit, perched on cushions behind his Remington and typing with his hands at eye-level, "thus causing him to appear to be boxing," and, in his downfall, with shaven-looking head, clad in stevedore's overalls and tennis shoes tied with string. A tropical fakir, he lives on after the book ends: one through whom lightning has passed, a lapsed idol, Varguitas' catalytic hero, who subordinated everything to what he called Art. His diction, as Varguitas notes, is exquisite: "in that voice not only each letter marched past in perfect order, without a single one of them being mutilated, but also the particles and atoms of each one, the very sounds of sound."

Like all books that gratefully celebrate life, and the way, it obliges us to invent fictions to live it through, *Aunt Julia* is about death and deterioration, in register both mild and minor (steady homage to age 50; the yellow Volkswagen, "overgrown with ivy and covered with spiderwebs"), but also in bold, overt comprehensive images that threaten to consume everything else. As master of disguises who can actually become the characters in his soaps, Pedro Camacho, "like a little electric robot," turns himself into a cardinal, a bigot, a beggar, an old lady, a judge, a sailor, a doctor, in a visual obbligato requiring only a few props—false mustaches, a white smock, false ears and noses, cotton bears, a biretta, a meerschaum, a crutch. While Aunt Julia and Varguitas watch him, "in openmouthed amazement," he fervently asks "What is realism...? What better way is there of creating realistic art, than by materially identifying oneself with reality?"

Travesty of a hand-me-down god, he personifies the genius of impersonation until, in a final act, he commits genocide upon the characters who have suffered through the catastrophes of his soaps, killing them off wholesale through fire, earthquake, car wreck, shipwreck, and wreck of train. At least a Samson, at most something out of Goya's notion of Saturn, by his very presence he transforms the novel into a pageant of the genuine heart among a festival of lies, of candor in the bowels of myth. And, whoever "Don Marito Varguitas" is, he must take some of the credit for the book's steady, tropical intensity, even before, towards the end, he gets everyone to drop the diminutive *ito,* marries his cousin Patricia, and comes into his own, a full-blown sorcerer living again in Peru after long years in Europe: a Peruvian novelist, Mario the magician.

Carlos Fuentes
The Old Gringo

CARLOS FUENTES is a man of parts with many roles. The versatility which is the hallmark of his excellence applies to him as a fiction-writer, too. There is Fuentes the discreet implier, concerned with special and not always definable states of mind, as in *Aura* and *Distant Relations.* There is Fuentes the voluminous, wide-handed visionary, for whom nothing is too small, too big, to go into his homage to the planet, *Terra Nostra.* There is the severely moving Fuentes of *The Death of Artemio Cruz,* who masters the forlorn, the poignant, with impetuous vivacity. There is the Fuentes whose work in progress happens to be told by a fetus, and there is the Fuentes of *The Old Gringo,* a cleverly conceived and crisply rendered book about Ambrose Bierce's mysterious last days, as an old man, in the Mexico of 1914.

The book's premise is that Bierce went to Mexico to die, in the army of Pancho Villa, because death is what Mexico is good at. It would be easier to explore this premise if Fuentes had come closer to Bierce's most hidden motives, but he backs off, only occasionally allowing Bierce to speak out, or dream forth, in his own words, in an idiom different from that of the novel's narrator: "This handiwork of man and beast, this humble, unheroic Prometheus, comes praying, yes, imploring everything for the boon of oblivion." The reader has to guess, wondering if indeed the old gringo saw a Mexican death as a fitting punctuation mark because death in Mexico, as distinct from death anywhere else, is more imposing, satisfying, incongruous or whatever.

After all, the author of "An Occurrence at Owl Creek Bridge" had a vested interest in death, its protocols and mannerisms. Shot, Fuentes imagines, in the back by a capricious junior general of Villa's, after making a solo horseback charge of indelible, reckless bravery, and after encountering too late for anything to come of it the exquisite and chaste Harriet Winslow of Washington, D.C., Bierce suffers a death every bit as enigmatic as his initial decision to go south of the border. Did Arroyo the general shoot him for being too brave, in other words for setting too high a standard; or for burning Arroyo's box of private papers? Take your choice. Or, better, shelve the question as if the novel were a movie (which it already is). Eye the events and decipher them as best you can in the absence of narrative help. I am not sure we aren't dealing here with an *acte gratuit* much as we find it in André Gide. At any rate, Bierce wanted his death, and got it, so for him the causation could hardly have mattered.

To some extent, then, this general Arroyo is a contraption, but contraptions fit well into Fuentes' highly schematic book, fraught with echoes, parallels, and doubles, almost like an enfolded rose. To both Harriet and Arroyo, the old gringo is a father figure. She has lost her father, at first thought killed in the war, but revealed to have run out on his family. Arroyo is the unacknowledged son of a grandee. In the end, Villa, himself a father figure to Arroyo, has Arroyo shot for shooting Bierce, but not before he has him dig up the old gringo's corpse for "execution" from in front by firing squad, to keep up appearances. There are other such patterns and their interaction, like something underwater as you sail through the clear prose element above, imperils and thickens the action, turning everything that looks straightforward into something indisputably richer and stranger. Fuentes understands how the mind, especially in his myth-rich native land, modifies whatever it attends to, and in this case he allows room for the accomplice-reader to become part of the sea-change itself.

What looks, at first, like an almost allegorical tale becomes something much less obvious, less fathomable. Old gringo, young gringa, young general, older general, begin to overlap more than they don't, and in a weird way their roles drop away from them until each—Bierce, Winslow, Arroyo, Villa—begins to get lost in the others, not on the level of character, but in a hortatory ballet, staged with phantoms in the neutral desert.

Looking back on it all, Harriet Winslow can hardly credit what she lived through, remembering best her mental affair with the old gringo, her intense physical one with Arroyo. She has discovered contingency, what Henry James called "the insolence of accident." She cannot separate the inevitable from a whole series, a concatenation, of flukes, which has nonetheless defined her forever. A traumatized survivor, she inherits the theme *"I cannot take it all in such a short time,"* and you wonder if, without realizing it, it is history she's talking about. Mantegna's Christ invades her mind, obsesses it, not least because she cannot link the old gringo as she knew him to the Ambrose Bierce who wrote the books. The man is dead before his name comes to life for her. On she goes, rehearing and rehearsing the monologues of ancient Mexico. The monologues seem almost as ancient as Mexico itself, although the events underpinning them were recent.

It's a haunting novel, easier to focus on with the second reading, and—although a blaze of fierce action—a book of interacting levels, one of which is contemplative: where the reader begins and ends, pondering the enigma of Ambrose Bierce, who became as baffling as Mexico in order to die at its visionaries' hands.

Alejo Carpentier
Reasons of State

NOT QUITE DEADPAN, he stares from the jacket with forbearing suavity. His cleft chin droops like a wattle and his left hand, advanced along his thigh to span its girth between thumb and forefinger, looks draped, vegetal, and, because so near the camera, oversized. Thus Jean-Pierre Couderc's photograph of Alejo Carpentier, as of a haughtier or exasperated Herbert Marshall; but what comes through most subtly of all in this extraordinary portrait is the fastidious, high-level canniness of a mind as much attuned to ephemera as to cyclical time, as much aware of time that is seasonal as of time that is mere chronicity. This is Cuba's UNESCO man in Paris (the very concept gives one pause), but also, and perhaps more than any novelist since Proust, Our Man in Continuum, whose chosen emblems— Haitian history; a voyage up the Orinoco; the Machado dictatorship; conquered Guadaloupe; time reversed seen as an exercise in optional thinking—have always more than a topical resonance and pluck at the mind's underside with irresistible energy, scotching roles and eras and taxonomies in the interests of a profuse contingency, a flux we never quite see whole or get accustomed to but endure while trying to relish it as the only thing that consciousness is offered. In a word, Carpentier implies an All. *Imply* means to infold, and that he does non-stop, with tough finesse.

What a spacious, noble view of fiction he has, proposing not chemisms, the darkling plain, the long arm of coincidence, the involuntary memory, the absurd, an E. M. Forsterian small platoon, or an "analogical consciousness" out of "Morelli" by Cortázar, but a vision of the horn of plenty forever exploding, forever settling in bits that belong together more than they don't because there is nothing else for them to do. In Carpentier the All and the One remain unknown, and suspect even, but the aggregate of the Many, gorgeous and higgledy-piggledy, does duty for them, never construable but always lapped up.

This is unusual, a far *cri de coeur* from the doting, philatelical, chosisme of Robbe-Grillet, say, or the infuriated listing (in both senses) of Goytisolo's Count Julian, or the voluptuous tactilities of Yukio

Mishima. It's akin to the optical illusions Claude Simon practices in *Conducting Bodies,* but altogether more voluminous, zestful, and more fun. A wild and whirling head has developed a flair for appetizing specificities, and Carpentier is a master of both detail and mass, of both fixity and flux. With none of Beckett's reductive extremism, little of Joyce's word-smelting multiplicity, he sometimes seems the only senior novelist today possessed of the view from a long way off: as if, during a sojourn on some noetic planet circling Barnard's star, he had seen mankind plain, and all our thinking, our births and deaths, our myths and structures and dreams, all our bittersweet velleities, rammed up against the anonymous doings of nature. Unlike Robert Graves, who once claimed that by holding a Roman coin in his hand he could transport himself back to Roman times, Carpentier uses astute vicariousness to guess what the coin would be like. He is one of the few writers of whom you can say: If we didn't exist, he would be able to imagine us (assuming he was the only human). In other words, he can not only describe; he can describe what no-one has seen; and, best, he seems to have the hypothetical gift of suggesting, as he describes, that his description—a text woven from words—is experience newly reified, made more available, more dependable, and more reassuring, than daily bread or daily trash.

How odd, then, to find critical notices of *Reasons of State* which chide Carpentier for anachronism or inaccuracy, or which regard the book simply as an exercise in quasi-historical portraiture, or politicist cops and robbers; yet no odder than the complaint, made against his previous novels, that he engages in heavy pondering and actually dares to hold up "the action" in order to think. The truth is that his fiction is ostensible, and his characters—Juan the Pilgrim and Noah in *War of Time,* the downhearted musicologist in *The Lost Steps,* Hugues the revolutionary in *Explosion in a Cathedral*—are pretexts. He has something more than narrative, or storytelling, in mind, and he uses it as bait (much as Eliot envisioned a poem's meaning as the poet-burglar's lump of meat provided for the reader's watchdog while the poem goes about its real business). What keeps on coming is the deluge of phenomena, against and amidst whose Niagara not only sentences and paragraphs, but mind and will themselves, are virtually helpless. And this is not only a theme in Carpentier's work: it is also a procedural mannerism evinced in thousands of exquisitely crafted sentences which, lovely in distension, threaten to distend further just because everything evokes everything else, and therefore all sentences are unsatisfactory surrogates for The Sentence, absolute and final, which unlinearly would render them unnecessary. Read in series, these sentences thrive on their own failure, an obbligato of also-rans: not so much near-misses as distant misses; and the drama, the action, in one sense, is less in the events than in this linear prometheanism which never gives up yet never succeeds, which exhausts itself in trying to exhaust the world (until the next time, the next sentence), and evokes a complementary opposite to the Eskimo fad of jubilant modesty—if you harpoon a seal, exclaim "I almost missed it!" Carpentier, always missing, creates a jubilant rhetoric of disappointment that includes, as part of elegant mind-play, the fiction of a near-hit. Doomed, of course, to miss, and to omit, he makes the trajectory thrilling, so much so that one takes the rhetoric (the harpoon work), as one must, as an end in itself: the ineffable and finally not historical but cosmic mental adventure against whose ground the more overt "adventures" of his books—revolutions, pilgrimages, quests—are merely invitational tropes. The agon of an articulateness born incomplete; the flirtation with the ghost of an articulateness born complete: these are his preoccupations, much as Beckett's failure to express, aggravating the need to express, is his.

At its most obvious, *Reasons of State* is a portrait of a sybaritic, cultivated Latin American despot, an absentee totalitarian who sows his wildest oats in Paris, from time to time steaming home to quell the latest revolt. Rum, venery, and lush rhetoric compose his life style; opera and paintings finesse it; and he somehow contrives to stay in power; stifling dissent and confiscating "red" literature (including *Le Rouge et le Noir* and *The Scarlet Letter*), at least until an uncurbable proletariat and some palace treachery dislodge him for keeps. He repines in Paris, wondering how single-mindedness, enforced by the military and a Model Prison full of electric chairs and wet-cement oubliettes, could have failed. "Yes," runs the hit tune of Jazz Age Paris, "We Have No Bananas." A banana republic has shed a skin and its naked-feeling despot dies, pulp for Eumenides of his own making.

But the novel is far from exclusively political or didactic: a big buzzing blooming confusion fills it, or at least a minor, fly-blown, withering chunk of window-dressing, in which Caruso, Nehru, Sarah

Bernhardt, flit like contraband moths through the chromatic parox-
ysms of *señor presidente's* vanity. Marble monuments, timely trains,
imported squirrels and reindeer and North American firs, gala
performances of *Marta* and *Rigoletto,* even Campaigns to Collect
Funds for Reconstruction, are of no avail. Fornication goes on in the
National Observatory; drunks invade the churches; skulls arrive in the
mail and funeral wreaths at houses where no one has died; a Steinway
ordered from New York arrives with a decapitated donkey inside it.
The Republic of Nueva Cordoba disarranges and disorders itself like
Rimbaud's mind, from stink bombs at the opera to a general strike led
by a stereotypical energumen called The Student. The comeuppance is
fizzy and satirically epitomistic.

But diverting and amusing as all this is, it isn't the novel's main
impact or the source of its perceptual zeal. Life's heterogeneousness
conducts us to intuitions of wholeness, and Carpentier, transcending
satire even while he creates a near-documentary album, conducts us
back—through and past matrices, regimes, credos, formulas, and
codes, so familiar as almost to seem natural structures themselves—to
an atavistic awe larded with unceremonious intrusions. Mind watches
mind evolving, and distraction keeps it at full stretch, as in the long
sortie that follows, characteristic of Carpentier's free-association
anthems:

> Now the Consul is showing me a rare collection of root-
> sculptures, sculpture-roots, root-forms, root-objects—ba-
> roque roots or roots that are austere in their smoothness;
> complicated, intricate or nobly geometrical; at times danc-
> ing, at times static, or totemic, or sexual, something between
> an animal and a theorem, a play of knots, a play of
> asymmetry, now alive, now fossilized—which the Yankee
> tells me he has collected on numerous expeditions along the
> shores of the Continent. Roots torn up from remote soil,
> dragged along, cast up, and again transported by rivers in
> spate; roots sculptured by the water, hurled about, knocked
> over, polished, burnished, silvered, denuded of their silver,
> until from so many journeys, falls, collisions with rocks,
> battles with other pieces of wood on the move, they have
> finally lost their vegetable morphology, become separated
> from the tree-mother, the genealogical tree, and acquired

breast-like roundnesses, polyhedric arms, boars' heads or
idols' faces, teeth, claws, tentacles, penises and crowns, or
are intimately connected in obscene imbrications, before
being stranded, after a journey lasting centuries, on some
beach forgotten by maps. That huge mandragora with its
fierce thorns had been found by the Consul at the mouth of
the Bio-Bio, close to the jagged rocks of Con-Con, rocking
in a hammock of blue waters. That other mandragora,
contorted and acrobatic, with its fungus-hat and bulging
eyes—rather like the "root of life" which certain Asiatic
peoples put in flasks of aguardiente—had been found near
Tucupita in the estuary of the Orinoco. Others came from
the island of Nervis, from Aruba, from the rocks like besalt
menhirs that rise amid the thunderous marine gorges near
Valparaiso. And it was enough to mention the name of a
port to the collector for him to pass from the root found
there to the invocation, evocation, presentation of images
brought to life by the syllables making up its name, or the
proliferative activity of the letters—so he said—a process
such as was foreshadowed in the Hebrew Cabbala. And
merely by pronouncing the word Valparaiso there were
plateaux of jurel-fish lying on seaweed, a display of fruit in
the church porch, the windows of inns showing the whole
counter covered in apocalyptic spider-crabs from Tierra del
Fuego; and there were the German beer-shops in the main
street, where reddish-black sausages spotted with bacon-fat
lay beside warm strudels powdered with sugar; and there
were the enormous public lifts, tirelessly moving parallel to
each other, with orchestras of blind men playing polkas in
the tunnels by which you reached them; and there were the
pawnshops, with a broad-buckled belt, a reliquary made of
shells, a scalpel with a jagged edge, a Negro figure from
Easter Island, slippers embroidered with Souv (for the left
foot) and Enir (for the right) which, when put endways on to
the passer-by, illustrated with amazing eloquence Kant's
Paradox of the Looking-glass.

What, that is radical in any sense, wouldn't fit into the contained
ampleness of that? Delving into phenomena, Carpentier finds every
sense-datum, every phoneme, a cross-roads, down each fork of which

he ponders his way, aware that the time-traveller's very presence modifies the space he's in. That long prose journey from "Now" to "the Looking-glass" exemplifies his way of making something infinitesimal exemplify infinity, something natural counterpoint something manufactured, something almost sacred something vulgar. Yet you can lose the whole thing, responding only to swell's augmentations rather than to swell's meaning, if you don't follow the allusion to Kant which at once undercuts and makes a triumphant finale. The passage is a triumph of style, of course, enacting in its movements—playful, dawdling, side-spill and eddy and full halt—its theme. And this reminds us that style for Carpentier is more than embellishment or panache, but a means of participating anew in the universe through the fixed physical configurations of prose rather than in some unwritten reverie. He writes amazement, even through the stunted sado-misanthropic mind of his anonymous head of state, whose sense of wonder is shallow and arrested, yet nonetheless there, and especially visible when Carpentier vouchsafes him the use of the first person, occasions on which outrage and indignation lead even that unevolved hobgoblin to a wider view in which more things are possible than before. But his mind seals itself, clenched around a few treasured obsessions, and he seems finally less interesting than his shotgun-toting consort-housekeeper, his foul-mouthed and intricately self-willed daughter, his mandarin literateur of a privy counsellor, even the part-Negro American consul who helps him escape. Behind them all, Carpentier the impresario of metaphors, the keeper of an entire zoo of assorted specificities, weaves and reweaves complex patterns of transcendence which are like light streaming through a pornographic stainedglass window. Yet if this is a moralistic book, I didn't find it so; a saint would have looked just as ephemeral, stymied, flawed, as this mythic head of state. All one can do is reflect on the barrenness of demagogical thinking.

Scattered saliences linger on: the reek of the seaport, compact of brown sugar, hot furnaces, and green coffee; the skeleton found in a jar in a cave (the description of which occurs twice, with the wording only slightly varied, a *déjà vu* sponsored by Nemesis); the master driller and borer who carves mountains into animals (thus, in his view, releasing a whole trapped bestiary); the Little German Train on which the head of state dotes ("As if it had just come out of a Nuremberg toyshop, gleaming, repainted and varnished"); and his horse, Holofernes, to which he daily feeds a pail of best English beer. Scattered throughout these saliences, a series of epigraphs from Descartes hedge the telling about with dualisms: individual and public notions of reason; space occupied and space not; deliberate and automatic behavior; the certainty that one exists and the uncertainty about how long; all culminating in "And deciding not to seek more knowledge than what I could find in myself" and, atop the last page, " . . . stop a little while longer and consider this chaos. . . . "

Can we, the book implies, know what it is we do not know? There is no knowing that, but one lifetime's opportunity to observe acquaints us with the beguiling insufficiency of what we do know. As Carpentier proves, no matter how skilled we are at speculative hypothesis, our knowledge of our ignorance is mostly retrospective, except for the big, cosmic questions. In between, however, between what we do not know we do not know and, say, What created hydrogen? there's much that's feasible, much of it being observation such as yields thick description, at which Carpentier excels, perhaps because he knows how thin our attentiveness can become once we realize we are the thickness while the thickness lasts. "In the Kingdom of Heaven," as we read in Carpentier's *The Kingdom of this World,* "there is no grandeur to be won . . . the unknown is revealed, existence is infinite." Or, as John Wheeler puts it, "In some strange sense, this is a participatory universe. What we have been accustomed to call 'physical reality' turns out to be largely a papier mâché construction our imagination plastered in between the solid iron pillars of our observations. These observations constitute the only reality." Imagination's role is to serve itself, as Carpentier has his tyrant confirm in his dying words: *Acta est fabula* (the tale is told).

Mário de Andrade
Macunaíma

MACUNAÍMA IS THE REAL THING. First published by the author himself, in 1928, it is the earliest effective attempt to weld Brazilian mythology into a single narrative lump. Sly, ribald and opulent in a hardheaded, buoyant way, the book is a classic, and you might never guess that Mário de Andrade had hit on the idea for its hero, Macunaíma, in the works of a German anthropologist. It's as if someone had unearthed Pan from the whimsical texts of Lévi-Strauss and orchestrated the result in the fashion of Villa-Lobos. A hallucinative poet suckled on Apollinaire and Laforgue, de Andrade takes in everything, ancient and modern, African and Italian, and creates from it a chirping icon, cosmic and undusty.

As stories go, and they come and go fast in this book, *Macunaíma* is that of a folk hero who sets out in quest of a charm he's lost. He has broken tribal law, so the gods punish him. In this sense, the story is that of the dispossessed young prince all over again. There is more than a touch of mysticism to the madcap knockabout, and the ending is truly poignant, as Macunaíma, seeing nothing worth staying on earth for, ascends to heaven, slaps the moon's face (cause of those dark blotches) and persuades the Father of the Crested Curassows to turn him and his belongings—"the cock, the hen, the coop, the revolver and the clock"— into a new constellation called the Great Bear. So much for the family of man, forever busy, forever evasive.

In the end we learn that the whole tale has been told by a parrot, full of sounds and fury, signifying more than most novels because it doesn't halt at the border of fiction or sociology or fable but becomes the rhapsody that de Andrade intended. What an amazing supple text it is, woven together from songs, curses, obscenities, tall tales, erudite letters and primitive improvisation.

It is almost beside the point to note that the book's content is just as varied as its manner, piling up with breezy receptivity the musician wren, a fortune in cocoa beans, a ship's wake of chocolate, a tree on which pistols grow and sometimes ripen, a cannibal soup "made from the body of a meat porter frozen overnight in a São Paulo cold storage," a sex change under rainbows, "that sublime village, Rio de

Janeiro," a man from British Guiana with a cold virus in his Gladstone bag and the golden-brown jaguar that fathers every Mercedes and Bentley. More urban paraphernalia would have enriched the mix; after all, de Andrade had a free hand in making this tapestry. Also some of the Britishisms in the translation ("peeler" for cop, "the horn" for a hard-on) should have been excised. All the same, the full tune, the ample flavor, of the original come through, reminding us that in this world of the subatomic, anything has the right to be next to anything else. Not many such chromatic romps will come our way.

As a novelist, I find the technique fascinating because it runs on sheer telling, with no effort to convince. The result is a free-associative consecutiveness which turns causation into a phantom and realism into a quibble. The myth is senseless and porous, a massive nub of fluidity done in an idiom glib and precise. You read it, you *should* read it, with gratitude for the open-ended fashion in which the hero's metamorphoses embody the universe he lives in: a fresh antidote to the anorexic provincialism of much that gets published today.

Sixty years after *Macunaíma* first appeared, de Andrade seems less the obscurantist musicologist-explorer-scholar-novelist than the Orpheus of the Amazon, but with a barbaric narrative drive and a full-blooded brand of wordplay. In the movie version of the book, Macunaíma teams up with urban guerrillas, reminding us that, when the Great Bear is a family member, the human family is endless.

In his lecture "The Argentine Writer and Tradition," Borges makes two points that are relevant here, claiming that the absence of camels proves the Koran an Arabian work (Mohammed had no reason to suppose camels were especially Arabian) and that South Americans in general are no more obligated to Western culture than are Jews, or than Irishmen to the culture of England. Just so: Macunaíma's patrimony is the universe. Andrade reminds us that the word "family" is from the Latin word for servant, and servants we are in his household of the All, along with monkeys, cowbirds, bushmasters, tacuri ants, Maceio mussels, pepper and cassareep.

It is interesting to compare E.A. Goodland's translation of Chapter Three with the one by Barbara Shelby in *The Borzoi Anthology of Latin American Literature*. Goodland, worth a novel himself, was a Cambridge-educated chemical engineer who traveled widely in Brazil, went on some tricky voyages by canoe on the Rio

Negro and made the translation of *Macunaíma* his labor of love during retirement. His labor was not lost, but Shelby has an American ear, although sometimes Goodland's Britishisms make the jungle seem even more exotic than ever, giving the swarmingness a touch of Victorian hauteur. De Andrade would have smiled, I think, and devoured the protean shift, if he had lived long enough to see the word *bandeirante* ("an armed band") become the name of a short-haul passenger airplane.

Osman Lins
Avalovara

DISTANT EXPLOSIONS make the crystal chandeliers tinkle, but the two lovers on the big pink rug don't look up. We are in the declining luxury of a parlor—faded damask, golden velvet—where someone called Abel and his perfect mistress meet repeatedly in this lush, ecstatic novel by an already dead Brazilian master. The plump, impossible she, whom Abel found after a lifetime's search and scarring liaisons with other women, has hair the color of honey and steel, is several women in one, and may also be imaginary, dead, or divine. Abel never says her name, but mentions her only through the ideogram ♉ , which cannot be pronounced.

Yet, in the other sense of that last word, she sticks out: less a character in Lins' novel than the novel is part of the universe she embodies. In very sense, she is Abel's newfoundland, physically, of course, but also mentally and cosmologically; and for Lins' narrator, openly trying to write the allegorical novel of paradise found—"several women and one man...a trajectory of which the protagonist is ignorant"—she becomes the source and symbol of all the cannot say, a liter for his thimble, a rune his linear ruler cannot measure. In a word, she is life, not just Dante's Beatrice, La Belle Dame *Avec* Merci and Garbo rolled into one, but everything—erotica, mystery, soul and by mathematical extension an infinite spiral which the narrator can't capture in his grid of pages. A nap or two apart, his dot-faced lady with the fuse-wire ears is inexhaustible in every way.

If all this sounds high-flown ("Avalovara" is a bird whose name seems to mean a Drinker Up of Eggs), Lins gets it across with sensuous, irresistible vividness, driving nonstop—almost as if it were a new idea—at the romantic yearning for an ideal Other, but also for the unknown as the scientist, the astronaut, the mystic know it. *Avalovara* is a novel of secular bliss, and ♉ (to use a phrase of Hemingway's) is what Abel has "instead of God." Maybe vice versa too, except that she can say his name and in that is earthier than he, as goddesses usually are. On the rug, but sometimes on a sofa or the concrete of a balcony, she and Abel adore each other, dawdlingly, fiercely, dreamily, stashing the past into a little summary (a "summula") and shutting out the life to come. She accepts him as he is, though with increasingly ritual ingenuity, but he is always trying to figure her out; after all, he's the narrator's proxy, and she is not. The narrator seems a man.

This narrator shapes his novel after an expression culled from Pompeii: "*Sator Arepo Tenet Opera Rotas,*" which means both "The plowman carefully sustains his plow in the furrows" and, more cosmically, "sustains the world in its orbit." The Latin saying he inscribes across a square divided into 25 equal sections, ending up with a two-way palindrome centered on two "Tenet"s crossed. With this diagram he plays his own variety of hopscotch in, as the book's last page reveals, Sao Paulo, from September 22, 1969 to December 1, 1972. Is Lins' dating the narrator's too? One cares because the cabalistic determinism of the square, printed right after an opening bouquet of five complex epigraphs, mocks the calendar of simple time (yet another grid), but also because it's overprinted on a spiral echoed in the narrative by carousels, bedsprings, wheels, clocks and galaxies. Meanwhile Abel and ♉ (you guessed it) are trapped in one right-angled shape or another—a room, a rug, a bed, a plaza—almost like Keats' lovers on the Grecian urn except that Keats flash-freezes them and Lins keeps them moving in fixed orbit, like the heavenly bodies they are.

Offered under such auspices, in prose at once deep and spectacular, this love story becomes an engrossing and haunting analogue for human maneuver in the face of the truly unknowable Unknown. What are we? she and Abel ask. Humans: but what are they? Things unfathomable, for which we invent sometimes unknown names such as "Yolyp." The scheme, of expressing creation's spiral in the humdrum square, is meant to fall and, in falling, to evince the superior magic of the universe, through whose spotty void we float, whether on "half-soiled" pink magic carpets or not. Lins' erotic novel of candid yet flawless good taste, full of saturated crescendos and rhapsodic rests, works on every other level as well: a divine yet profane comedy, a tragedy in which the lovers are the cosmic spiral's sacrificial offering to itself, a hymn of celebration in which the brain runs riot, and a continuum of freely-sculpted prose that sometimes feels like an auroral display pent up in a bell jar.

"I won't even live a thousand years," she says, "my life is quick, a scratch on time, just as one day a fish leaps up over the vastness of the sea and sees the Sun and an archipelago where goats are moving among the crags, that's how I leap out of eternity." So, says she, "Come, Abel. Penetrate me and make me grow. I am obsessed with sponges . . . " Off her pour the aromas of ripe oranges, burnt lavender and sulfur. The crocodile and the rabbit in the rug's pattern come alive and join in the love-play as if ravished by Scriabin. There are scores of such moments.

Two of Abel's other women, aloof Roos and bisexual Cecilia, drift in and out of this walk to the paradise garden, figures who might be dominant in any other novel, but here are subordinate and minor, almost noises offstage (like the Orff music that plays in the parlor), and less real than that mythic unmockable bird of contentment, Avalovara, which flies and cries "Raah!" during human climax, only to vanish, or the long-historied grandfather clock which chimes Scarlatti.

Osman Lins, a banker turned professor and novelist died at 54 in 1978, known only in his native Brazil, Germany and Spain, yet surely, on this showing of his third out of five novels, one of the most majestic prose stylists Latin America has ever produced, sumptuous, original, impenitent, and gravid with mellow power: the Villa-Lobos of the novel.

Julio Cortázar
A Certain Lucas

E SPECIALLY FOR THOSE OF US aghast at the tofu fiction spawned and favored in North America, Cortázar epitomizes the celebrant who fires on all cylinders, who lets fiction be itself, lets it flow and evolve. Suppleness, elasticity, metamorphosis are some of the words that come to mind on pondering his oeuvre, as well as not just the notions of magical realism but the magic of realism itself, the magicality of the real, the verbal and mental reality of the imagined. Partitions and compartments attracted his metabolic gaze but never fazed him; his imagination traveled in all classes, from Concorde to steerage, simultaneously, and the *volupté* of the journey was more important than any Stamboul train's ending up in Istanbul.

Play. Doodle. Conjure. He did all three, and mostly with sleek ebullience, as if his life, his mental health, depended on it, as for some of us it must. He dreamed. He fooled. He raised the category *verbal* to exponential maximum, yet kept a naturalist's senses on the axolotl, the dance hall, the tang of the maté, the apparition of faces like petals in a budding grove that grew from Buenos Aires to Paris. When he evoked Charlie Parker's saxophone, he divined the door which a certain hitherto unplayed sound would pass through like an acoustic neutrino. He was something of a witch doctor among quantity surveyors, a sedate dervish among deadheads.

So there's a homage to pay, elegiac as never before, yet without getting him wrong, without homogenizing him. He sometimes had the chutzpah to do things straight, exercising the imaginant's privilege of daringly going the other way, even if that meant no more than feeling obliged never to report things as they are unless you can imagine yourself imagining them into being from the start. He was not all Rimbaud, all Genet, all Joyce, all Lezama Lima; he held back as they do not, but that only makes him more complex, many-sided, a virtuoso with a straight face in his bulging repertoire. He made other imaginants (the word is his) feel less alone. Belonging nowhere, and only belatedly a citizen of France, he functioned in a limbo of gift where it doesn't matter what language you craft in or whether you hail from Belgium or Xanadu. Everness, Borges calls it. I call it The Invisible Riviera, where

invention reigns, and what Coleridge called imagination—the "esemplastic power"—weaves a woof unindebted to sectarian ethos, where
the mind is its own place, the Arabian palace of the individual.

Most of all, although he was political, he knew that language is not
an intrinsically moral or sociological thing, whatever liberals, puritans,
bigots and drones may say. Language is the thing that exceeds us all,
being not merely conduit or message, but a placeless frieze of timeless
resonance, a maze of etymology in which its ancient users and misusers
whisper to us with dead glottises. Other fires' embers are in its fire. It is
really the country of quite a number of us, scattered among the
Americas and Europa Nova, and whether we write in Spanish,
Portuguese, German, French, Polish, Czech or English, we ride a
glacier that transports us all, aware of noises off as of noises within,
aware even in face of life at its grimmest ("Worstward Ho," as Beckett
says) of something cognate with tonic sol-fa or pigment: the transcendent mixtures of a lifetime's stylishness, which death cannot mar and
which, if one is lucky, end up on the lips, and in the heads, of other
communicants. Passionate, articulate interiority set down, this is the
gift of ourselves to the watch on its birthday (remember his "Preamble
to the Instructions on How to Wind a Watch"). This is how to make the
corpse of Eva Perón, long after the epileptic musical and the ghosted
autobiographies have vanished into silt, go on bloating underground
and infest the whole of Argentina. I don't know if he ever published that
sometimes-mentioned work, but it lives nonetheless, much more than a
jeu, a trope, a *sotie:* worth nibbling on and appropriating for some
harpy of our own.

II

As soon as I heard of his death, I thought of a dozen still living,
whose demise one might have wished, on aesthetic grounds anyway;
but it was Cortázar who had been stopped, and then I thought of a
bunch of students with whom I had discussed *Hopscotch.* They were
most bewitched by the ironic Morelliana in the appended chapters.
Look, I tried to explain, these are the fudgings of a novelist who can't
write his novel: Morelli can theorize about the thing he cannot do, but
he can't get it to lift off. No, they found the notions more exciting than

Hopscotch itself, and I understood how little serious thought about advancing the horizon of fiction goes on in American academies. That there were Argentinian novelists at all, imaginary or real, amazed them.

Anyway, I thought: No more *liber fulguralis,* whether that Latin mouthful is ironic or not; no more lightning book. But I was wrong of course, *A Certain Lucas* (Ediciones Alfaguara, 1979) was on its way to us, and other things were in the wind. Yet I persisted in thinking: The gods kill first those whom literature needs, and I wondered about the quick mortal shift that comes when the author dies as you are reading, or reviewing, his or her book. Do you adjust toward the generous? Or at last discern a pattern? Or do you go about your business as if nothing has happened? My own response has usually been that death is a supreme fiction by means of which the destroyer of delight tries to snatch attention from the book, the author. And, in the case of Cortázar, obsessed by doubles always, the dead one was the same as the other, except perhaps that I lingered on the finitude and finality of each word. *A Certain Lucas* is that kind of book anyway, distilled and reduced, eclectically terse, less a jigsaw puzzle than an assembly of slices and glimpses promising an oblique self-portrait in a mirror as badly scratched as the plates of E. J. Bellocq, who photographed the whores of Storyville. The mood, cheerful and didactically playful, evokes *Cronopios and Famas,* but the book has more meat than that earlier assembly and, in its patient delineation of selected aspects, favored characteristics, recalls Beckett's *Watt.* Lucas too is an imposing conundrum; but, before you get him into focus, you have to come to terms with a number of centrifugal squibs which, through sprightly ridicule, imply serious points about imagination as a force that likes to keep up-to-date.

One of these, popped into a *jeu* called "Texturologies," invokes those opponents of the new who, of course, do not ride in horse-drawn carriages, seal their letters with wax, or fix their colds with leeches. The point comes well from Cortázar, who was not that experimental a writer, but happily combined matter-of-fact sentences with a hands-off attitude to imagination: What imagination wants, imagination gets. Like Lola. The sea-changes in his work are conceptual, not typographical or organizational, but that is only to say he conferred maximum license on what matters and didn't bother much with the marginal fripperies. What you find in Cortázar is the fluidity and elasticity of the mind, allowed to deform and run riot where it has to, but in the main crafted into a pellucid consecutiveness you might just as readily find in Erasmus, Lucian or Suetonius.

Turn the first pages, and Lucas the Hydra, bumpily presented with here an *oof,* there a *Hmm,* here a *no sir,* there an *etc.,* gets on and off the phone, goes shopping in his pajamas, forgets what he has gone out for, adopts the anthropomorphic view of an octopus, stays at home rather than go out to concerts (from which he was usually ejected for behaving badly), teaches at Berlitz (which took him on "half out of pity"), opts for the urban over the pastoral, and gets into some languorous soliloquies through which the ghost of a narrator self-consciously interferes with Lucas as Lucas talks to himself. Quite often, this Lucas—a certain Lucas from among the many-headed Lucas-Hydra— seems to be answering back, but to a narrator who has withdrawn to a seemly distance. Such elastic overlap complicates the book in a useful way, reminding us not only of identity seen as a bunch of irreconcilable particulars, but also of the incalculable aliases that a reader, who is not a static he or she, assumes in the act of reading even the simplest text. If Lucas were to add up to anything at all, to a certain fixed Lucas as distinct from all those Lucases, he would become a prop rather than a process. You never know where the book or Lucas in and with it is going next; like the American Constitution, it is a living document, and the things it rubs your noses in—contingency, arbitrariness, the polymorphous diverse, the ephemeral and the gratuitous—remind you how even daily living, every bit as naive as Husserl said it was, is in fact a creative, a self-creative, process, never mind how absentmindedly or obliviously undertaken.

Halfway through rehearsing a certain memory, Lucas decides "to remember how at that hour he would shut himself up to read Homer and John Dickson Carr, loafing in his little room to avoid hearing again about Aunt Pepa's appendectomy." Even if he doesn't remember whom he shut himself up to read, the memory is part of who he is today. Things trivial, like things serious, float into permanence, disturbing the neat grids upon which we choose to assemble the detritus of who we are. The book makes the point of identity poignantly.

And it makes it by confronting us with a spasmodic process depicted in a spasmodic way. Mutability goes on in front of us, as it must in fiction of all kinds, most of all in the type that, pretending to have in it people with names (although there abandoning the analogy with folks we know), runs headlong into the quicksand of identity. The result is that you have to try to put the pieces of the book together as best you can. If you fail, then it is as if you have grappled with something nonverbal. If you succeed, then you have profitably triumphed over the uncertainty of not knowing if you could.

The book is both a whole without parts and parts without a whole—an impossible object akin to such works as Uwe Johnson's *Speculations About Jakob* and Max Frisch's *Man in the Holocene.* As they pile up, the luminous and sometimes prankish little essays that compose the book's chapters tend to fray and vanish. You are almost always adding a new something to a diminishing incomplete recall. Some of the congeries gets lost, but no more than gets lost in straight narrative that (unlike, say, in Dickens) fails to repeat itself. Much of the book has the tone of fast amphetamine musing and is none the worse for that; the feel is narrative, but the motion is circular. You end with an uncertain Lucas-ishness shown pell-mell.

On the one hand, you get direct allusions to Lucas's dreams and cures, friends and songs, his stays in hospital and how his shoes get shined, and a steady enough portrait emerges without ever being hard and fast. On the other hand, you get sentences or paragraphs so lissome, and so opportunistically adroit, that you tune in to the old Cortázar beat, recognizing how the prose style embodies almost as a ritual the charms of free association. As in this:

> In the center of the image are probably the geraniums, but there are also wisteria, summer, maté at five-thirty, the sewing machine, slippers, and slow conversations about illnesses and family annoyances, a chicken suddenly leaving its calling card between two chairs or the cat after a dove that's way ahead of him.

After the chicken, anything could happen, mainly because the rhythm works as an *ave* to the cornucopia; even though the sentence ends soon after, you sense it could go on, limning an everything that's like the dove the cat can't catch. Cortázar's mellow incantations have always had this effect, more useful in the short story than in the novel. If you can imply, you needn't ever tell in full. Hence the success of *Lucas,* a short book rammed with intensely suggestive snippets evincing a complex, unintegrated life unsuitable for "a mysteriously multiform measurement that in the majority of cases fits like a well-cut suit."

If, however, you tire of the plural Lucas, you can always warm up on a smaller version of him proffered as that lesser hydra, Jekyll and Hyde. Here, the former knows who the latter is, but "the knowledge is not reciprocal." So we have to contend with "Hyde's ignorance," or, in another figure, the presence of a corpse as "the silent co-pilot." Take your choice between a predicament easily summed up as *Who Am I among so many of me?* and *Which of the two me's is me?* Or a lot of lemmas versus a dilemma. It would be hard not to settle for not merely the safety in numbers but the variety too, whereas Jekyll always having to bear the strain of an unreciprocating Hyde makes the whole thing a one-way song. Voices in the head is not a new phenomenon in literature, but a voice aimed at a numbskull is rarer, and the whole object of this book—if I divine it right—is to celebrate the joys of pluralism.

True, there are some eerily Beckettian moments, when a certain Lucas (meaning one or another of the Lucases) in "Ways of Being Held Prisoner" resists the narrator, Hyde-like perhaps, and lets rip:

> . . . I reject this text where someone writes that I reject this text; I feel trapped, annoyed, betrayed, because I'm not even the one who's saying it but rather someone who's manipulating and regulating me, I'd say that he's putting me on as well, it's clearly written; I'd say that he's putting me on as well.
>
> He's putting you on too (you who are starting to read this page, that's how it was written above), and if that wasn't enough, Lil, who doesn't know not only that Gago is my lover but that Gago doesn't understand a thing about women.

How even to describe such writing may be a problem: when point of view breaks down and, at least as far as is possible within the confines of a linear art, floating integers cancel out the text as it advances, except that you are always left with something like flotsam, which can only say: Hereabouts is the imprecise locus of where something tried to be said. *Trompe l'oeil? Trompe l'oreille,* rather. Mingled voluntaries coming out of nowhere, yet presumably sponsored by J. Cortázar, these are in several senses generations of words. Words generated by words. Successive ages of families of words. Simultaneous generations of words generated by people made of words. You don't have to be voraciously observant to detect the emphasis on words, behind each unique combination of which there hovers nothing that corresponds to them exactly, unless what corresponds to them is the mental image each individual reader makes of them. In other words, there is no antecedent for such formulations, and no simultaneous equivalent; but, as soon as a reader has read them . . . *now* there is. It's an old game, of course, elegantly staged here through tables that lift a leg when alone, telephones that are really cats and drink milk, ears that grow on the faces of intent listeners, slippers full of snails, swimming pools full of gray grits, and the act of "climb[ing] up an adverb."

Usually, the verbal nature of literature—its being made of words—bothers nearly everybody save those with souls born phenomenological, who don't worry if appearances correspond to something else, but who entertain appearances—phenomena, manifestations—in their own right. For instance, someone in this book coins the word *Adbekunkus,* and then wonders what it stands for; says to it "Now shut up, you distasteful Adbekunkus," and then wonders at this "name of a lesser devil, of a sad goblin. . . . I ended up accepting the fact that Adbekunkus was not attached to any conscious element . . . the phrase demanded silence of something, of somebody, who was a perfect void." How wonderful to be back in the Garden, with Adam, doing the naming from scratch all over again. No, not quite; coming up with names for eventual use. In this case, Adbekunkus "would never be quiet because he had never spoken or shouted. How could I fight against that concretion of the void?" Is this Hyde, mouthing and mumbling, only to be construed by vigilant Jekyll, to whom all things make sense because his skull is a poem-drome full of mnemonic ricochets and explicit chirps?

One wonders, then turns to *Being and Time* (another old pseudocouple) to find: "He who never says anything cannot keep silent at any given moment." In one sense, the thing that has no name cannot say anything to us; yet, as soon as it has a name to be called up with like a dog, it cannot keep silent. It is always saying itself. And it never says anything else. That is what bothers Cortázar: the premature, final husk on things. It bothered Beckett enough to make him have his Watt elect, prefer, to call a pot a shield or a raven (an uncommon privilege to be sure). We are dealing here with reversed order, of course, when the name precedes the thing, when science precedes nature. Yet not so fantastic after all, given the tendentious nature of language, the prophetic-divinatory nature of physics. Joyce had the word for quark before quarks were known, and the human throat-mouth-nose combination was making sounds for what ailed it before it knew what ailing was. Out of our involuntary mumbles comes something as fancy as the word *phenomenon* itself. What fun, and what a liberating enterprise, to have at least a few authors who look at the process both ways: *prior* and *post.* My own equivalent for Adbekunkus is Areemayhew, coined when I was six, I think, mainly to see how the combo sounded, but eventually my name for the red-hot devil that chased me up the cellar steps. Yet, did not the word bring the devil into being lest a good word go to waste?

Couple this with another piece. "Lucas, His Partisan Arguments," and you see what is going on: "There are no known limits to the imagination/except those of the word." The converse is true too, says Jekyll, who knows all about these things. For every sayable seeking its word there is a word seeking its place. What, then, of the words that come into being and never find a place? Are there any? Are they just so much babble? If, say, we came up with *mrok,* and couldn't find a thing to fit it to, would we willy-nilly harness it sooner or later to something else? A hitherto unnamed phenomenon, discernible but never put into a pithy noun? Say the sunset, "sleeping in its long canned spiral"? I think so. *Brillig* always seems to me to have gone to waste when, surely, the military at least might have picked it up to laud an explosion with— which might be appropriate both denotatively and connotatively. But would we ever, simply because we couldn't get the word out of our heads, plant it on a humpbacked inkwell, a lizard-faced fern or an eye that grows where once a nipple was?

Here we enter slang, and, for extraordinary naming, the realm of the Hopi, which Cortázar did not come upon, and more's the pity— what might he, with his developed sense of the double and the plural, have made of verb forms and change not according to the subject but to the *object?*[1] To toss one thing is *te'va,* to toss several is *ma'spa.* This is the world of objects coming after you with a vengeance, things getting their own back on the word *via* the mind. Again, when you knock on a Hopi door, and are alone, *two* will be invited to enter (if at all); the other is your spirit *Dopplegänger,* who however will not be invited to sit. Either spirits do not sit or they wait outside in perennial polite invigilation. How well Cortázar's own terms—"fictionant, imaginant, delirant, mythopoietic"—match that view at its profoundest. What you think is there is nowhere else.

III

It is instructive to look back at a first novel so straightforward, yet so fraught with anticipations, as *The Winners.* The luxury-lottery evokes Somerset Maugham, but the book includes sustained scenes of psychological revelation, and it remains a compelling parable, as if F. Scott Fitzgerald at his least shallow, least gesture-ridden, had redone *Ship of Fools.* The winners, losers all (in the vaster scale of things), have no idea of their destination. Essentially they are the "ordinary people" evoked in the novel's epigraph from *The Idiot:* "It is impossible to leave them out of fiction altogether." *Is* it? Anyway, the interchapters thickly and suggestively confront the reader with the absolute Sargasso Sea of speculation, providing a plane on which, through some grand-slam feat of holistic bravura, Cortázar does a *Lucas* type of thing more elaborately, less feyly. The amazing maze of the prose is a delight. In a sense, he never got better than this, maybe because in *The Winners* he was writing with an unmitigated abandon he knew the glossy plot counterpointed and, as it were, walled in.

It is okay to make prose Hundertwasser or Villa-Lobos provided you sandwich it in between wads of what ordinary folk want to know about ordinary people. Lucas is both ordinary and extravagant, whereas those who in *The Winners* want their winning-ticket's-worth are as predictably present and as predictable in their ways as some of those in *Hopscotch.* Cortázar learned to push ordinary folk to

---

[1] *Hopscotch?*

extremes, but he also learned not to water eccentrics down for suburban consumption. Middlebrow as he can be, he relishes the exotic butterfly, the mambas in the Métro, the birds of paradise meddling in remote attics with the prose of their diaries, which to them is the very fabric of the universe.

Cortázar, gone with almost Gothic prematurity, abides our question, but the most inimitable thing about him remains his free-associative, centrifugal paean to the world as a juxtaposition, not an osmosis. Jekyll knows this, Hyde does not. Persio knows it too: "If I simultaneously saw everything that the eyes of the race, the four billion eyes of the human race saw, reality would no longer be successive, it would petrify in an absolute vision in which the *I* would disappear, completely annihilated." It's the simultaneity that gets him going: "the polyfaceted, the ten-thousand-eyed." Should he, then, let himself be guided by *"the stars, the compass, cybernetics, chance, principles of logic, occult sciences, the boards in the floor, the state of his gall bladder, sex, character, palpitations and presentiments, Christian theology,* Zend Avesta, *royal jelly, Portuguese railroad timetables, a sonnet,* the Weekly Financier, *the shape of Galo Porrino's chin, a papal bull, the cabala, necromancy,* Bonjour Tristesse, *or simply by adjusting shipboard discipline to the encouraging instructions found in all packages of* Valda's Coughdrops?" Confronted with the inexhaustible, Cortázar's sentences always fall short. The All eludes him, but, through rhythm, cadence, pile-up, epitome and radiant abstract, he limns it until it comes after him and sucks him back in again. It is too easy to be Hyde.

Gabriel García Márquez
1: *One Hundred Years of Solitude*

TO PUT IT ONE WAY: this is a chronicle of the Buendía family, whose successive generations have lived and died in a mythical Latin-American town called Macondo, and its framework is a family tree (printed at the front of the book) which shows that the astounding progenitor José Arcadio Buendía married Ursula Iguarán and thus produced Colonel Aureliano Buendía (who married Remedios Moscote), that José Arcadio married Rebeca, and that—out there on a limb of her own—Amaranta married nobody at all.

But this extraordinary novel obliterates the family tree in a prose jungle of overwhelming magnificence, even to the extent of only infrequently letting the people talk in their own right. I haven't read this Colombian author in his native Spanish, but Gregory Rabassa's translation is a triumph of fluent, gravid momentum, all stylishness and commonsensical virtuosity.

Above all, García Márquez (*via* his translator) feeds the mind's eye non-stop, so much so that you soon begin to feel that never has what we superficially call the surface of life had so many corrugations and configurations, so much bewilderingly impacted detail, or men so many grandiose movements and tics, so many bizarre stances and airs. So I find it odd that the blurb points to "the simplicity, ease, and purity" of García Márquez's writing while a quoted review of his previous book, *No One Writes to the Colonel*, mentions its "serenity" and "understatement." That's like calling a mammoth a moth.

Take García Márquez at his mildest:

> He sold everything, even the tame jaguar that teased passers-by from the courtyard of his house, and he bought an eternal ticket on a train that never stopped traveling. In the postcards that he sent from the way stations he would describe with shouts the instantaneous images that he had seen from the window of his coach, and it was as if he were tearing up and throwing into oblivion some long, evanescent poem: the chimerical Negroes in the cotton fields of Louisiana, the winged horses in the bluegrass of Kentucky, the Greek lovers in the infernal sunsets of Arizona, the girl in the red sweater painting watercolors by a lake in Michigan who waved at him with her brushes, not to say farewell but out of hope, because she did not know that she was watching a train with no return passing by.

It's a prose that's always controlled, but it expresses a vision full of lunges, spurts, mild or maniacal hallucinations, preternatural heavings and bulging gargoyles. Tracing the growth of Macondo—from jungle village into a town served by a railroad and then into ghost town—García Márquez is rather like an infatuated god watching a planet seethe and bubble, settle and cool, and then develop forms of life that finally annihilate themselves. The town, of course, is made of prose, as is the ever-encroaching jungle; and, such is the prose's dense physical immediacy, you have the sense of living along with the Buendías (and the rest), in them, through them, and in spite of them, in all their loves, madnesses and wars, their alliances, compromises, dreams and deaths. The book stages a process in which naming doesn't matter so long as the characters rear up large and rippling with life against the green pressure of nature itself.

In other words, you feel magnified, anthropologically enlarged, by having to fight for air and space and sanity against: José Arcadio Buendía who, against the day when all memories have been lost, hangs a sign on the cow explaining what she's for and thinks about a spinning dictionary with a man lying along its axis; José Arcadio the giant who, with a religious medal around his bison neck, his arms and chest tattooed all over, and a belt twice the width of a horse's cinch, eats sixteen raw eggs on waking; Colonel Aureliano Buendía who organizes thirty-two armed uprisings and loses them all, who has seventeen male children by seventeen different women (and loses *them* all in one night before the eldest reaches thirty-five), who survives fourteen attempts on his life, seventy-three ambushes, one firing squad and a dose of strychnine in his coffee fit to kill a horse, and who finally draws a chalk line round himself so that no one shall come too near; a vast woman called the Elephant who at an eating contest consumes a whole side of veal without breaking a single rule of table manners and thereafter polishes off two pigs, a bunch of bananas and four cases of champagne; José Arcadio Segundo who locks himself up for six months with seventy-two chamberpots; Gaston who waits years for a small biplane from his past to arrive above the treetops; and the Aureliano, last of the line, whose newborn son has a pig's tail extending from his coccyx and, only hours after birth, is dragged away by millions of ants. It's not often that you find a Technicolor tableau of fools which, got up as a family saga, stretches the mind by cramming it and reenacts paradise found and lost as a version of Latin America's own history as well as of (I suspect) one man's love-hate feelings for his own bombinating imagination. Knowing his material inside out, García Márquez writes it large without losing sight of its true size or of the inexorable truths that hold good for all lives everywhere. The verbal Mardi Gras which is his mode of narrating invokes a before and an after (birth and death) which no hyperboles, his or ours, can alter. Like the jungle itself, this novel comes back again and again, fecund, savage and irresistible.

2. *The Autumn of the Patriarch*

ONE WAY OF SETTING the stage for comments on a new novel by García Márquez is to reaffirm that, in the English-speaking countries at any rate, the anti-style rabble is still with us, waiting to pounce, in its crypto-puritan fashion, on any piece of writing it thinks flashy, flamboyant, exhibitionistic, exaggerative, or voluptuous. The same goes for any writing that seems to draw attention to itself as distinct from its 'content' (as if that rancid old dichotomy made any sense in the first place) or ventures, heaven forbid, into areas not "traditional" to the novel, such as science, instead of the ups and downs of little people with mortgages and fireplaces that leak smoke. Anyone who has been called "pretentious" for involving his or her narrative with something as outrageous as the genetic code, will understand what's meant. The novel has certainly come of age, but its readers by and large have not. I have written at length elsewhere about the preposterous situation in which, through some unwritten agreement between pipsqueak readers and the pundits who pronounce *thou shalt nots* to them, thinking has nothing to do with art, certainly not with fiction, and the novelist is somehow duty-bound not to trespass into areas that form the domain of any intelligent mind. "The Milky Way!" exclaimed one novelist of my acquaintance, upon being told I had written a novel making structural and thematic use of it, "I could only write about such a thing if a piece of it fell on my characters while they were in bed." Rather than try to argue I content myself with the thought that whatever fell on them would be part of the Milky Way anyway and couldn't be anything else. Deep down, this attitude (if it has any depth at all) is homocentric or homo-chauvinist, quite failing to see that *homo sapiens* is special because he has occurred in a context that's unthinkably bigger than he is, or ever will be. Even in the third third of the twentieth century, with our robots working capably and at MIT a gene synthesized that is able to function inside a living cell, the parochialists insist that we do no more than rewrite The Forsyte Saga or *The Mill on the Floss* (I speak as one who writes in English, but I imagine Latin American novelists hear an equivalent litany). I can only say that such lack of a sense of wonder increases my own sense of wonder still further and makes me thankful for the novelists I do read.

Once upon a time (as well as under it, and through it, and beyond it, such is García Márquez's elastication of the arbitrary category called 'event'), a dictator had a double who was assassinated.... What is supremely interesting here, and more so than anything in *One Hundred Years of Solitude,* is García Márquez's *modus operandi,* which a merely cursory description would have to call a voluptuous, thick, garish, centripetal weaving and re-weaving of quasi-narrative motifs that figure now as emblems, now as salient samples of all the stuff from which the world is made (at least the Caribbean one), now as earnests of a dominant presence who might be the dictator's wife Leticia, the dictator aping his double, the double aping the dictator's aping the double or the dead head of either or schoolgirls, or even an indeterminate chorus of voices all of whom have something to contribute to the burgeoning mythos of one distended career in honor of which, posthumously, someone created for him the rank of "general of the universe," with ten pips on the epaulette.

Hyperbole is the keynote, of course; even when it isn't on stage it is hovering, off, ready to be exploited. But what lodges in the mind after you finish the book is a technique I'd call horn-of-plenty bravura, not so much hyperboles amassed as Caribbean phenomena keenly registered non-stop, so that what you read is a flood, a crop, a spate, all the more poignant because, as often as not, it's the general's vision of "life without him," by and large going on as if he had never been. It's the copious version of Abram Tertz's austere one in *The Trial Begins,* when a character looks at the chair by his bed and sees that it will survive him, so he begins to loathe it. A great deal of García Márquez's book, therefore, is construable as posthumous present, with the constant implication that, insatiable as it is, the observing eye takes in the merest fraction of available phenomena and has to make do with, in fact, next to nothing.

Such is my own reading of this technique, at any rate. Crammed with data, the book is a bulging elegy for the unseen, the not-experienced. We're told about the perfumed volcano of Martinique, the tuberculosis hospital, the gigantic black in lace blouse who sells bouquets of gardenias to governors' wives on the church steps, the "infernal market" of Paramaribo, the crabs that came from the sea into the toilets and onto the tables of the ice cream parlors, "the solid gold cows on Tanaguarena beach," the rebirth of Dutch tulips in the gasoline drums of Curaçao," the ocean liner that passed through the hotel kitchens of the city center, and much, unthinkably much, more. Isn't, someone asks, the world large? And not just large but *insidious* as well? And "the whole universe of the Antilles" is a mere speck, although unassimilable. The evoked theme is ancient, a fusion of *carpe diem* and Husserl's "More than anything else the being of the world is obvious." ·Not that García Márquez lists things; he does, but he assembles them in such a pell-mell fashion that the movement from one item to the next becomes almost a narrative kinesis in its own right, while the items themselves, far from being mere entries in a stock-book, are epitomes of action: people, animals, plants, waves, clouds, captured in moments of characteristic and definitive doing. The effect is extraordinary, creating a textural narrative to counterpoint (even abolish) the story line that involves an air force, a league of nations, an assassination, and ambassadors Kipling, Palmerston, Maryland and Wilson to a tyrant aged between 107 and 232. Try to figure out what is happening and you end up with a better knowledge of event's context than of event itself. It just isn't that kind of novel. Its point is its precision-studded vagueness. Its content is a mentality, a sensibility. Its power is that of what I think radio technicians call side-band splash, when to receive one thing you must receive another. And that means the novel is all accretions, almost like a language being spoken century after century until, at some point, one asks: *What was Indo-European like? When?* What follows those questions is the work of sheerest hypothesis; such a proto-language must have been there spoken by such and such a people, maybe the Kurgan people around 3,000 B.C. Much the same applies to the plot of this novel: you have to move toward it through what it has generated, and when you get there it has gone, and you are encountering an hypothesis of your own.

So, then, this volcano of Proustian saliences is a demanding book to read, yet only as harvests are hard to swallow down. García Márquez's forte is that he always provides enough material in the next twenty syllables, and always in greater detail than most novelists can muster. Something Keatsian is going on here, in that he not only loads every rift with ore, he also evokes an obsolescent Hyperion trying to figure out why one set of gods has to give way to another. The book is an ode to "the uncountable time of eternity" that always comes to an end, whether we call it autumn or the general's reign. For example, we see this:

> Leticia Nazareno moved aside the herniated testicle to clean him up from the last love-making's dinky-poo, she submerged him in the lustral waters of the pewter bathtub with lion's paws and lathered him with *reuter* soap, scrubbed him with washcloths, and rinsed him off with the water of boiled herbs as they sang in duet ginger gibber and gentleman are all spelled with a gee, she would daub the joints of his legs with cocoa butter to alleviate the rash from his truss, she would put boric acid powder on the moldy star of his asshole and whack his behind like a tender mother for your bad manners with the minister from Holland.

Wrenched thus out of context and flow, it's not as effective as its reinstated version, but notice how the general, at once baby and sexually deformed adult meets the world's substances on a primitive level. In fact he is learning how to read and write at the same time as, in the world outside, the black vomit is thinning out the rural population, except that no one dares tell him. At almost any juncture in the book there are as many different things going on; the compound ghost of the narrator speaks with mouth full. An effect of marmoreal amplitude is what you end with, not least because this is a book of no paragraphs, few sentences, and many, many commas, all toward a cumulative surge of the whole, Beckettian in rhythm yet full of all the stuff that Beckett leaves out, Nabokovian in its appetizing abundance yet quite without his mincing, dandyistic sheen.

It is such a book as, at the lowest level, would teach a fiction student how to write, what to keep on doing; every sentence, every phrase, *has enough* in it. At a much higher level, it's a book which raises the ghost of something truly unnerving: the chance that, after all is said and done, literature has nothing to say, no message, no interpretation, no answer, but only a chance to catalogue what the senses find and cannot do without.

José Donoso
The Obscene Bird of Night

I F THERE IS A PRIZE for epigraphs, José Donoso deserves it for his
quotation from Henry James Sr. writing to his sons William and
Henry Jr. and concluding thus:

"The natural inheritance of everyone who is capable of spiritual
life is an unsubdued forest where the wolf howls and the obscene bird of
night chatters."

Certainly, the forest of this long novel is unsubdued (it could
advantageously have been thinned out) and the feral cacophony within
it is unstinting. Yet there is, embedded as a figure in the luxuriant
ground of the whole, like a witches' Sabbath in a greenhouse, an
outrageously brilliant novella about a Chilean grandee who secretes a
deformed son on the remote family estate and combs the world for
other human sports of nature to keep him company. I know of no more
compelling stretch of prose in modern Latin American fiction. I just
wonder why Donoso added so much to it, muffling and weakening it. If
he felt it gained through contrast, he was surely mistaken; we supply
our own contrasts to anything gruesome, freakish, willful—indeed,
self-styled "normality" needs no boost in its smugness. Not that any
part of this book is badly written (or badly translated); it just has so
exceptional a core that what I suppose is the shielding seems a bit
humdrum and sometimes superfluous. In other words, pages 187
through 328 embody a commanding, dynamic imagination that works
best when dammed up but, given chance to sprawl, sometimes goes to
sleep, elegantly and comfortably, but to sleep all the same.

After Don Jerónimo de Azcoitía has bypassed the urge to kill "the
loathsome, gnarled body writhing on its hump, its mouth a gaping
bestial hole in which palate and nose bared obscene bones and tissues in
an incoherent cluster of reddish traits," he has all vestiges of the outside
world removed from the estate, and the mansion itself he redesigns to
face inward. By the pond he installs a statue of the Huntress Diana
carved with a humpback, acromegalic jaw, and crooked legs, as well as
an Apollo that's an image of what the boy ("Boy") will look like in
adolescence. To this enclosed bear-garden, at a high price, come
dwarves, Miss Dolly (one of the fattest women in the world), girls with

the extremities of penguins and ears like bat wings, hypertrophics of all kinds and, after a while, a quorum of the world's stunted, clamoring for admission. (The only missing ones seem to be the protagonists of certain recent German novels.)

But there's a refinement: Humberto, a frenetic blocked writer who is also a retainer, is appointed to run the whole thing and create a class system at the bottom of which are defective or deficient bakers, milkmen, peons and so forth. Ostensibly the only normal person, he becomes a freaks' freak, Boy's vision of what is monstrous, and from that point of view has to write the history of Boy's world. He stays blocked, though, and no wonder, insulating himself in a staggering variety of mental evasions, from fantasies of cuckoldry and miscegenation to others of deafness, dumbness and immolation. An eminent surgeon, Dr. Azula, arrives, not to beautify Boy but to normalize his metabolism and physique (excluding his legs, since he mustn't wander off the reservation). Things get out of hand, anyway, with Boy bloating himself on meringues, ice cream and candied fruit, and all the time watching his enormous penis grow. Orgies, however, don't suffice to blot out his first memories of the world, and he asks Dr. Asula to cut out that portion of his brain containing his first five days, and then the portion that includes his father.

Underpinning this *tour de force* are two related schemes: voodoo and metaphysics. The first appears through a graphically updated folk tale about a lacerated witch's being floated out to sea lashed to a tree trunk for trying to create *imbunches* (Dr. Moreau-type human mutants with all orifices sewn up and their hair and nails proliferating), the second implicit in the willed heterocosm in which Boy never hears the words *why, when, outside, inside, before, after* and a bird flying over must by prescriptive definition be flying from nowhere to nowhere and have no other existence. The fusion of lurid atavism with the proscription of inferable concepts enriches the book no end, especially the Boy sequence.

There must be a score of other characters, nuns and whores and hair-slicked losers, all garrulous and superstitious, as vivid as expendable. In the long run, only Humberto is Boy's weight: "Humberto had no talent for simplicity. He felt the need to twist normal things around, a kind of compulsion to take revenge and destroy, and he complicated and deformed his original project so much that it's as if he'd lost himself forever in the labyrinth he invented as he went along that was filled with darkness and terrors more real than himself and his other characters, always nebulous, fluctuating, never real human beings, always disguises, actors, dissolving greasepaint... yes, his obsessions and his hatreds were more important than the reality he needed to deny... " Demented ringmaster, he lets his mind swarm until it becomes the zombie of its own black magic.

Augusto Roa Bastos
I The Supreme

A UGUSTO ROA BASTOS is himself a supreme find, maybe the most complex and brilliant, the densest-textured Latin American novelist of all. And *I the Supreme,* his lavish novel—the first of his works to be translated into English—makes me wonder, not just about the familiar and seemingly endless fecundity of Latin American imagination (which shows up in many more than a few fashionable novelists) but about the givens of Latin American life over the past two centuries. What a political demonology these novelists inherit, of ready-made, eccentric, monstrous tyrants such as they might invent only if they didn't otherwise exist. The price of admission to this Satan's gallery, however, has often enough been the right to reside in one's own country. For the past 40 years, for example, Augusto Roa Bastos has been exiled from his native Paraguay and living in France, teaching at the University of Toulouse until 1985.

What is it that makes Latin American tyrants, more than others, so usable—for Latin Americans, of course, such as Alejo Carpentier *(Reasons of State),* Gabriel García Márquez *(The Autumn of the Patriarch),* and Roa Bastos? To my knowledge there is only one good novel in English about even Hitler: Beryl Bainbridge's *Young Adolf,* and that is hardly epic in scope or proportions. We still await a commanding novel about Mussolini (though movie versions have been attempted, with disastrous results.) The Spanish novelist, Juan Goytisolo has written about Spain rather than directly about Franco. And the tinpot tyrants of Central Europe go begging—are they too dull to figure except as remote and inscrutable prefects?

Some streak of inventive madness seems missing in all but the Latin Americans, something that perhaps only tropical Catholicism can breed, something sadistically daffy that might fit well into Suetonius' *Lives of the Caesars,* something that appears a virtual monopoly of countries south of the border, where the mix of superstition and megalomania turns bloodily festive and charmingly ridiculous at the same time. I am thinking of tyrants whose mothers wish their sons had learned to read, tyrants who double as playboys in Paris, tyrants who "sell" part of the ocean, tyrants who, like the one Roa Bastos writes about, suspend all mail service with the outside world.

Perhaps the answer lies in something peculiar to Latin American imagination itself; unobligated to European and North American models, to logic, to what's verifiable, and perhaps the only continental imagination *capable of inventing* the weird things it finds on hand. Perhaps, in order to do such novels as *I the Supreme,* you have to be able to imagine what it *would* have been like to create that ostensibly "supreme" being yourself. Knowing that, you do a kind of reverse obeisance to the facts you then exploit, murmuring *I could have invented you all, all the time.* The confidence generated by that hypothetical triumph of literary creation carries over into the semi-documentary writing feat. Knowing you could have cooked up The Supreme, or Amin, you pillage his image with cogent vigor and so have energy to burn on minor matters, vesting them with unusual intensity.

As here. Put at its barest, *I the Supreme* imagines its way into the head and heart, the life and times, of José Gaspar Rodriguez de Francia (1766–1840), who in 1814 contrived to get himself declared Paraguay's "Supreme Dictator for Life." But that is like calling World War II an upset, an oak tree something invented to cast a shadow, a book a paper tile. Roa Bastos not only reconceives the life of tyrant Francia, but also makes Francia reconceive that reconception. At some point before beginning, Roa Bastos has all the "facts" in order; he knows what happened in history. Then he lets Francia, his own creation by now, play fast and loose with those facts expressionistically, at the same time that he plays fast and loose with Francia himself. Indeed, Roa Bastos tampers not just twice but three times, handing over the facts to

Policarpo Patiño, the tyrant's longtime secretary, who notes down (and alters) Francia's deathbed ponderings about his childhood in a Spanish monastery, his fellow tyrants in other countries, the egotistical sublimity that denied him family, friends, intimates, and the massive meteorite chained to his desk for having turned its tail on its place in the cosmos. (Is this the Paraguayan version of García Márquez's jungle iceberg?)

Between them, Francia and Patiño turn the old romantic notion of the infinite I am into a literary carte blanche, calling into question the beguiling array of smudges we like to call facts. If you read this book very slowly, you see things mutating in front of your eyes, not merely *Rashomon*-style with various conflicting accounts of the same event, but also in a timeless kaleidoscope whose import is: The world as perceived by humans is nothing but arbitrary images that correspond to nothing but themselves. We live amid a welter of glimpses we arrange and interpret in almost helpless subjectivity.

The book is littered with warnings: "I don't write history," Francia says, "I make it. I can remake it as I please, adjusting, stressing, enriching its meaning and truth ... *the order of the facts does not alter the product of the factors* (my italics)." Roa Bastos writes with a cylindrical white-ivory pen containing a "memory lens" that turns everything into metaphor, which of course is what the five-page footnote describing the pen does to the pen itself. This footnote's author is someone called the Compiler, whose task is to join several modes of writing into a readable whole, from an outsized ledger called "the private notebook," some pages of which are burned, torn, illegible, crushed into a ball, worm-eaten, stuck together and petrified, or written in a hand other than Francia's, to a text that Patiño calls his "Perpetual Calendar," which at first sight seems more of an attempt at reliable, official narrative, but isn't. Rumination blurs both ledger and calendar just as incessant, engrossing footnotes blur them, not to mention ukases found nailed to the cathedral door, rough drafts of documents, excerpts from a logbook, bits scrawled at midnight or in The Tutorial Voice, loose leaves, and a list of toys.

The effect of all such textual sea-changing, as you gradually get used to the Compiler's ways, is that of a familiar-looking constellation rising and setting in the wrong order, at the wrong time. Pieced together from a thousand disparate pieces, this *Supremiad* samples all the ways there are of revealing someone through his miscellaneous writings. Indeed, the Compiler doesn't always identify his sources, so there you are, a willing accomplice among the motions of a mind learnedly overheard, and you are obliged, like all the king's horses and all the king's men, to put Humpty Dumpty Francia together again.

What a glory of echoing voices this Paraguayan portmanteau is, more Joycean than Cortázar's *Hopscotch,* every bit as volcanic and visionary as Lezama Lima's *Paradiso* or Osman Lins' *Avalovara.* If the "Boom" of the Latin-American novel's world pre-eminence is over, then this novel begins the Boomerang, arriving 12 years after its publication in Spanish in Argentina, the second volume of Roa Bastos' trilogy. Demanding our time and indulgence, *I the Supreme* is a work of graceful, volumious genius, an Everest of fiction, astoundingly predicated on a simple idea: Shall 19th-century Paraguay be itself or vanish into Argentina or Brazil?

The novel gives you both everything you think would come to mind apropos of that question as well as everything you think would not. Figure and ground merge together amid a blaze of puns, tirades, and dreams. "In Paraguay," we read, "time is so hard-pressed that it slows way down, mixing up the facts, shuffling things about, mis-placing them. . . . You see that over there. No. It no longer exists. It has become an apparition." Strange to relate, this is very much the mood at the end of Samuel Beckett's *Molloy* ("Then I went back into the house and wrote, It is midnight. The rain is beating on the windows. It was not midnight. It was not raining.") When nothing is certain, everything matters, at least if you intend to write a novel; otherwise, nothing matters, and the novel vanishes into a cult of silence.

I the Supreme is vastly helped into our view by the superb translating of Helen Lane, who turns the impossible into child's play—and that into a miraculous feat of lexical magnificence. It is beginning to look as if the novel, instead of coming back to North America and Europe after the Latin America and Europe after the Latin American domination of the past 15 years or so, is to remain in those wizardly hands after all. Of magical realism we have perhaps only so far seen the tip. The iceberg refuses to melt or go away. Roa Bastos has trapped *his* meteor.

Ariel Dorfman
The Last Song of Manuel Sendero

T HE BOOM MAY BE OVER but, south of the border, the sun still
shines on literary innovation. While North America staidly
wonders if Philip Roth in his latest book has at last grown up, if
minimalists have moral reasons for writing as feebly and drably as they
do, and impudent academics try to leach the subjective element from
literary response, Latin America is going ahead, still pushing to new
extremes, imagining itself where and how it wants to be. As if the
quality of life depended wholly on personal invention within the wild
country of the soul. All this means is that Latin America continues to
avail itself of fictional privileges as old as those exercised in the
literature of ancient Araby.

The most recent virtuoso to use these privileges against both the
novel and social norms too is the Chilean, Ariel Dorfman, author of
The Empire's New Clothes, How To Read Donald Duck, and
Windows. To call *The Last Song of Manuel Sendero* a tour de force
would be like calling *Finnegans Wake* an obituary notice. The
conception is brilliant: a revolt of fetuses who, aghast at the political
mayhem in their unnamed country-to-be, refuse to be born. The son of
Manuel Sendero begins the revolt, and the rest follow, putting the
future on hold. No more children, no more victims, no more tyrants, no
more parents, and in the end no more country either.

The trouble with this absolute stance is that like all new and fertile
ideas it is subject to talk. The fetus who says *I will not serve* has
volunteered to become, if not a solipsist, at least an underground
person, an intrauterine scold, aware perhaps but also impotent,
confronting human problems with almost theological obtuseness.
Arguing among themselves by means of a convention we need not
explore, the fetuses begin to think they should get out into the world
after all and do something about the mess.

Needless to say, once out they conform, lose the Wordsworthian
gleam, and at last the son of Manuel Sendero is left alone, in perpetual
gestation, getting on in years, fidgety and horny, yet still immured in
mucosa, sealed away from his heritage. It matters little if the reader
concludes that the birth never happens: the whole world seeps into the

womb, as does the seductive presence of Pamela his beloved. Clearly
one has to revise all notions of the womb as a stamping ground, a
waiting room, and let these almost 500 pages radiate and flow,
surpassing place and time, locus and track, doer and done to. It would
be hard to think of a novel more destructive of old dualisms and
dichotomies than this, always reminding the reader that it's made of
words.

Dorfman joins the big league of rhetorical transcendence that
includes the novel of Carlos Fuentes spoken by the fetus of Christopher
Columbus; Beckett's thirteen *Texts for Nothing,* and Louis MacNeice's
poem, "Prayer before Birth," that begins "I am not yet born; O hear
me." In Mr. Dorfman's case it is not just a matter of asserting that these
things are so and not otherwise, take it or leave it; he weaves a
shimmering flexible web that keeps everything related and responsive
to everything else. Everyday criteria fall away and we are left with a
whole new range of libertine cosmologies fleshed out with the density of
monuments. The commonplace survives only to serve as a backdrop
for the preposterous which, it so happens, begins to undergo
seachanges when examined thousands of years hence by archeologists
to come, whose job is not only to edit the texts they find but also to
figure out the conundrum within Dorman's basic metaphor, almost as
if the folk he's writing about were Mayans or Aztecs.

It's a wonderful idea to fabricate this timeless microcosm and then
have savants of the future try to make sense of it. I am reminded of an
equally startling, prankish novel, by Arno Schmidt: *The Egghead
Republic,* in which an American journalist goes aboard a jet-propelled
island to learn about brain transplants and the freezing of geniuses.
Dorfman's special skill, however, is to make the basic metaphor so
structural he needn't insist on it in the texture. We do not easily forget
that the country he is writing about is a Catholic one and that brand-
new casuistries beset it, not the least of them being: Between
contraception and abortion, where does indefinitely and deliberately
prolonged gestation fit? If wholly fictional, can it have sociological
import at all? And so on. The whole novel is fraught with wonderment,
at its subtlest in the long passages of fetal extravaganza, at its most
explicit in the sprightly dialogues of David and Felipe, displaced
Chileans who argue their way through Mexico and Europe homesick
for what they can't abide. "Chilex," the novel calls their country, so

Chilexians they must be, unlike another character, Carl Barks, an ancient North American innocent invited to tour Chilex by the Chilexian ambassador.

The writing is just as vivid as the characters, sometimes even more so. We read about a baby within "the savory rumba walls of his mother" and "the misty keyhole of the umbilical cord." Manuel Sendero's song "wasn't exactly a sound, but rather an exaltation of a different light, as if the touch of a blind man could make itself heard," certainly something less dynamic than the "soft stampede of antelopes in her underbelly" evoked elsewhere. We look back on "Dragon Pinchot" as if he were as distant in time as Attila the Hun; and, while scholars named Appel-Muus, Ferrowell, Kalki Gregor, and Dubrovsky-Pérez do their best to construe the thirty-thousand-year-old text called the *Dialogue of David and Felipe* (at last sorting out what *a visa* was), we ourselves may linger on such a sustained episode as that of the bakery delivery man riding his bicycle:

> Deaf, irresponsible, carefree, he just kept on pedaling. The wind was with him, the bicycle was a jewel, and he was anxious to put distance between himself and the scent of jeep, bullet grease, and sergeants, to cast off with his little boat laden with bread fresh from the oven and to sail, his shirt unfurled whitely behind him, down the street.

Until the sergeant shoots him, in full view of the newspaper vendor, and the bicycle

> swayed first toward the curb, then incredibly it righted itself and, swinging, its wheels spinning and dancing, its pedals chasing the shadow of the shoes, it was an animal that took its rider in tow in the middle of the desert, as if nothing serious had happened, and the distributor of bread was only resting for a few minutes, his head and chest bent confidently over the handlebars.

The aftermath is all crumbs: "like the shining eyes of the dolls and teddy bears that keep us company in the dark when our parents turn out the light, green and violet crumbs, bouncing and rolling among the soldiers' boots, trying to fall far beyond the reach of the sergeant, who held them up at eye level like someone examining a manuscript."

Mr. Dorfman's slight and sometimes homely distortions do more for his novel than a whole host of force-fed hyperboles would. It isn't so much a novel as a compulsive recitative full of voices who overhear other voices in other wombs. Another way of doing the book would have been to expand the basic conceit, rather than distracting us from it with the more humdrum David and Felipe stuff, but Mr. Dorfman goes his own way with burly finesse, limning a portrait of the tuneful fetus as an Oskar Matzerath betrayed not by Rita Hayworth but by Mother Courage.

Hermann Broch
The Sleepwalkers

HERMANN BROCH considered himself a thinker rather than a novelist. He disdained "mere literature" in favor of a literature that tried to put the world to rights. Addressing himself to "the loss of the Absolute," to "the apocalyptic consequences" in the presence of a "gigantic Machiavellianism" that originated in the mid-19th century, and explaining that "what I don't get into my epistemology, mathematics, etc., turns into the novel-structures," he played into the hands of two groups who—the one because it wishes all literature were philosophy, the other because it wishes all philosophy were literature—have ignored the virtuosity of his technique.

True, the philosophical digressions in the third volume of *The Sleepwalkers,* his monumental and idiosyncratic trilogy of German life, reappear in the second volume of his collected essays, but too much can be made of this. It is enough to recall that Broch was a metapolitical crusader and that his homiletic zeal sometimes made him write badly. At his best, almost in spite of himself, he was a brilliant, innovating craftsman, and it is to this Broch that we should attend, disregarding his self-disparagement and what philosophical or literary purists have made out of it since 1951, when he died in a cold-water apartment in New Haven, still toiling at his *Study of Mass Hysteria.*

First published in 1932, *The Sleepwalkers* won immediate acclaim. Colossal, said critics; Broch is with Proust and Joyce: he has sweep, grandeur, conscience, a meticulous eye, a delving and elegant intelligence, a keen sense of the absurd and—something rare in novels of such documentary weight—a gift for suggesting the ineffable.

The critics were right. Aldous Huxley found *The Sleepwalkers* conducting him to "the very limits of the expressible," limits which Broch, in a later novel, *The Death of Virgil* (1945), transcended altogether through the anecdotal massiveness of the dying poet's imagination. Of these two works by which Broch is best known, *The Sleepwalkers* is easier to get into but harder to stay with. You cannot breeze through it or skip, for Broch gradually disorganizes it to stimulate the disintegration of values that was the prelude to Naziism. By tugging the mind in several directions at once, he makes chaos not only explicit but felt; and gradually he accomplishes for the first time what he always wanted—the "polymath" or "epistemological" novel.

On a less portentous level, *The Sleepwalkers* is an instructive historical document, personifying as it does three crucial years through three major human types. Pasenow, the hapless and inhibited Junker hovering and fumbling amid the mendacious rituals of a doomed class, is *The Romantic* (1888). The petty-bourgeois bookkeeper, Esch, with not even a lie to live by and dominated by the tidy-minded outcast's rage for "justice," is *The Anarchist* (1903). And Hugenau, the complete Machiavellian who destroys them both, is *The Realist* (1918). Taken together, these three volumes have all the ironic, labyrinthine impact of the novel of manners without adding up to such a novel at all. The reason for this is Broch's total willingness to please himself, and the result is a procedural *tour de force* not Joycean, not quite Proustian, but as if Gogol were rewriting Kafka's *Amerika.*

The Muirs' translation beautifully conveys the alternating bite and blather, the faintly muffled vernacular of the ontological sorties, the malicious hyperbole of the page-long portraits and the shameless relish for such simple phenomena as the ammoniac warmth of a cowshed or the texture of whitewood planks. Broch dotes on such particulars. But above all, *The Sleepwalkers* is an omnium-gatherum of humor: humor sly, scabrous, macabre, cerebral, rustic, sick and blasphemous by turns.

It is joyless humor such as only a racing, disabused mind can extort from the discordances of everyday life packed together against the blankness of heaven. The somnambulism Broch diagnoses is akin to the passion of Don Quixote. Men need something stable to live by, even if it is only an illusion or (as with Hugenau) the perfection of moral nullity.

In the first volume, Pasenow, on the brink of sleepwalking backwards into marriage with the gelid Elisabeth, visits "the Kaiser Panorama" of India in which you no sooner see one view than you find it "sliding away while another view comes sliding after it, so that you feel almost cheated." Nothing stays. Life is a flotation of fragments which *The Sleepwalkers* traps and stills until (as Broch requires) you feel sickened, resenting the stillness as much as the flux.

As you read on, lurching and skidding, and certainly after you begin the third volume, you can sense his dissatisfaction with mere sequence. He interpolates irrelevant chapters about a "Salvation Army Lass in Berlin," and most of these in verse; he preaches and theorizes on "The Disintegration of Values." The novel suddenly scatters into a one-man symposium of the divided mind, and Broch finds he can connect nothing with nothing or everything with everything. Even Hugenau, who is a magnificent, haunting conception, ends up "feeling that he was sitting in some pit or dark cavern looking out . . . while life streamed in distant pictures over the dusky firmament." He has found the cruelest version of the Kaiser Panorama.

And ourselves? Can we read Broch on his own terms? The answer must be a guarded affirmative, guarded because the mockery with which he presents Pasenow filters into the rest of the trilogy and contaminates his own earnestness. The satirist cannot afford to resemble his targets. That is the precept by which this thoughtful, indisputably imaginative work has to be judged, and by which it stands or keels over. Now and then Broch's disregard of art impedes the arrival of the thing he cares about most: his message. He becomes the oblivious performer whose doctrinal preoccupations link him to his own Virgil, who pleads that the *Aeneid* be destroyed.

Even so, as Broch unobligingly says at the end of the first volume, "the reader can imagine for himself." Broch's sociological passion is the least interesting aspect of his intense, careful humanity, and I do not think we have to accept his preference for it over the novels. With *The*

Sleepwalkers, The Death of Virgil and his neglected novel on Hitlerism, *The Tempter,* inside us, we can imagine the tracts. No one who has read and admired, say, Mann's *Doctor Faustus* or Günter Grass's *The Tin Drum* should miss his turn at the *Brochenspiel.* All it takes is a disregard for theorizings that is as strong as Broch's own coyness about literary art. Seen plain, he is one of Europe's major novelists: dismaying and enthralling, eloquent and egregious, and wholly attuned to the compulsive disorders of our time.

Hermann Hesse
The Glass Bead Game

W HEN HERMANN HESSE died in 1962 at the age of eighty-five, a *New York Times* obituary dismissed him as "largely unapproachable" for American readers; and it was true that his ruminatively lyrical fictions, some of which are so slow they make someone like Walter Pater seem a charging rhinoceros, ran counter to the realism then dominant. He was awarded the Nobel Prize for Literature in 1946, but in 1949 he was still an unknown in North America. Time unitalicized, however, has made amends: Hesse's *Steppenwolf* is one of the few modern European novels which a teacher can count on his students' having read (sex, drugs and jazz sent up with an irony they tend to miss); some of them even know such solemn dollops as *Demian* and *Siddartha* (which offer, respectively, pacific dropping-out and a mystifying Buddhist mysticism); and now a new translation of Hesse's last major work, available since 1949 as *Magister Ludi,* with Hesse's original title restored and a useful introductory essay by Theodore Ziolkowski. "Sublime" was Thomas Mann's opinion of the book, but discerning readers will find ironies and jokes both on and beneath the surface. For, essentially, *The Glass Bead Game* is a rebuke aimed at the aloofness and the solemnities of Intellect, and that includes all earnest readers of Hesse's other novels.

What worries me is that Hesse's ironies and jokes are as solemn as other men's solemnities. Knowing what his fun is for, he tailors it and very nearly choreographs it, so there are few irresponsible-seeming spurts of wit, few Dickensian detonations of gratuitous fatuity. The book's main plea—for unsecluded imagination to keep our minds receptive and fresh and flexible—I find most congenial: Hesse says this as well as anybody except perhaps Wallace Stevens, whose view of imagination (as the violence from within that opposes the violence from without) he closely approaches. The glass bead game is an imaginative, although insufficiently dynamic, metaphor for imagination itself, which Coleridge called the "esemplastic" power (i.e. all-unifying) and Hesse saw as building "the *Unio Mystica* of all separate members of the *Universitas Litterarum.*" Played in Castalia, an unlocated spiritual province named after the Parnassian spring sacred to the Muses, the Game is a strict mental flexing that brings together all the virtues of all the ages, winnowing Culture and Sweetness and Light from Barbarism and Anarchy and Dogma. All very well, as if Matthew Arnold and Irving Babbitt and Jakob Burckhardt—any synod of culture-mandarins—were to found a Chase-Manhattan of the Spirit; but not so good really, as Hesse found, as getting it altogether critically without retreating to a Castalia at all. The most human pastoral is that which dung quickens. In the avid joiner find the fanatic in embryo.

Initially, Hesse intended this novel to express his idea of "reincarnation as a mode of expression for stability in the midst of flux" through "a man who experiences in a series of rebirths the grand epochs in the history of mankind." It sounds a fascinating idea, this private-eyeing of an unprophetic and un-nostalgic epic revenant; but in the event Hesse shifted his hero, Joseph Knecht, into twenty-fifth-century Castalia for most of the novel and relegated his first three incarnations—in prehistory, in the Golden Age of India, in the early days of the Christian church—to an appendix to stand alongside some tart poems as samples of young Knecht's prentice-work. A pity, because *The Glass Bead Game* as we now have it is suety and monotonous, whereas Joseph Knecht cantering through the ages might have set up contrasts strong enough to survive the numbing touch of Hesse at his heaviest.

What we do have is an account of how Knecht, whom Hesse partners with the erratically brilliant Tegularius (Nietzsche, it seems) and Tegularius's spiritual opponent Father Jacobus (Jakob Burckhardt, it seems), rises to become Master of the Castalian Game but finally defects, exchanging ivory tower for the common ground on which most folk stand (and, in fact, suffering accidental death while swimming). The point—the active life as superior to the pensive one— is only just worth making, even in ironic terms, and certainly not on behalf of an everyday world of the senses (of which Hesse was only dimly aware) against inveterate habits of intense intellectuality (which give the lie to Knecht's defection). Knecht moving out into the vulgar world is rather less dramatic than a monk sending out for a newspaper.

The whole novel is too diagrammatic, too aloof in manner for its matter to matter much (a visit to a slum, a mental home or a cancer ward is more convincing). He who collects enough chamberpots may one day find the Holy Grail, which somehow makes better sense than collecting Grails in the hope of finding a chamberpot. Desperate men will reverence chamberpots or relieve themselves into Grails, as Hesse knew, he being above all an expert on the degrees of self-deception involved in surviving comfortably from day to day. Platitudes we all need, but not as largely or as laboriously writ as this elongated parable, pre-wrapped in a winding-sheet of courtly tedium.

Günter Grass
Dog Years

O F ALL THE THINGS Günter Grass has taught us in his ribald, voluminous homily, the one that sticks—sticks perhaps in the throats of hopeful liberals who envision the Great Society—is that nihilism can be virtuous and books expressing it can be fat. Grass has still not got over the guilt and the awfulness, the turpitude and the tantrum. He is still in deep shock and still, with obsessed acerbity, going over the same ground with the same thoughts in mind, and especially the thought that the German tragedy was the result of each individual's lack of faith in his fellows' readiness to support him in a decent refusal. Grass's is not the *non serviam* of Stephen Dedalus; it is, rather, the bleakest sequel yet to Thomas Mann's "I do not have much faith in faith, nor do I believe very much in faith, but far more in a goodness capable of existing without faith and which may even be the direct product of doubt."

This much became clear with *The Tin Drum*. And here, boldly woven into another iconoclastic tapestry, is the identical theme, writ shambling large again and counterpointed by the presence of dogs, scarecrows and the Vistula River at Danzig. Brawny Walter Matern is a muddled Slavic German, both well meaning and despicable, self-hating and amoral. As a Nazi he helps beat up his maladroit, half-Jewish friend, Eddi Amsel, the scarecrow-maker, who (according to the minor deviltry of boys' rituals) was once his blood brother whom he taught to play a fair game of *schlagball;* after the war Amsel, mysteriously transformed from fat boy into Brauxel, the thin mine owner, tries to talk Matern out of the self-loathing into which he lapses. *Dog Years* is a work of dialectic, dialogue and parallels, whereas *The Tin Drum* is one of heroic monomania.

And yet, once the Matern-Amsel friendship has settled down into what is visibly the book's theme, Grass, who has his own perverse way of doing things, begins with beautiful indirection to blur it. Quite early he explains that "it will be necessary to subject the Matern-Amsel friendship to many more trials," and he really puts the pair of them through it. But the main trial they undergo is that of his method, and this has two effects. First, they become less characters than magnificently animated motifs in a swarming, knobbly host of images. And, second, although they grow into men, they seem arrested in boyhood. So what we get is history moving forward from the twenties while Matern and Amsel, alternately meek and infernal Tweedledum and Tweedledee, look back to the ham-fisted autos-da-fé which have not only formed them irrevocably but supply Grass with the most poignant, most farcical version of his anti-Nazi theme.

Setting out to de-demonize the Nazi cult, Grass chooses to dwarf it: not, as in *The Tin Drum,* by creating a monster of halted development (which is the arithmetical or plane way of doing it) but by creating two complementary characters whose growth into adulthood turns them only into enlarged boys adrift in a copiously noted landscape. This, I take it, is the algebraic or spherical way of handling the theme; and *Dog Years* is much the more deliberate, more controlled of the two novels. *The Tin Drum* is like improvised jazz, whereas *Dog Years,* for all its cavorting ribaldries and alluvial excursions, is a boldly orchestrated microcosm, amazing in its stylistic variety and yet indefatigably *ad rem.*

Part One not only deals with Matern and Amsel as boys but also records the beginnings of Harras the dog, who sires Prinz, the *Führer's* favorite pet. See how Grass puts it, naming the hound who will come from behind and surpass not only his contemporaries, human and canine, but even Amsel's super-scarecrow, "Potrimpos, the forever laughing youth with the ear of wheat between his teeth." "But," we learn, "Amsel never designed a scarecrow in the image of a dog.... All the scarecrows in his diary, except for the one with the milk-drinking eels and the other—half grandmother, half three-headed willow—are likenesses of men or gods." In this first part (to borrow Grass's own words) "elements of fantasy mingle with immemorial folk ways; delightful figures, but gruesome ones as well, may be standing in surging fields and in gardens blessed with abundance." The three strands of Matern-Amsel, dogs and Vistula—now seen with a dreaming omniscience, now with shocked incomprehension—conduct us firmly into a humdrum-awful, festively demented world that Grass has made his own. Sometimes the treatment is dead pan, with truckfuls of raw data dumped into the stanzalike paragraphs to thicken the texture or ballast the extravaganza. Sometimes the verbal sounds go running on while the sense—the original drift—remains intact. Sometimes Grass shuffles his feet, but usually in preliminary for a raucous shout; and sometimes the personages fall into slow motion, like Mardi Gras grotesques or, in Grass's phrase, "tin soldiers against magnifying glass." He doesn't waste a rhetorical trick.

Yet it is a sanely purposeful pandemonium he makes, and his narrative survives its garish, baroque burden of data. It survives what amounts to a caustic ecology of his native region, an ecology alive and unnerving with eels that suck the cows' teats; a miller who does a worm-and-beetle census of his flour by auscultating the sacks; headless knights and nuns; the scarecrow called the Great Cuckoo Bird which induces goiter, swivel-eye or miscarriage; Grandma Matern buried with her hairpins still in place; young Walter belting frogs with his *schlagball* bat; and a whole cacophony of tough chatter by tiny guys who have arrived here by way of *Cat and Mouse*.

If *Dog Years* stopped even at page 113, where the first part ends, it would be a dazzling feat of imaginative audacity. Somehow the facts about boyhood float apart and drift lazily sideways like exhaust in the sky until, suddenly, you have the feeling that Grass has managed a total image almost without trying for one. Something happens which gives extra life to, draws extra life from, every particle of the material read to that point. It's nothing to do with epiphany. It's a total articulation of the human maxima and minima, adapted from Danziger folklore and travestied by Amsel's scarecrows. I don't think I have read any other postwar novel in which this diligent sense of life's interrelatedness and unity has been set down in such iron sentences or, through patient assembly of the fruits of exact examination, made so stark. Grass has managed this—and it cannot have been easy for him—by foregoing some of the gratuitous fun which enlivens but sometimes muffles *The Tin Drum*. This first part is incomparably well done, especially for the sense it gives of humanity blocked when, say, the miller listens to his sacks or Amsel eats newts' tails and then vomits them up (having passed the test). The actions bear on everyone and everything, are endlessly relatable, and gather to themselves layer on layer of significance without ever becoming meaningful. Grass shows us a region every bit as vivid, as tactile, as Yoknapatawpha. County or Dylan Thomas's Wales, and reveals the inhabitants stretching after something that isn't merely human, rural or manufactured. They end up with folklore pushed to its limits, but blocked off from God (or whatever), with Amsel's scarecrows uninformative and stillborn against the dunes and the same uncaring Vistula. All overtures to mystery end by being answered by men. So it is safer, perhaps, to order one's life by the shifts at the mine or the *schlagball* periods in school. And all the time the dogs go about their business, couple and yelp, unscared by scarecrows and little heeded.

The narration of Part Two falls into the hands of the ingenious creep, Harry Liebenau, a younger member of the Amsel-Matern generation, and assumes the form of "Love Letters" to his cousin, Tulla (fresh from *Cat and Mouse*). When Tulla was born, Harras was 14 months old. Grass whips things along, portraying the middle dog years with ferocious honesty but somehow letting his characters become mere representatives. Once the coruscating documentation of boyhood and youth is over, things fall a bit flat. It's not that people become less imaginative as they get older, but that Grass treats his characters in much the same way as Mann treats Hans Castorp: with didactic intent so strong as occasionally to deprive him of his own already established identity. It is as if Grass' heart looks back while his mind dutifully gets

on with the painful job, alertly on the trail of Amsel (now manufac-
turing scarecrows that parody goose-stepping S.A. men, of whom
Matern is one), the war, and Prinz, who deserts Hitler. The effect is a
radiant, bony knottiness, but weakened because the calamities seem to
be happening to people almost as arrested as Oskar Matzerath in *The
Tin Drum*. True, Grass may want just that effect of the unspeakable
marionette, but surely he could have secured it by giving us the
contorted psychology of people sacrificing themselves to the stench of
Zeitgeist (I am thinking of how Broch does this in *The Sleepwalkers*).

As it is, the cruelty and turpitude of the boyhood games carry over
into the second part only to animate a brilliant diagram in which Amsel
and Matern, instead of festering inwardly, fade somewhat and begin to
add up to a compound ghost. Grass triggers everything into colliding,
dissonant activity which overpowers even the two girls, vicious Tulla
and gentle Jenny. The materiality of farce takes over and the
psychological point partly vanishes under a landslide of reportorial
debris. So you feel sorry for the characters in the way you feel sorry for
the sorcerer's apprentice or for children whose pets have got out of
hand, and not (as I think Grass wants) sorry for adults who are fellow
traveling with Peter Pan. One paragraph beginning: "Who does not
rub his eyes when he looks on at transmutations, but is unable to
believe either his eyes or the snow miracle?" puts it exactly. I was
rubbing my eyes all through the first part, such were the transmutations. But the second part is like Tussaud or Disney; you marvel at the
fecundity of the artifice but have no invitation to the interior. If this is
the way the world almost ended, then where are the whimpers of
conscience, the bangs of anguish on the brainpan? This central part
should have been *penseroso* as well as *scherzando*. Then the curious
round-and-round effect which it creates, with themes and images—
rats, bone piles at the camps, raspberry drops, Tulla's miscarriage from
jumping off a moving streetcar, Jenny's knitting, Heidegger's jargon,
kennels and black shepherds—convecting like rice in boiling water,
would have seemed less smart, less a feat of nothing but virtuosity.

Having blamed Grass I unblame him. I have to. Look what
happens when German tries to do interpretive psychology: *Doctor
Faustus, Steppenwolf, On the Marble Cliffs, The Man Without
Qualities*. This way is better. It is, in both senses, a tattoo, both ornate
and percussive. Grass is right to reduce to bestial puppetry the

antihuman antics of a whole generation. I think it might be imprudent fictional technique, but it is a reduction with both poetic and historical justification. One catastrophe-quiet, shame-laden sentence almost at the end of Part Two sets things to rights and reminds us of some of the reasons: "All are eager to start out fresh with living, saving, letter writing, in church pews, at pianos, in card files and homes of their own." The rest is yelps from the machine of the economic miracle.

"Materniads"—scabrous semi-philippics—compose the third part. Matern, released from an English anti-Fascist camp, inherits Prinz whom he first thinks of calling "Shit" but finally names Pluto (shades of Cerberus). He embarks on a tour of revenge which involves infecting the wives and daughters of his former comrades in the S.A. with venereal disease. While he does so the novel, like Matern and his lewd hosts, Sawatzki and his Inge, sleeping three to one bed, develops a "yearning for intricate harmony: so many arms and legs!" But things do come together, as when Matern and Sawatzki accidentally touch fingers while exploring Ingepussy from different sides of the common bed. One touch of Matern's clap makes the whole nation kin, and not until his vengeance is complete does he cure himself by urinating into an electric socket. He swyves on, however, unable to resist the hungry Inges, and five times more has to resort to electricity to rid himself of "his lordship's cold."

He begins to fail while, all over Germany, the meal worms (those born survivors) take over and the novel becomes a bombinating parody of the *Wirtschaftswunder* through which, on their six legs, Matern and Pluto stumble vengefully, clad in patches of Joycean prose. A radio script partly in verse falls into the narrative like a curbstone, and Matern ends up visiting the infernal region of Brauxel's mine, where countless mechanical scarecrows called rage engines now await the invasion order from above. As Brauxel observes, "A cardinal emotion that promotes the grinding of teeth can't be a passing fad." *Sic transit* Eddi Amsel.

No two ways about it: the book is a marvel, no matter how cantankerous, willful, filthy, tedious, brutal, nihilistic, long-winded, importunate, self-conscious or Germany-obsessed you find it. If execution can be lyrical, then *Dog Years* is that. But the hangman is far from affable and, it is worth pointing out, this is the second time he has formally executed this body. Never has a dunghill been reported with such a consummate sense of its pageantry or the violence of racism smacked dead with so savage a hand. Matern and Amsel are both to blame, both to be felt with, neither to be excused. To be human is not to be excused, but only to make excuses when confronted with a censor as drastic as this.

Heinrich Böll
Group Portrait with Lady

R EALITY," ACCORDING TO Heinrich Böll, "is a task ... It requires our active, not our passive attention. What is real is fantastic." Of course, and Böll dutifully addressed himself since the end of World War II to the configurations of German society, always subordinating extravagance of imagination to accuracy of report. A soldier returns by train from furlough to the Eastern front in 1943. A group of German soldiers retreats homeward from the Balkans. These are the preliminaries, after which we have a telephone-operator husband deciding to live apart from his family, followed by two adolescent boys, from contrasting backgrounds but alike in lacking a father, who study the emotional starvation of their mothers. Next, a young man who repairs washing machines loses his mediocre materialism when he falls in love. In *Billiards at Half-Past Nine* (1959), three generations of a German family of architects embody phases of an in-depth historical panorama. *The Clown* (1963) is a portrait of indignation, with the main character reviewing his past while telephoning various friends and acquaintances. At odds with society the narrator of *Absent Without Leave* (1964) transfers his wholesale coffee business to his son-in-law and devotes himself to his memoirs, looking back in semi-euphoric torpor.

Such is Böll's gist. A humane man writing about men whose main concerns have been, are, or will be home and family and ethics and tradition, he consolidated almost to perfection a doctrine of neighborliness, hunting in commonplace places for a human probity without which daily life becomes an automatic charade.

Communicating thus, Böll communed, and urging he no doubt

persuaded, more or less on the same plane as Ignazio Silone once appealed for the dignities of "companionship," which is grounded in the humble ritual of taking bread together: *cum paanii.* He belongs with Saul Bellow, except he couldn't have written *Henderson the Rain King,* and with George Gissing, except he's more ironic and seemingly less helpless.

So far so good. Hum's Tin Drum, he is almost too good—virtuous and well-meaning, that is—to be true to the kaleidoscopic extraordinariness of the times. Not only does he not concern himself with such impersonal marvels as the snowflake or any given amino acid, or hummingbirds or the moon, thus reducing his context to one of *hm* rather than of awestruck wonder; he's pretty short on autonomous imagining—play, daub, doodle, idol, cartoon, supreme fictions— maybe because this eidetic side of things belongs to his Catholicism and has already been taken care of. As it is, he has more in common with E. M. Forster than with Günter Grass, and almost nothing but the trains motif with his unjustly neglected contemporary Arno Schmidt. Böll is a weevil, a grayish and long-snouted beetle, to Beckett's shamming opossum, Borges's peacock, Nabokov's bookworm.

Group Portrait With Lady is that, but almost as much is Lady With Group Portrait, or Portrait of Group Lady, so vivid and dominant is Leni Pfeiffer, and so various that she seems not one woman but half humankind's epitome. The novel opens, with ostentatious and ironic helpfulness, by describing her: "forty-eight, German: she is five foot six inches tall, weighs 133 pounds (in indoor clothing), i.e., only twelve to fourteen ounces below standard weight; her eyes are iridescent dark blue and black . . . " The further Böll goes, the more he reveals; the more he reveals, the more she becomes a multifaceted Ur- mother, a female Figaro trapped in linear time, a Tess of the Über- Alles, unwilling to talk about herself and in quest of whose story a fictitious author, who throughout dubs himself "Au," plods from person to person like Father Brown spot-checking the Almanac de Gotha, the amassed West German telephone directories and *The Rise and Fall of the Third Reich.* The leg-work is only a come-on for the nudging, shuffling patience required to fit together the pieces of the Leni Pfeiffer puzzle. It's almost as if Böll had taken a hint from Uwe Johnson's *Speculations About Jakob,* about a signalman who is killed and about whom numerous people speculate in parochial obliquities.

Leni is at least alive, and her taciturn presence gives the novel a structural slyness. Will she, won't she, speak out? No indeed, otherwise Au. couldn't get so vexed and so grubby, or be able to mount inquisitiveness into a mnemonic possession which in the long run leaves him better informed but none the wiser. Leni still "sees" the Madonna on TV, the only clarification of that habit being that the Madonna is herself, "appearing...because of some still unexplained reflections." And who finds that out? Au.'s life has not stood still during this protracted investigation; his informant is a redheaded nun he's converted from convent to the joys of extramural living.

Paraphrase fails before such a labyrinthine quest, and even the list of characters at the front isn't much help. Böll's swarm includes eight Pfeiffers, six nuns, four other family groups, as well as 12 "other informants" and seven "other characters." Some come into immediate focus and remain in the mind as idle roomers, even when Böll has shelved them; whereas others never in focus obtrude fuzzily and might easily have been treated eclectically and through allusion: a splinter where a wedge is, a wedge for a monolith. But this isn't Böll's way, and such is the penalty of his merits. For him, character is almost all, and his tribute to Dickens in an early essay tips us off.

It's Leni, diligently recovered, who commands the memory. Almost like Beckett's Watt, she seems never to have understood the world (who ever does?), and to life's puzzle she adds her own enigma variations. Her sex life has been minimal, but she gets her kicks from being a breakfast-roll fetishist and plasters the walls of her apartment with color photographs of human organs. Her major enterprise is to paint "a faithful picture of a cross-section of one layer of the retina" using a child's paint box: six million cones and 100 million-rods (nice analogue for the pointillism of the novel itself).

As for Au., the encyclopedia-addict and expense account fanatic, he's refreshingly square, haunted by a caricature of himself, of, say, losing all his buttons while smoking too much at the Clay-Frazier fight. His prim civilities frame the swarming group which, more than a photograph, is a mosaic of ants on the move. With so many characters, and with such an appetite for Jonsonian humors, the telling *has* to be conventional, so the plethora can transcend it.

Uwe Johnson
Anniversaries

A FTER GROWING UP in East Germany, where he wrote his first novel, *Speculations about Jakob* (1959), which the authorities prevented from being published, Uwe Johnson shifted to West Berlin, but there refused to don the mantle of the classic defector. Then came a two-year stint in New York City, where he wrote part of *Anniversaries.*

Clearly, Johnson is his own man, even to the extent of not worrying overmuch about national membership and he joins those other expatriate writers—Beckett, Nabokov, Borges, Jakov Lind, Cortázar—who have focused their material the better by leaving it behind or have discovered new material of more ecumenical clout. If Johnson has an abiding theme, it is deracination; and if he has a typical mental movement it is that of emigrating in the mind—as he did in West Berlin when, after reading Faulkner (banned in the East), he Yoknapatawpha-ed *Speculations,* entirely recasting it. Overland, or in the mind, he is a novelist of transits, borders, hinterlands, spatial simultaneities, and, above all, history lodged in the head like contraband.

Yet he is far from being a novelist of fragments, a rootless experimentalist, as *Anniversaries* proves at some length. He does permit himself a certain scrambling of narrative procedure—unexplained tilts from voice to voice, or from one time to another, or from *I* to *we,* even from a plural-feeling *I* to a singular-feeling *we*—but these are far from innovational, and he emerges increasingly as an orthodox novelist occasionally given to mystification and quaint chronic overlap, as if Mann's *Buddenbrooks* were being ghostwritten by the Faulkner of, say, *Requiem for a Nun.*

This new novel, the first of a two-volume English translation of Johnson's own abridgement of the four-volume German original, retrieves from *Speculations* a character named Gesine Cresspahl who, in her time, has helped NATO and the CIA. A defector from the East, she finally comes to New York (West 96th Street) with 10-year-old Marie, her daughter by the Jakob about whom all the speculations were (he was a signalman killed as he crossed the tracks one foggy morning in 1956). Tape-recording a diary, Gesine shuttles between

Jerichow, a small German town, and her job in a New York bank. As the diary furls and unfurls, Jerichow becomes a magnified image of Nazism on the rise, and New York an appendage to that prime synecdoche, its *Times,* a paper which Gesine not only reads compulsively but comes to regard as a crotchety, right-minded relative she calls "Auntie" (as some British call the BBC).

Thus, while Gesine's mind roams back on tape, or breaks off to respond to Marie's precocious questions, the front-page news (mainly Vietnam—the war there, the protests at home) piles up on the novel's doorstop. Point finds counterpoint. Or is meant to. The Great Society, though crass and defiled, wasn't the Germany of the 1930s, and Gesine takes comfort. But New York City isn't America either, and the view from, say, Oxford, Miss. might have been more telling. As it is, Johnson hymns a city that, in theory, is no man's enemy, and pays a tribute which, keen-eyed and copious as it is, blurs and impedes the novel's point.

This wouldn't matter so much if Gesine came through as a woman vitally interested in herself. She's not; rather she's an abstraction, a device, a reportorial revenant, whose virtue seems impersonal and whose presence is faint. In consequence, she exists as much on the level of historical overview as on that of fictional events, and one ends up wondering why, since this is less a novel than an evocative montage, the thematic contrast is so lopsided: representative small German town, unrepresentative American city. It's a matter of scale and congruity that wouldn't matter if her story sucked us in as what happened to a person; a Moll Flanders, a Carrie, a Nancy Mannigoe.

In other words, in reading his dense, allusive, mighty intelligent book, I felt my head much exercised but my pulses moved only by the pulsations of history. Johnson's grave plethora is that of a pensive, moral, intact man who prefers speculation to the known and is given to longwinded trance. Nothing wrong with any of that; but, as several speculative novelists have shown (among them Claude Simon and Cortázar), the multiple choices in the enigma-novel need to be at least twice as vivid, as garish even, as the established facts in the novel that gives what's-known-for-sure. It's odd that Johnson, in the mold of the chronicle-novel, has created a long work in which what happened next seems almost irrelevant to the heroine's life. She's a fine mirror, even as a distorting one, but for insistent, integrated presence she doesn't compare with the woman in Böll's equally complex *Group Portrait with Lady.*

Arno Schmidt
The Egghead Republic
and *Evening Edged in Gold*

T HE CLOWN PRINCE of contemporary German fiction, Arno Schmidt, died in 1979, the author of some twenty novels, a satirist who first wrote rather straight, pessimistic, intensely visual allegories of post-Nazi society, with excursions into the time of Alexander the Great and A.D. 541, and then soared into tight, allusive wordplay that translates uncommonly well into English. Although a couple of his other untranslated novels might have been a more prudent introduction to his work, what we are now offered takes us right into Schmidt at his feistiest, his most ingenious, and his most captivating.

Much of *The Egghead Republic* (1957) is sheer, complex fun, the book's time being the year 2008, when an American journalist, Winer, visits two secret regions of the globe: an Arizona desert reserve, complete with mutants and experimental hybrids (centaurs, for example, and spiders with human heads), and an island afloat in the Pacific which serves as a ghetto for intellectuals. In Arizona the flippant Winer, having fun while compiling his report, learns the arts of love from Thalia, a centauress with an ashblond mane who is "24 Gowchromms" old and who gives him supplementary tuition in the aphrodisiac uses of stinging nettles. On the jet-propelled island he learns about brain transplants and the art of freezing geniuses, neither of which gives him half the kick of the centauress' huge tongue in his mouth ("tasted good and warm; of grass-seeds") or watching centaur calves crack eggs with their hooves.

The reader may sigh for a less convulsive, less telegraphic prose style (supposedly Winer's fault of course), and fewer entities so close to cartoon, as well as wishing the egghead island weren't routinely polarized between East and West; but there is enough snazzy stuff to keep you cheerful as you flash forward from paragraph to paragraph (each with its topic sentence or phrase in eye-catching italics), assimilating puns ("moronsters," "inconsolubly," "I wasn't Her Cules after all") while overhearing Winer report on centaur soccer, a boy in love with a butterfly, the island's being made from 123,000 steel chambers riveted together, novels written by a committee called "Cadre 8," the "brain-sized dollop" of mashed potato you get in the greasy spoon near the transplant clinic, and, the quaintest epiphany of all: "If a strapping 30-year-old had her brain transplanted into a young man she could spend one or two nights with her own other-brained body."

Perhaps the sprightliest (and least overtly exploited) jape is that Winer's ostensible report, done in 21st-century American, has been punitively translated by the authorities into German, by then a dead language, from which we now have a retranslation back into 21st-century American, based on the text known as "Specimen No. 5 (Valparaiso)." If the tenses bother you, tempting you to recast "has been" into "will have been," they should; this is a prophetic novel, spawned by insecurity and especially by nightmares of impermanence, such as the one in which 2008 and 2009 never come, except in fiction.

Whereas *The Egghead Republic* is a textual freak, a forward anachronism, *Evening Edged in Gold* dramatizes the fluid phase in a text's history known as the Final Draft. Weighing 10 pounds, measuring 17 inches by 13, and hard to manage manually unless you have a piano to rest it on, *Evening* takes the form of a reproduced typescript, thus reminding you that it might never have been published at all (and in one sense it hasn't, not at a price beyond the pockets of most booklovers). Presumably any paperback edition would also have to have the same format: wide, wide lines, which excitingly lead the eye much farther to the right than usual, pages divided into two or three columns to convey a slewed simultaneity and pose the mesmerizing choice of which column to tackle first, other pages designed to be read from bottom to top, while still others sport important or trivial information set off in the margins or in boxes. Deletions, maps, postage stamps, clippings from magazines, diagrams, quotations, doodles and asides drag at the eye all over the place, signs not of a book gone wrong but of a book going fabulously well, a book which reveals the author's mind in the fine frenzy of cooking things up, attempting different versions of one phrase, and most of all auditing a tumult of language which is the backdrop against which the novel's compound voice will finally come clear.

Such is the narcissistic side of an engrossing superbook, superbly and creatively translated, whose title page says, disarmingly enough, "Materials gathered: 1972–75," as if the whole thing were an idiosyncratic album of folk songs, nursery rhymes, graffiti, or curses: unique but unintruded into. In a sense that's true of this last book, in which Schmidt voluptuously spreads himself over a continuum of voices heard and overheard, misheard and unheard of, awash with lubricious puns and preposterous echoes that bring back all the dead folk behind the words in the dictionary. Fifty-five scenes in 20 acts over three consecutive days, it transforms humdrum material into golden garrulity. A couple of girls go to swim in a pond early in October 1974, and a couple of days later take a shower together, but are you ready for this?

"The swimming-hole by Klappendorf, a bawling of color on green (:'You are ev'rything to me, 'cause I love you 'xclusiv'lee: Micae-la-a-a'), in the afternoon lite. Very warm for the 1st of October (24°!): little white clouds, pasturing themselves, ('The aviong's leaving trayls' Ann'Ev' remarkt; but Martina: 'Aw c'mon. The wind's doing 0.03; kdn't thro a bee from a buttercup.')"

Or this, in the shower, where "2 smooth creatures" are "saponifizing each other" and Ann'Ev' says "Do y sents it, too, when the forbidden wishes a men gather about you! What does your mutsch feel & say?; (tss; ought t be briter lite-bulbs in here. . . . "

Other prosaic material—oldsters taking breakfast on the terrace, dreaming of infinity, gathering elderberries, digging for treasure—yield Joycean fugues no less rich, and, once your eye has settled down to Schmidt's typographical ways, no less comprehensible. True, a few of the dozen or so characters are offbeat to begin with, one being a double amputee from the thigh down, another an 11-year-old already a widow several times over, but the rest are average sensual creatures—very sensual indeed during one three-columned sequence, really a three-ring sexual circus, in which the middle column, spoken to each other by Martina and Ann'Ev', turns into high voyeuristic lyricism whipped up by the bawdiness that flanks it. It's as if the two girls have read the words on either side of them.

What is so wonderful and welcome in this masterwork is how the voices, the narrator-cum-stage-director's among them, transcend themselves nonstop; what the reader hears in the mind's ear, never mind from whom, is the human heart of all the ages lustily or dreamily talking loneliness and boredom to a standstill. Or, contrariwise, fixating on bodily pleasure, in which this book abounds, until the mind almost (but never quite) gives up.

Christa Wolf
The Quest for Christa T.

INTENSELY FELT without gushing, and economical without being skimpy, *The Quest for Christa T.* is the sort of novel not often written in English. More than that, it's essentially German in its fusion of cerebral insistence with a gunmetal broodingness, and its reticences seem not so much those of someone practicing on literary grounds the tact of omission as of someone practiced in finding obliquities that might defeat the censor—Christa Wolf lives in East Germany. I can think of only one novel (written in English) that it resembles, and that is William Golding's *Free Fall,* a novel loaded with enigmas and incertitudes and suffused with muted hosannas the reader just has to accept. The difference is that in *Free Fall* Sammy Mountjoy reviews his own past whereas, in *The Quest,* the narrator explores the life of her friend, Christa T., who died at thirty-five, through diaries, letters, and even her university thesis on Theodor Storm. In the one instance, Sammy Mountjoy feels too close to himself, whereas Christa Wolf's narrator feels at too great a remove. The one is Narcissus almost failing to discover (and therefore interpret) himself, the other is the intimate detective discovering herself in the act of looking for someone else.

"The quest for her: in the thought of her," Wolf begins, and adds "And of *the attempt to be oneself.*" It's a highly abstract opening, but the problem is clear: the Christa T. of the documents isn't the one whom the narrator remembers, and the counterpoint between these two *personae* beautifully sustains itself throughout, each threatening to cancel the other until, in the moving last section, the body of Christa T. goes into the Mecklenberg soil and they somehow float free and complement each other, united in the very consciousness that has been writing the book. In other words, the narrator's dialectic yields an eventual synthesis nicely pitched between the notion that no-one knows anyone in full and another notion that to perceive anything, anyone, is to distort it, them. The narrator's consciousness, in which she herself takes a healthy but sceptical interest, proves catalytic (she's the same woman throughout) and lingers in the mind—mine at least—as some meticulously observed alembic whose every act of refining, changing, or purifying gets recorded. Christa T.'s argument with herself produces both rhetoric and poetry whereas the narrator's produces facts, even though these are bedded in, without being smothered by, qualifications, riders, and elegant dubieties. The whole book is an exercise in consciousness' being acutely conscious of itself, but without coyness, jargon, or whimsical casuistries.

All of which might persuade the non-European—non-German, non-East-German—reader that *The Quest for Christa T.* is a dry and rather solemn slow-motion amble around the heads of two highminded female highbrows, one dead, the other waiting to be born. I confess I found this aspect of the book just as absorbing as the mental gymnastics. Wolf brings Christa T. into vivid and abiding focus: tooting through a rolled-up newspaper as she walks down the street; watching a glider (launched by village lads) sail over her house with her name on the wings in big black letters; owlishly writing in her notebook *"The pilot who dropped the bomb on Hiroshima has been taken to a madhouse";* reliving the moment when she sat in a munitions truck in a snowstorm looking at a new grave; noting *"I can only cope with things by writing";* swigging beer with her students after the potato harvest; feeling her spine chill when, for a bet, a boy twice tries to bite off a toad's head; taking a taxi with her fiancé to a new restaurant in the Stalinallee where they order a mixed grill and ice cream; as wife and mother bearing a dish crammed with roasted cuts of wild boar; looking up the disease called panmyelophthisis, of which she will die.... Thus she grows and in growing realizes that, if God *is* love, best get it in writing.

Caught in history too, she has made her accommodations with it, as someone reaching adolescence in Germany during World War II would have to: going along with the Nazi order and then coming to her mature senses in a ghost country occupied by Russians. That progress of the spirit alone would make this an instructive novel, but Christa

Wolf has made it more than that; it's a both analytical and lyrical conspectus of the life and death of a woman too intelligent to accept other people's reasons for doing things and yet mordantly critical of her own. Wolf so arranges things that successive images of totalitarian polity reflect the totalitarianism of the universe itself, a universe that stamps out the gross and sensitive alike. She has one phrase—"floating equipoise"—which exactly describes the narrator's method; it's a method which makes the book itself seem only just to have edged itself into being. Constantly tempted as the narrator is to lapse into silence or speculative diffidence, into defensive games with tenses and points of view, she does well to express so much within her self-allocated span.

This is a book written on a knife's edge, with never a mention of the dangers inherent in Christa Wolf's own staging of the quest for Christa T. They are present nonetheless, like omitted parts of text which leave their pressure on what remains. At one point the narrator says, "a person must never be asked to take over someone else's liabilities, except perhaps in some circumstances." Reading between the lines of this obliquely cast declaration of independence, you learn the real force of those last five words. I am reminded of Citizen Kane, for whom there was also a quest: the key to the life and times and torments of Citizen T may well be the "red poppy" offered on the last page in the future tense—a counter-ideological rosebud in its way and, although much less grandiosely arrived at, just as poignant, just as haunting.

Peter Handke
1: *A Sorrow Beyond Dreams*

AMONG CONTEMPORARY WRITERS, Samuel Beckett has made an honorable specialty of composing a text and then cutting it, or shrinking it, beyond bare bone to the marrow, in the end producing something that feels like an irreducible minimum but still evokes its ampler versions. Beckett's *The Lost Ones* is one such text; Peter Handke's new book is another, though Handke offers the reader considerably more than Beckett in the way of colorful phenomena to hold on to and linger over. Easier to read, it has something of the same self-generalizing force as *The Lost Ones,* however; and the dreadful poignancy of the theme—the suicide of the narrator's mother—suffuses a maze of particulars which both scald and sustain him. A gentle, candid searching-out of her life develops into a tough inquiry as to what a writer, and a compulsive one at that, can make of grief, shock, and indignation.

One answer is: as short and as loaded a book as possible; no fat, no *longueurs,* no self-indulgent melodrama. Another is to recognize in the act of writing, as Handke's narrator (Handke himself?) does, that objectification or getting something off one's chest is impossible. Objectified, the hurt becomes a groomed presence the more upsetting for being out in the open. One never gets the text off one's chest. As the narrator says toward the end, "It is not true that writing has helped me . . . the story has not ceased to preoccupy me." Earlier, he explains that he "experienced moments of extreme speechlessness and needed to formulate them," only to discover at the halfway point the twin evils of over- and under-stating. These "two dangers" slow down his writing "because in every sentence I am afraid of losing my balance." In fact, as he says, this story is "really about the nameless, about speechless moments of terror," and it's impossible to read it without sensing in every sentence an ontological vertigo. From that faint but sovereign impetus comes a text that feels wrenched-out, choked on itself, self-rebuked.

The mother's life rears up as an entity as it rarely did for her while she was living it. She begins high-spirited over boiled beef and horseradish sauce, runs away from home to learn cooking at a classy hotel. In her second phase, the death of her brothers, the privations of war, and several self-inflicted abortions reduce her to an organism, with none of her old chic and élan. Almost a human darning egg, she turns into a sexless and niggardly cipher.

Then, in phase three, with her husband and her two children, she leaves the eastern sector of Germany for Austria. Life picks up, picks *her* up. She smokes, reads, wins a prize at a masked ball, goes in for bowling and eggnog, and becomes an untidy individual. It's as if she has burst into flower. And then, in her final phase, excruciating headaches begin, the result of a strangulated nerve in her neck (why didn't her doctor prescribe a collar?). Told she is having a nervous breakdown, she visits the seashore for the first time, sits in a garden fanning wasps out of her coffee, even thinks of adopting a child.

In the end, tormented by a nervous system that refuses to serve, she puts on a pair of rubber pants, two other pairs as well, and takes a hundred sleeping pills. Her farewell letter to the narrator includes instructions for her funeral.

It is a profoundly affecting story, counterpointed throughout by the narrator's offended hesitancy and his weird but utterly comprehensible pride in what she's done. A giggle here, a self-conscious image there ("In these tempests of dread, I become magnetic like a decaying animal"), only sharpen the impact. Some day, the narrator promises himself, he'll write about the whole thing in greater detail. One hopes not. Subtitled as it is—"A Life Story"—*A Sorrow Beyond Dreams* not only implies an alternative genre, the death story, but also crams two lives into one death. Brief as it is, the text seems radioactive, professionally unprofessional in its abrupt, blurted pain. The writer is almost as much at a disadvantage as, say, a lion-tamer or a TV repairman who has to express grief entirely in the idiom of his calling. A better developed, less panicky, book wouldn't be half so disturbing.

As it is, we have here some mordant death-chamber music from an Austrian writer who gets better all the time, and whose quirky, fastidious German is firmly registered in Ralph Manheim's English. The titles of two previous Handke novels. *The Goalie's Anxiety at the Penalty Kick* and *Short Letter, Long Farewell,* strangely prefigure this new book: it's not often you find the elegist's anxiety at the elegy so naked and concise.

2: *A Moment of True Feeling*

C OMPETENT LIVING entails inattention to things no doubt worthy of scrutiny, such as gradual changes in clouds, foliage, the texture of one's skin, the apparent slow wheeling of the night sky around us. Yet only when bored, convalescing, or doomed do most folk register much of life's gamut in all its intricacy and shading. A pity: the good citizen stands a good chance of dying back into a universe that's gone largely unnoticed.

You do not have to be a glutton for phenomena to discover this. You only have to realize once, like Gregor Keuschnig in Peter Handke's novella, that perceivership is a boon, the key to the One's many-sidedness, the basis for dying not wiser, perhaps, but better informed, more abundantly attuned, or fatter-souled. What Keuschnig, for a bizarre reason, sees all of a sudden is that his life as press attaché to the Austrian embassy in Paris is both automatic and null. Awakening from a nightmare in which he has murdered an old woman, he abruptly opens up, seeking "a moment of true feeling," and rejects his sham self.

The ironically banal title thus signals his aspiration to join the twitchy revulsed or alienated protagonists of absurdist literature from Jarry to Gide, from Kafka to Camus. Against the conformisms that stunt you, the formulas that deny you, there is only the resolve to put yourself at your own disposal all over again, or for the first time, which sounds just fine—graced with overtones of rebirth and with doors of perception opening up all over the place—until the crunch.

Which comes when you swap cozy anesthesia for the desolating sense that nature too is automatic and heeds you not. The facts have not changed, but you have become more aware of their fabric, and that is all. You can regale yourself with a richer sum of phenomena, but you cannot add it up. You are using your sensory equipment better, but it gives no answers. All this Keuschnig finds, moving at speed as he does from a compulsive Rousseauistic otherness to sensuous glut ("What a lot of things there are!" he says aloud), and from that to a resolve "that he would not go on living," thence to a randomly made assignation, in his new cheap light-blue suit and yellow shoes, at the Café de la Paix. His wife has left him. He has left his mistress. He has actually lost his daughter in the street. And, suitably enough, the fat writer who's been dogging his steps all day (and has found the daughter) has walked away from him, saying, "I have no further use for you." Instead of a bang or a whimper, a dying fall or an uplift valediction, Keuschnig just dwindles, via three terminal dots... into a flux of mere chronicity which has no seasonal or meaningful times, and in which "events" merely occupy a blank.

Yet Keuschnig never quite reconciles himself to the sameness of things. He goes on believing in the one "insignificant detail which would bring all other things together." So he's a choosy epiphanist, willing to scale a pyramid of data, weathercock in hand, and this makes him interesting beyond measure, a person who, like all of us, evinces the ingenuity of matter, but keeps a warm place by his mental hearth for a sign that life, having taken him thus far, might take him further. The long-term gist is that the mind fudges up its own miracles, for which, according to our degree of insecurity, we credit other sources.

Everything in turn becomes a salience, from the flannel smell of suits hanging in a sunny open-air market, to the puckered skin on his mistress's elbow, from the vapor forming in cellophane packages of crepes outside a bakery, to hazelnuts in their "rufflike carpels." But a salience of *what?* Thingness? The "seductive taboo" of materialism, or selfishness, or indifference? All four form his mood, make him strip naked in front of company, copulate with a secretary—a total stranger—on the floor of her office, and conclude at the outset that, "To be initiated had become absurd, to be taken back into the fold had become unimaginable, to belong had become hell on earth." In the end, though, choosing to live absurdly in an absurd world, he baas his way back into the hell of other people. One, as he finds after Brecht, is none. A full head can be an empty gesture.

It's an elegant, solid story, underpinned with wit and loaded with the pageantry of everyday. Maybe it's too short, as if Handke had lost interest; but to track Keuschnig further would be redundant. Doing whatever Keuschnig, "panoramic coward with the eyes of a glider pilot," encompasses "the downward-curving surface of the earth in a single glance" and makes "the kind of sound one might make to frighten an animal, but now it was addressed to everything in the world." Bah, maybe, instead of baa. A portrait of the press attaché as sacrificial lamb gives way to a glimpse of him as the high priest of his own impermanence.

Jakov Lind
Numbers

R EADERS OF JAKOV LIND'S autobiography, *Counting My Steps,*
will not easily have forgotten his account of how, as an adolescent
Austrian Jew, he maneuvered his way to safety through pogrom, air-
raid, and unpredictable deployments of land armies, at one point even
conning his way into a job in the aircraft industry in the lion's mouth in
Germany itself. For Lind World War Two was traumatic, inducing
him to adopt a variety of aliases, but also useful in that it schooled him
in an inventive duplicity akin to creativity itself. He survived, or rather
all of his successive selves did, and his writing has tended to become a
roll-call of the pieces, a gathering-up of spent entities. In his fiction he
seeks to exorcize horrors through expressionist hyperbole, in his non-
fiction to make exorcism itself yield a code to go on surviving by, in the
face of a different enemy.

But in vain. The horrors abide, more present for having been fixed
in prose, and the self remains unstructured, a compound ghost lacking
a wasteland and ineligible for the complacent snakes-and-ladders of
peace. *Counting My Steps* is less a linear, consecutive narrative than an
album of vicissitudes which permits thought to separate itself from
events, from chronology even, its ultimate effect being more that of a
mentality paraded than of a wartorn Europe exhumed. And *Numbers,*
deliberately evoking the homelessness and faith-lost plaints of an
identically-titled book of the Bible, resumes the same mode, more
extremely in fact, and should not be read without a preliminary
training spell with *Counting.* Being about pax, anti-climax, and the
inevitability of taxes, it sardonically swaps the earlier book's question—how to survive?—for another of less heat—what to do for a
living?—which boils down to what living can there be which isn't a
form of dying? Clearly, to survive is only to postpone. There's a music
that's played while Rome cools down as well.

No wonder *Counting* opened with a concise metaphysical bar-
rage, an abstract policy statement from he author, and no wonder
Number opens with epigraphs from that book of the Bible and
Bertrand Russell's *Mysticism and Logic* followed by an inductive
catechism which ends "God is not primarily a moral issue but a way of

looking at things, and the best way to love Him." It sounds facile (and even a bit ungrammatical), but it isn't, having been earned in a holocaust that also taught Lind that "When you are dead you cannot enjoy the knowledge of good and evil either, so why presume it's easier now?" This author, we gather, is an optimist; he tells us so and that is the mark of the optimist. Both books are demonstrative, not so much exemplifying a thesis as emphatic and gesturing in mood. The upshot comes first, the facts follow, and the actual process of interpretation gets left out—which may account for the obliquity and the elliptical strain of Lind's aphorisms and may also leave the reader helplessly trying to connect the memoir with its introductory meditation. There is only one way, and that is to accept that the broken eggs of this Hamelette are very broken indeed. Lind's picaresque adds up, just as 2 + 7 + 1/2 + 1/72 = 9 37/72, but how that total comes to equal "optimism" we don't know.

But we do get to know this man well, almost as if all things happening to him happen at the same time. Anti-intellectual yet creative, drop-out who justly claims he was never in, he makes love to his occupation of war-orphan (as well as indefatigably to juicy-sounding women from all over Europe). Like Jean Genet, he embraces a role thrust upon him, fantasizing himself into "the empty space in a long stippled line of warriors, horsemen and nomads. Inside was neither Jew nor Gentile, neither male nor female, but all of them simultaneously, or the absence of all. Inside was something which could not speak for itself yet as it was in a constant state of change, without either a body or a soul." And this unracial, androgynous, inchoate anachronism of an abstraction inhabits his body from Vienna to Stockholm, the long way round, the whole point of the vagabondage being "to be alive for the sake of fun and pleasure and not because we came out of the gas chambers." Not *sur*vival, then, but *vival* pure and simple, an experiential maximum both anonymous and uncaused, as if Lind were stealing flames from the center of the Reichstag fire. Lind the layabout becomes Lind the odd-job man unloading lard or Vichy water, a semitic Autolycus bluffing his way across the big hardening scab of European quietism, then Lind the emigrant, the student of Stanislavsky the would-be writer, all of these however true to his maxim, "One good-looking audience in bed is worth two thousand in an auditorium." (Which, of course, as well as evincing Lind, rebukes

Adolf Hitler, virtual creator of the Lind we know.) Averse to settling down (though *Numbers* suggests he does so quite regularly), he cannot forget that "whatever happens, it happens right in this brain . . . on top of this neck, on top of this face . . . two fistfuls of gray gooey matter." *There*'s his sticking-place, and the whole postwar palaver throbs in it as an optional distraction to his main concern: out of war into woman, out of the pit into the pudendum.

Incidental exhibits therefore don't have quite the same force as they would in a less existential book. A dildo made of buffalo hide, oiled with sesame oil, "and spiced with ginger for taste," seems only a gloss on the generic tupping, while the Viennese habit of watching you talk without listening to what you say pales beside Lind's own habit of watching himself live without wondering why. Uninvaded England's rigidity, and relativistic America's importunacy ("ready to tell a stranger the color of their bowel movement of that very same morning"), figure as improvised gargoyles, while the Swedish girl who eats paper for breakfast is as much a trope as a snapshot. Lind's novelties never displace him, never obscure his presence as the presiding demon. Of all his expressionistic images, though, the last is the most haunting, both realistic and strategically conjectural: he shovels snow for a living, one eight-hour shift earning him a good meal. Except when it rains. It rains in Lind's head as well, and *Numbers* is unnerving to read, like a shower cubicle turned into a Caligari cabinet. To come clean is to vanish and to stay put is foul play.

Lautréamont
Maldoror

IF ISIDORE DUCASSE (1846–1870), self-styled Comte de Lautré-amont, had published *Maldoror* for the first time in the present year it would either have been ignored, as it was in the 1860s, or have fared much worse than it did in the 1890s, when Huysmans, Maeterlinck and Remy de Gourmont enthusiastically rediscovered it.

Why? So many American commentators on books are dismally

old-fashioned, and you don't have to hunt to discover academics who want literature to stand still while they polish pontifications about it, or the schoolmaster *manqué* who chastises innovative writers as if they were ungovernable brats, or the bigot who blathers against writers' playing God (the truth being, of course, that God knew what he was about, was an innovator, not a critic). The fact is, in a country so ill-supplied as this with serious review media (compared with England and France), the forces of reaction have things pretty much their own way, and it wouldn't be too much to say that too many "review" media function as organs of exclusion and suppression, and that a whole developing branch of literature exists without the reading public's knowing anything about it. Vis-à-vis 20th-century writing, in fact, the public is in roughly the same position as thinking the biplane the newest flying machine or the fountain pen the only writing tool.

All of which is much the same as saying the battle of surrealism (like that of expressionism, of symbolism, even) has to be fought over and over again; not so much with the public as with publishers, editors and reviewers. Amazing when you think of it: the present century is pretty well along, but most people's taste in the arts is way behind, arrested at the Dreiser, Rachmaninoff, Wyeth stage. And *Maldoror,* at once ghoulish and hallucinative and defiant, reappears as a 100-year-old novelty, a fillip to cognoscenti, but to most so-called "opinion-makers" an object of less interest than the last prose apple pie baked by any minimalist. One says these things less in the hope of prevailing than to register a needed attitude in the mode of a lament.

Born in Montevideo of French parents, Ducasse was haughty and remote, suffered from migraine, wrote nocturnally at the piano (at which he "chanted" his lines, punctuating them with chords), and died at 24. His works—*Maldoror* and some prose-poem fragments—have worn well. To be sure, there's a certain amount of unfocused rant and over-epitheted invocation loaded with dud similes, but his prose at its best is graphic, caustic, and ferally alive. Maybe the finest thing in *Maldoror* is a sustained tale of how God, bored or overcome by procrastinated lust, comes down to a noxious whorehouse and leaves behind one hair, which Maldoror perceives as a man-high "flaxen pole composed of interlocking cones" that thrashes about against the walls and the floor. Time and again in these "chants" (symphonic tirades, I'd call them) Ducasse depicts turmoil in such commanding images, and

others even more detailed: a wedge of flying cranes; the webbed-footed
sea-bear; an omnibus full of zombies; an aerolith falling into and
through a field of corn. And it's just as well, because they punctuate and
crystallize his otherwise lurid pandemonium of gibbets and giblets,
saliva and pus and blood and sperm, toads and lice and scorpions and
tarantulas and octopi, scabby drabs, flayed elephants, disemboweled
children, and tremulous hermaphrodites.

In other words, Ducasse is a first-rate imagist locked inside a
compulsive cliché-monger; at his best he evokes Beckett, at his worst
the pulpiest porn. He wasn't a nice man, any more than Céline or
Montherlant, but that's no reason for not recognizing and admiring the
uniqueness and pioneer caliber of his imagination. Nowhere else in the
mid-19th century have I found so closely anticipated Beckett's *Watt* ("*I*
know not how to laugh"), Cortázar's metamorphoses ("the fig eats the
donkey"), the imaginative impotence of Genet and the self-conscious
alienatedness of the modern fabulator ("A man or a stone or a tree is
about to begin the fourth canto"). Had he lived longer, he would surely
have beefed up the precisions, cut the fustian, given us more of the
playful but strategic subtlety that suddenly sets up the first five-sixths of
Maldoror as a "hybrid preface" to the announcement, "Today I am
going to fabricate a little novel of thirty pages." As it is, Maldoror,
stalking Paris like an arthritic gangster marooned in a moonscape,
becomes an irresistible figment, a surgically-minded apostate as eager
"to feed the minotaur of his perverse instincts" as to commit the
definitive act of hubris. His mind aflood with bizarre combinations—
Australian boomerangs, cylindro-conical bullets that will pierce a
rhino-skin, the aerial cavatinas of a pet canary, the elasticity of wood, a
hermit-crab large as a vicuna, the dome of the Pantheon—he zeroes in
on his victim, "Mervyn, that son of flaxen England," and leaves him a
withered skeleton roped to the Pantheon's cupola.

Visibly, this isn't your run-of-the-mill good read (as the English
say), and it's only just a bit more a narrative than a monologue, more
dream than mosaic, more self-regenerating than self-destructive. It's a
lurid contraption concerned with its own precarious status. Ducasse
disappears, as do Maldoror and Mervyn, yet they reappear, as it were,
heraldically fused in the monstrously intimate impersonality the book
assumes as you look back on it. It's like a coat of arms designed only for
someone who, like Ducasse, decides to oppose the universe by precisely

re-imagining it. Or perhaps a better image comes, in an aphorism, from Ducasse himself: that of an "intellectual manchineel-tree," skin-blistering and poisonous.

You may lose your patience with him, feel either rejected or humiliated, but it's impossible to miss the ferocity of his sensibility, the hypnotic novelty of his image-making, his resolve to demolish merely by exercising to the full his own mental fecundity. "Anyone could contrive a literary luggage for himself," he wrote, "by stating the contrary of what has been said by the poets of this century. He would replace their affirmations with negations. And vice versa." Of course, he went far beyond such mechanical swaps, eventually developing into a literary polity the notion that what people have been used to getting isn't the only thing they can have.

Alexis Lykiard's translation is both subtle and earthy; he effectively brings Lautréamont's many puns over into English and, basing his version on the final text that Lautréamont polished, claims to have restored a book "previously mutilated and misrepresented." Quite so; this is the best translation now available. For example, concerning a master mariner who's been at sea for 13 months and arrives home to find his wife giving birth, his own translation reads: "his wife, still lying-in, had given him an heir *to whose affiliation he could lay no claim.*" Not bad; the French is "à la reconnaissance duquel il ne se reconnaissait aucun droit." He offers a pun of sorts, whereas John Rodker's 1924 version runs, "to recognise which he recognised no right" and Guy Wernham's 1943 New Directions version, "to the existence of which he could make no just claim." Lykiard's implies something sardonic, whereas the other two miss altogether. There are some useful notes, including a reference to a movie of this book begun by Kenneth Anger in this country, 1951–52. I wonder what became of it.

Blaise Cendrars
Moravagine

BLAISE CENDRARS (Frederic Sauser) is not a familiar name to the reading public or, for that matter, to many people of advanced or specialized taste. The publicity machines have done nothing for him since the Twenties and Thirties, when, in fact, he published himself with a satanic gusto that's rare even today. Having fled from his parents at fifteen, he sampled Russia, China, Persia, New York and Paris, then joined the French Foreign Legion and lost an arm in World War I, always refusing an artificial limb. Thereafter he conducted his harum-scarum career with even greater panache. He commuted regularly between Paris and South America, taking along an Alfa Romeo racing car whose body had been designed by Braque. He got himself painted by Leger, Modigliani, and Chagall, and helped "discover" jazz, Negro art, Henry Miller, and the innovative music of Les Six. Proudly one-handed at everything except, perhaps, the clap, this ferocious Swiss-Scottish literary nomad was one of the most original and anarchic of the surrealists, and ranks among those who have made a career of their temperaments. He died in 1961, aged 74.

Moravagine, first published in 1926, is an extraordinary and unnerving fusion of rant and pensiveness, plot and schizophrenia, impassioned luridity and deadpan itemization. It's a short history of the world embodied in a magniloquent ogre called Moravagine, a convicted murderer horribly stunted in physique who pours out his soul in several languages in a manner both farcical and odiously poignant. Sole descendant of the last King of Hungary, mad, and an anarchist as well, he enables Blaise Cendrars to compose an alias autobiography as well as to hold a distorting mirror up to the first decade of the twentieth century. The result is farouche, hypnotic, and deliciously vile, for if Cendrars felt anything steadily (beyond the urge to shift about and the compulsion to test his physical prowess) it was modern civilization pullulating all round him while he tried to wolf it down. Modernism flows into Moravagine's head like a sargasso from Hades; he cannot resist it, but, Canute-like, tries to, only to end up submitting completely to the destructive ecstasy it provokes in him. Moravagine is the man who ate *Zeitgeist* and died of it.

The novel opens with a garotting and ends with Blaise Cendrars's "discovery" that the Nazis have destroyed the cache of his hero's manuscripts. In between, as it were in demonstration of Remy de Gourmont's dictum that "a brain isolated from the world can create the world for itself," the narrator explains how he helped Moravagine escape from an international sanitarium (where he first saw him, in the act of masturbating onto a goldfish in its bowl) and toured the world with him for ten years. The whole thing takes place in Cendrars's head, and Moravagine is just as much in touch with the world when incarcerated as when out on the run.

All that is lacking is the commonplace or, rather, a commonplace response to it: Moravagine—who once cut the eyes out of his family portraits and his dog, who became sexually involved with a stovepipe and a lead ingot, and then disembowelled his mistress—now enrolls at the University of Berlin, there combining meditation with exploits worthy of Jack the Ripper. Then he and Cendrars are in Russia on the eve of the 1904 revolution, forever retreating along some Trans-Siberian Railway of the mind that eventually gets them to the Finland Station, Liverpool, New York, New Orleans, Arizona, the Gulf of Mexico and thence, through shipwreck, up the Orinoco, where they encounter Blue Indians (who all suffer, as they're almost bound to in a Cendrars novel, from a skin disease of syphilitic origin). Then they are back in Paris, with Moravagine planning to fly round the world while Man-Friday Cendrars enlists in the French army. Their odyssey ends in 1917 when Moravagine, believing he is on the planet Mars, dies in the same room as did the Man in the Iron Mask.

These picaresque ballistics are exhilarating, but the book's appeal is in Cendrars's indefatigable mental exhibitionism, lugubrious and caustic, bigoted and visionary, in turn. He spares nothing—women, politicians, psychiatrists, the law, Jews, paper money, Sarah Bernhardt, funerals, the French family, the USA—and yet in his tirades is always grateful because his very antagonism warms his mind, as do thoughts of the bellies of aphrodisiac honey ants, "these Sacred Heart medals, these Lizst rhapsodies, this phosphate, these bananas," an early airplane ("the most beautiful possible projection of the human brain"), a large reddish orang-outang clad in white flannels and a Byronic shirt; Alfred de Vigny's *Poet's Diary;* morphine and madness, vowels and vertigo, and *Kay-ray-kuh-kuh-ko-kex* (the only word in the Martian language, at least according to Moravagine).

Existence, Cenrars wrote, is "idiotic, imbecile and vain" while consciousness is "a congenital hallucination." And yet, as this pioneering novel shows, he recognized the virtues in the fact there is nothing else to turn to, and so developed an intricate relish for the All, evil not left out. *Moravagine*—the very name is like a hell, coupling as it does the Latin for delay with the Latin for sheath to produce a slow birth— *Moravagine* is a demented hymn to Creation, a seminal work in which a semi-gangster mentality anticipates many of the ironic-fantastic literary modes of our own day with a bumptious, carefully deployed bitingness no one has quite equalled.

Louis-Ferdinand Céline
North

L IKE AN EVEREST thick with soot, Céline is there, daunting, implacable, and more alluded to than grappled with. Perhaps reading him, like Everest-climbing, is a specialized activity requiring schooled nerves, a predisposition to metaphysical anger, and maybe even a certain amount of mania. In my experience, you don't find many people who have read *Journey to the End of Night,* that fictional bombshell of 1932, in which Ferdinand Bardamu went lunging in search of himself through World War I, the slums of Paris, the jungles of Africa, and the auto factories of Detroit. Your mature reader dismisses Céline as a barfing werewolf (antihumanist, antihuman, self-obsessed, crypto-war-criminal, etc.) and your student reader prefers the pompous naïveté of Hesse. In this age of dewy-eyed righteousness, in which the evil geniuses of power politics are supposed to vanish at the repeated cry of Love!, there seems little room for this man's almost voluptuous *saeva indignatio* in which satanic improvisation contends with an almost saintly self-disgust.

More's the pity. There are few enough writers around with his ferocity, his ability to be mordant while being voluminous, his to-hell-with-it-all panache. What's admired is the way Kafka reports the absurd without losing his bourgeois cool; the Velveeta whimsy of

Tolkien; Brautigan's pretty froth—a far cry from Céline's lived fusion of pessimism and Bosch. It was André Gide, maybe more than anyone, who stated the essence of the man's writings, explaining that "It is not reality which Céline paints but the hallucinations which reality provokes," to which one might add an idea that Gide advanced with no one particular in mind: that of a man writing a novel in a rage. It fits Céline exactly. In the circumstances, then, all credit to the publishers for bringing out *North,* which slams across our imminent *fin-de-siècle* pieties as a raw and dangerous abomination as unlikely to cheer anybody up as to inspire yet another deliquescent fit of Woodstock togetherness. Man, it emerges from this continually backfiring novel, isn't nice; neither was Céline; but both can be engrossing, even for their vices.

I like *North* and the badman it contains, and I suppose many people will find liking it or him at all an enormity. Let them, there is always Edith Wharton on the shelf, there is always John Galsworthy with his Nobel Prize for Civics. "The North," Céline wrote in *Journey,* "will at least preserve your flesh for you. . . . There's very little difference between a dead Swede and a young man who's had a bad night." That is pretty much the mood—bleak, gloatingly mock-worldly—of this book, which recounts the journey made by Céline and his wife and cat, together with an actor friend, across Germany in 1944 and 1945, their destination being Denmark, where Céline had stashed away some gold bars (the same gold he'd gone daily to watch being weighed at his vault in England). A cold, caustic going they had of it, all the way from Baden-Baden and its stranded oblivious aristocrats to a Berlin almost paralyzed by Allied bombings, thence to Sigmaringen and the famous castle over which, on October 1st 1944, the prudent refugee colony hoisted the French flag.

Simply as the tale of a picaresque ordeal interrupted by stopovers in various havens, with the Allied armies on the Céline's heels and Germany falling ever faster into disarray, *North* is fascinating and fizzy, but what makes it so potent a document is the "remarkable sensibility" that Gide commended. The prose has a dense inconsecutiveness brought about in part by Céline's favorite device of the three dots . . . (which both invite you on and trip you up), but also by his flair for letting his imagination range further than his analytical mind wants to go. Thus, nonchronologically, you read the book by vaulting from one salient image to another, from a wheelbarrow full of eyes to an outbreak of measles in the 17th century in the Faroe Islands, from climatized tunnels in the "basement of Kilimanjaro" to a pastor who keeps bees in the wings of downed planes, from the "silent" wing of Dachau to a one-armed sergeant obsessed with "Parisian vagina," from a corpse found in a manure pit to Céline's being denounced as the muse of the charnel house and his self-description as the "foremost living stinker from Dunkirk to Tamanrasset." In other words, he counterpoints the book's rambling chronicle with a set of images about which the book might have been structured, but isn't.

At the end you are left with an ephemeral tale and a temperament that feels timeless, a temperament that (to borrow Céline's own words) doesn't so much "harmonize every conceivable ruckus" as let things fall where they may "in the course of this drawn-out pensum." The Beckettian overtones of that last phrase are in tune with the book's being a region rather than a structure and the man's being an aggregation rather than a type.

Samuel Beckett
1: *Texts For Nothing*

ESPECIALLY ON HIS BIRTHDAY, Beckett seems the consummate pessimist waiting it out, waiting to be proven wrong. Over the years since *Waiting for Godot,* his plays have seemed, though bleak, less bleak than his fiction, maybe because theater, a group sport, thrives on the gift of gab and keeps you company. The voices in his plays break the silence, but those in his fiction enforce it. Fans of *Godot* and *Krapp's Last Tape* recoil from the savage, reductive dumbshow of *Molloy* and *Malone Dies,* which teaches us only that the mind can't think itself to a halt. Reading such books responsively is like being brought back to life in an ecstasy, glad to be burned at the stake near the North Pole. Because the fiction corners us, its impact is keener, more intimately humbling; its prose is right on top of us, daring us to look at it again in a fit of delighted dismay.

One balefully obvious thing his fiction has always said, or always implied. "The mortal microcosm," as he says in his majestic essay on Proust, "cannot forgive the relative immortality of the macrocosm." Relish the punch of the word "relative"; the time scheme is vast. Whatever becomes of the macrocosm, we know some things for certain about the humans in it. If human life endures at all, it may get more comfortable for some, but we will end up dying as before. And if human life dies out, it will certainly get grimmer toward the end, plunged into nuclear winter or incinerated by our old friend the sun turned into a red giant. In this context, Beckett gears us for the worst, defusing the unthinkable into the familiar. It is hard to resist thinking that, even if death no longer came to us, Beckett would only reluctantly admit that fact, drawn as he is to extremes, of which his basic metaphors are made. He writes almost as if he himself had created human life, somewhere in Ireland, behind a bar or a toolshed, and botched it miserably, yet finds it—a poor thing but his own—a source of violent hilarity. His *miserere* for all humankind, extolled in the Nobel citation, yields not creature comforts but a diagnostic horse laugh. Somehow the creator of the fiction chides himself for Creation at large. In his skewed but profoundly affecting novels and stories, first things and last afflict us with not only enraptured horror, but with shame and guilt as well: for birth and death *we* take the blame.

Of his drastic and enigmatic fictions, none seems more about birth and his birthday than his sixty-five page sequence, *Texts For Nothing,* composed in the personal and creative misery following his mother's death in 1950 and the completion of the Molloy-Malone trilogy with the volume ironically named *The Unnamable.* Almost a sardonic hymn to gestation, to the phase in which we are nothing or nobody, *Texts* deals triumphantly with *Nothing*-ness by treating it as something: a something, though, as we say, that is next to nothing. Like a wad of microscope slides held up to the light, these thirteen pieces show faint specks amid a translucent delirium intoned by uncoordinated voices. Obliged to sing or to say, this chorus has nothing much to express save a sense of desolation comparable, for sheer mellifluous sadness, to Richard Strauss's dirge-like study for twenty-three solo strings, *Metamorphosen.*

On a less sublime level, what are these texts woven from and around? An amazing amount. Number 8, for instance, includes a sand pebble, a ventriloquist's dummy, no's knife cutting yes's throat, Aristotle, a white stick and an ear trumpet, a bowler hat, a pair of brown boots. Lost amid the cautious dither of the voices, these things loom large, like relics, fossils, statues from some Easter Island of the mind. Mostly the texts merge into a kind of atmospheric surf, and as a result you fall upon what is hard and definite and devour it, glad of something fixed where all is seepage, glaze, and flow.

And so to the birthday in question. Beckett has always insisted that he was born on Good Friday the 13th of April, 1906, carefully tuning his legend to the highest pitch of bad luck. But his birth certificate says the 13th of May. Whatever the truth, the April date is more imposing, not least because it interacts dramatically with the *Texts*. Friday the 13th is unlucky to begin with, of course, but if you count back from it at the rate of one text per day, you land on April Fool's Day. More bad luck. Surely these *Texts* evoke the last thirteen days in his mother's womb and repeat one of his favorite themes: that of expulsion from a lodging place. In fact, his mother's name was Mary, her nickname May, so one can see why, looking back to his birth, he did not wish to be born in the month whose name was his mother's nickname. He did not wish to be born from, or gesture in, a mother newly dead. Or, for that matter, on Crucifixion Day, from or in a mother properly named Mary. The tug of April is clear.

Images and echoes of birth float expendably through the prose, though there is no crescendo from 1 to 13 (which Beckett himself calls a coda). Instead we find something like a recitative of being unborn, all the way from "You can't stay here" to the final sentence's "were there one day to be here...born of the impossible voice the unmakable being...it murmurs." In between there is much about departure, not knowing where to go, being frightened to be born, being a dead infant in a dead mother. A pent-up antlike entity hovers on "the brink of shrieks," labors in the pump of the womb, in a waiting room, beholds "great sights, peeping down," says peekaboo, and comes into this world.

This year, 1984, the 13th of April is a Friday, an appropriate occasion for noting that, while Beckett's histrionic use of the calendar and of popular superstition is hardly recondite or subtle, it is bold and poignant. The work develops a new lease, an indelible fresh face. The author has given himself to the text for its birthday. What happier return than that?

2: *The Lost Ones*

B ETWEEN 1946 AND 1949, in the most productive period of his life, Samuel Beckett wrote the trilogy composed of *Molloy, Malone Dies* and *The Unnamable,* as well as *Waiting for Godot* and the 13 *Texts for Nothing* He was neither well-known nor likely to be popular; he refused to submit his work himself and Mme. Beckett did this for him, but the major French publishing houses declined his trilogy, which he insisted must not be broken up into separate books. Eventually, however, Jérôme Lindon, who had taken over Les Editions de Minuit, read *Molloy,* liked it, and signed; and (in three separate volumes, after all that) the trilogy was published between 1951 and 1953. The rest is literary history (as well as a lot of Beckettian silence), with Beckett the fictioneer *diminuendo* after *How It Is* (1961), extruding a succession of ever-smaller and more exiguous texts in which the urge to write seemed only miminally larger than the urge not to.

In such a context *The Lost Ones,* begun in 1966 and averaging out at nine pages a year, looms as an almost mammoth tome. One surprise apart (Beckett is using verbs again), it resumes that severity for which he is famous and confronts us with a flattened cylinder 50 meters round, 18 high, in which 200 "lost bodies roam each searching for its lost one." There are 15 ladders, various niches and tunnels, and not much else, which by Beckettian standards amounts to a crowded scene.

Yet the image is potent enough, evoking womb and spaceship, test tube and Klein bottle; at its faintest a clean but ill-lit peopled brainpan, at its most vigorous a *summa claustrophobica* in which the "aerial surf" still sounds but within a biobox made of "solid rubber or suchlike." If the pensive reader attends, this image resonates and goes on resonating in his mind, something between allegory and the deliberate enigmas of *Watt* and the trilogy ("things of great formal brilliance but indeterminable purport"). *The Lost Ones* (the French title, *Le Dépeupleur,* means The Depopulator) is no riddle; yet the connoisseur of Beckettian enigmas, who relishes indecipherable images in their own right, won't be disappointed: the ghost of something called "harmony" mysteriously stalks through these pages and leaves one wondering about the music and the mathematics of it all.

In short, Beckett has added to his panoply of epitomes an image that both invites interpreters and vindicates enigmatists. For all its being comma-less, this book is easier to read than much of the fiction Beckett has published since *Murphy* (1938). Yet, it titillates hermeneutic appetites it refuses to gratify—more so than even Beckett at his most riddling, as in "Imagination Dead Imagine" and "Ping."

At first sight, Beckett's account of the two doctrines concerning a way out of the cylinder seems readily construable: one school of thought "swears by a secret passage . . . leading in the words of the poet to nature's sanctuaries"; the other "dreams of a trap door hidden in the ceiling giving access to a flue at the end of which the sun and other stars would still be shining." Hell or heaven? Hell and heaven? The hot bowels of the earth or the airless cold of space? Safety in a fall-out shelter or exposure to fatal radiation? The more you think about these seeming complementary opposites, the less explicit they are; what is certain, though, is that the former (downward) is fractionally losing ground to the latter (the trap door up). This teeming precinct is in fact a dead end, a stultifying life-sentence that echoes in the book's forensic sentences, sometimes rising to concise elegance, more often lapsing into a monolithic stiltedness.

Beckett's purpose is now much bleaker than heretofore. "For in the cylinder alone," we read, "are certitudes to be found and without nothing but mystery." And those certitudes are barren, monotonous, incontestable, easier to write about than Nothing and therefore less likely to provoke invention for invention's sake. Among the most vivid of the certitudes are the squatting defeated woman who represents north in the cylinder and those lost ones who brain themselves with rungs from the ladders. What's lacking is culture, with which we occupy ourselves while serving our sentence. In girder-like prose Beckett sums up what can't be pared further without the material's becoming transparent.

In this his latest purgatorial igloo the only dignity left us is in being articulate, after surrender, as in his concluding sentence, halting and cautious as its gait is:

> So much roughly speaking for the last state of the cylinder
> and of this little people of searchers one first of whom if a
> man in some unthinkable past for the first time bowed his
> head if this notion is maintained.

Maintain it he does, scrunching much of Dante into Plato's Cave, much of his own life's thinking into 60 pages. Once you have factorized life, and are able to dwell as remorselessly as this upon the factors, there seems little point in multiplying them together again. Hence the depopulation, the only question that remains being how to get rid of the 200 survivors without falsifying history. After all, 200 can be said to have some representative power, stand for the race in some measure: 200 on behalf of 3,580,000,000 is acceptable enough, whereas none on behalf of the same population isn't.

Michel Tournier
The Ogre

A FABLED MAN-EATING GIANT or monster, or anyone heinously cruel, brutish or hideous: such is the ogre in fairy tales, but not in Michel Tournier's absorbing novel, winner of the Prix Goncourt. True, the towering Abel Tiffauges who dominates *The Ogre* is a bit callous, especially when on the prowl with his camera, but he doesn't otherwise fit the mold. He does, however, have in him something of Dostoevsky's Underground Man, which reminds us that "ogre" comes from Orcus, god of the underworld. Tiffauges's main passion, far from man-eating, is a hyperbolical one for lifting up children, for savoring them while he holds them up. All in all, he's a gentle unjolly giant, with a grand appetite for coincidences and avid for anything that enhances his stature. Semi-mythical to begin with, he mythologizes himself in his own first-person sections of the narrative and readily swells under the same treatment by Tournier's third-person know-it-all.

In the first section, "Sinister Writing of Abel Tiffagues," Abel is a garage-owner who, one day in January 1938, having injured his right hand, begins to compile a diary with his left (hence "sinister") and is soon pouring out an antic tirade about his ex-mistress, his school days (the school fat boy made him eat grass), his big hands and his shortsightedness. The very act of composition makes the world richer and more mysterious for him, most of all when he looks back on his wrongful arrest for child-rape and his being freed into the French army as World War Two gets under way. Vicariously identifying with the guillotined (and left-handed) multiple murderer Weidmann, he recounts his present passions for raw meat, for dunking his head in the toilet bowl, for tape recording children at play and then repeatedly replaying the tape like a symphony buff. Avid for "meaning," he find none "in this world covered in hieroglyphics to which I haven't the key," and instead affiliates himself with Atlas, the porters of Les Halles, Hercules Pedephorus, and Rasputin, "the greatest phoric hero of our time" (to whom, in fact, Tournier dedicates the entire novel). *Phoric?* It means "bearing," as in St. Christo*pher,* which it so happens is the name of Abel's school.

This careful and indeed elaborate embodiment of the theme at various levels—the coincidental, the allusive, the historical, the metaphorical, the mystic—is Tournier's principal strategy, and it serves him well; in fact enriches and complicates his novel beyond the point of allegory, and keeps the reader busy synthesizing as he advances. Abel becomes an army pigeon handler (for one sickly one he first masticates its food himself), then, as a POW in East Prussia who remains free to wander around in the woods, the tamer of a blind elk. Not long after a 2000-year-old peat-bog man is dug up, Abel finds himself employed on Hermann Goering's private game reserve, mounted on a horse he names Bluebeard. We next find him serving as an aide to a mountebank geneticist who, studying a corps of Hitler Youth quartered in an old fortress, dreams of creating a Golden Man to partner that "masterpiece of Chinese creative biology," the goldfish. A hulking double Cyclops with a savior complex, Abel finds coming his way what he calls "a continuous stream of warm, quivering creatures," of whom the last is an emaciated youth from Auschwitz, whom he tries to carry to safety ahead of the Russians.

What is exceptional here is the gradual accumulation, through parallels and overlays, of a resonance which gets you into the mood for "meaning" but never delivers it. The novel builds, broadens out, in an exciting way, yet you are obliged to feed your excitement back into the images themselves, which thus become intensely charged while remaining beyond explanation. There is a dignity of emotive inventiveness in these pages that transcends the old habit of making things make sense and sets up, in fact, a fabricated entity, Abel, who evokes a vast amount yet corresponds to nothing, and in the long run can only be regarded with awe.

I have only one quarrel with Tournier's complex mummery: in the first section of the book (the best), he assembles a perfect basis for extrapolation and parabolical flights, but he goes on squaring what he might have cubed, held back maybe by some flickering devotion to realism. It's odd to find him re-presenting, rather longwindedly, in terms of Hitler's youths, qualities of Abel he much earlier on made patent among schoolchildren. It's as if he were reluctant to shift from the improbable to the impossible: a strangely suburban flaw in such a mythic-minded writer. Never mind, *The Ogre* is engrossing, poetic, and profoundly eventful, like a Celtic ode to the biological tropism best summed up as the raising, not of Cain, but of Abel-with-child.

André Schwarz-Bart
A Woman Named Solitude

ANDRÉ SCHWARZ-BART, who won the Prix Goncourt in 1959 for *The Last of the Just,* and then waited 8 years before bringing out his next novel, *A Plate of Pork and Green Bananas,* is a selective and economical sensibility incapable of being stampeded or seduced into output for output's sake. Rather, its motion is patiently to distill experience until an epitome has formed that transcends him, thus permitting him a degree of impersonality unfamiliar in French novelists since Camus. No anti-novelist, Schwarz-Bart is more a meta-novelist, for whom fictional artifice exists only to record and dramatize his conscience. Anyone looking for narcissistic squeeze-and-tease à la Robbe-Grillet, or for mathematical infra-puzzles à la Raymond Queneau, should leave this book alone: far from being à la mode, it has something timeless to it, and nonspatial as well.

On the other hand, anyone looking for some kind of sequel to *The Last of the Just* (which explored the continuity of Jewish martyrdom through the ages) should get into this book at once. An echo, a pendant, it's about the mulatto daughter of a West African slave who, as the epigraph (culled from a history of Guadeloupe) informs us, "was executed [guillotined] on November 29, 1802, immediately after the delivery of her child." No matter that I reveal the ending, it's in that epigraph after all; and the execution is the merest punctuational drumtap, a formalization of a lifelong putting-to-death as Solitude is shuttled back and forth between proud (or not-so-proud) possessors, who re-enslave her while seeking, for bizarre and maybe psychopathic reasons, to promote and polish her as well. She emerges a tantalizing but stunningly graphic fusion of Mother Courage and Alice in Wonderland, a woman into whose psyche Schwarz-Bart enters with gracious ampleness and osmotic subtlety. It's a portrait that might have been mawkish, doctrinaire, or simply righteous, but it isn't, thanks to the force of the literary imagination at work here, which seems to benefit from being dammed up for periods of several years.

French reviewers haven't failed to point out how this new novel renews Schwarz-Bart's commitment to the walking wounded of history, to martyrs and victims, and how it supplies an overt analogy between the tragedy of deported slaves and that of persecuted Jews. All true; but the book's appeal (and major virtue) isn't historical, ideological, or even moral, but psychological—as if, say, Georges Bernanos (one of Schwarz-Bart's favorites) had re-created a character of Amos Tutuola's, and the result is something (someone) eschatologically exotic, rippling with nuance and prepossessing openness. Solitude, as she calls herself, is more vivid than even the culture amid which she toils; her physical presence doesn't fluctuate, even within a prose that can enliven and intensify itself nonstop with such colorful native sayings as "how delicious are your hind parts cooked with almonds" and "don't blame God for creating the tiger . . . thank him for not giving him wings."

In other words, Schwarz-Bart continuously sets Solitude in relief against a rainbow context: "She moved soundlessly among the runaway blacks, like a soap bubble revolving in the mansions of the sky . . ."; "she saw herself changed into a sugar statue, which the Frenchmen of France were slowly eating far far away at the other end of the world, first breaking off her fingers, so thin and long that they seemed unreal." Her story he could hunt out, as well as do his homework on Guadeloupe; but her mind, zany flashing shuttle that it is, he had to invent, and he has done that well. (Although, to my mind, in the first quotation above, "in the mansion of the sky" weakens the image by etherealizing it: a vice he doesn't often succumb to).

Quibbles aside, Solitude, supernumerary and sibylline human flotsam on the tide of the colonial impact of the French revolution, assembles in the mind while the vicissitudes that compose her "story" fall away. With a white hen placed on her head to determine the status of her virginity, the frenum of her tongue slit in a vain attempt to cure her of her stammer, and "a chilling absence in her eyes"—one dark, the other light green—which have "a mineral life of their own" like suspended glass globes, she is given as a *pet* to a girl about her own age. She tries to kill herself by swallowing her tongue. Afraid of turning into a dog, she barks in her dreams, turns into a genuinely wild child instead. In elaborate costumes that give her the absent exotic look of a parrot, she endures. She leads a band of rebellious blacks (in her abstracted, intermittent way) with a machete. Ancient at 30, she walks to execution raising her knee high, and her last utterance is in "excellent French French."

Italo Calvino
1: *Cosmicomics*

F AMILIAR WITH THE FICTION of such Italian writers as Moravia, Silone and Pavese, the North American reader heard little of the Italo Calvino who, immediately after the war, launched out with realistic stories about the Italian poor and then turned increasingly to fable and fantasy. After *The Path to the Nest of Spiders* (1957), a book much influenced by Hemingway, he came completely into his own with two idiosyncratic, sportive novels that are well worth sampling. *The Baron in the Trees* (1959) deals with a contemplative perfectionist of a nobleman who, at the age of twelve, sickens of life at ground level and elevates himself a few yards above it. There he stays; take it or leave it. The hero of *The Non-Existent Knight* (1962) is dissected in battle but manages to continue his earthly life.

Just as curious (indeed, curiouser and curiouser), this famous collection of stories, whose very title specifies Calvino's fondness for superhuman oddity, gives us a hero as old as the universe itself. Provisionally called Qfwfq, he sports and springs about among the galaxies as a protean prototype who remembers how the universe evolved from a single point and whose relatives—whom he reports upon with gossipy pertness—are formulae or primitive cellular structures. At one juncture, after his girl friend Ayl has fled underground from the newborn first colors, he pleads, "Come, let me take you outside"—and that, really, is what Calvino is saying to orthodox readers of orthodox fiction, inviting them far outside the usual social and economic, moral and psychological matrices into what is, in effect, the first biography of all: a poignant, freewheeling account of Creation itself.

Calvino's aim, it seems to me, is both praiseworthy and responsible. Talk of *the* "dying" novel has all but mesmerized us into repudiating the diversity of fiction, and Calvino is heeding Aldous Huxley's last words: "Our business is to wake up." Imagination, as he shows, was given us not solely or even principally for the purpose of imitating the everyday world, but rather for purposes of exploration and (something we have almost lost) play. He raises imagination to its exponential maximum, and that is praiseworthy—doubly so, in fact, when we admit how staid and category-bound the publishing industry is.

But there is more here than a publisher backing an author's dedication to principle. Calvino's execution of his preposterous aims is responsible in the sense that he presents the fantastic in "realistic" ways, so much so that we accept before we puzzle. Take some examples (or rather take them on trust, because you have to concentrate on the *texture* of the stories and not so much the outline). "When the moon was very close to the Earth," Qfwfq says, he used to land on it by ladder with bucket and king-size spoon to collect "moon-milk" that formed between the scales on the moon's underbelly (itself having an aroma of smoked salmon). One day, while the nebulas were condensing, he tripped for the first time (over the first solid he'd encountered). After making a mark in space, he waited 600 million solar years for it to reappear; but, when the time came round, he saw another mark in its place (pity the cosmic Crusoe). When, he tells us, the universe was a single point, there was no scandal; everybody was necessarily in bed with everybody else. As a child, he played marbles with hydrogen atoms (always allowing, of course, for the curvature of space). Endlessly transformable, he left the waters and used his fins as paws on the land; as the last dinosaur he found his own son non-dinosauric and "caught the first train out." As a mollusk he dispassionately discusses his natural narcissism; he discovers identity when bizarre signals such as "I saw you" appear on a quasar 100 million light years away; and he discovers cosmic feedback when the closing Wall Street quotations begin to arrive from an inevitable future.

Far-fetched? No, it was all at hand all along; Calvino has simply had the complex wit to identify it and make it relevant. In *Cosmicomics* he imaginatively reclaims for us vast tracts of time from which we have evicted ourselves, and, thereby, instructs as in the merits and joys of writing graffiti in the margins of Genesis:

> And so now, after five hundred million years have gone by, I look around and, above the rock, I see the railway embankment and the train passing along it with a party of Dutch girls looking out of the window and, in the last compartment, a solitary traveler reading Herodotus in a bilingual edition, and the train vanishes into the tunnel under the highway, where there is a sign with the pyramids and the words "VISIT EGYPT," and a little ice-cream wagon tries to pass a big truck laden with installments of *Rh-Stijl,* a periodical encyclopaedia that comes out in paperback...

Thus muses Qfwfq, the ex-mollusk who sounds like a radio station's call letters, and without whom we would none of us have ever been.

2: *T Zero*

T ZERO picks up where *Cosmicomics,* its immediate predecessor, left off. Qfwfq, the protean hero who is just as much at home in the protozoic slime or sporting among the galaxies as he is on a cloverleaf where the superhighways begin to fan out, reappears unchanged (inasmuch as he is still constantly changing himself at will), but with a new obsession. Whereas, in the earlier book, he told about the fun he and his contemporaries used to have collecting milk in buckets from the surface of the moon, now he suffers from something we ourselves might have experienced only recently: moon-nausea. His partner, Sibyl, who stares all day through an observatory telescope, tells him the moon is coming closer and closer to the earth: and then, from the porch of his suburban home, he sees the moon begin to melt down on to the earth, depositing "a matter composed of gelatin and hair and mold and slaver." Ugh, thinks Qfwfq, champion of the "clean" clinical world of plastics, steel and cement, and ugh again when he looks at Sibyl herself, "fat, disheveled, lazy, greedily eating cream puffs."

In manner and subject matter, "Soft Moon," as the story outlined above is called, would fit congruously into *Cosmicomics*, as would the one about the reptilian first bird, who sings "koaxpf" in anachronistic homage to Aristophanes' frogs, and the one about Qfwfq's yearning for the old days when each substance was concentrated into a single large crystal—whereas, now, he has to work among the glass slabs of Manhattan whose Tiffany's enshrines the splinters of a vanished kingdom.

Reading such fictions, one's mind must flex itself continually in order to keep pace with all the offered possibilities: the long-since extinct alongside the newest synthetic fabric; the way various species evolved alongside the ways they didn't; and the simultaneous modifiability of everything through imagination, so that whatever is trumped-up is just as "real" as what is not. It's a kind of genetic opportunism in which it is impossible to make mistakes. Calvino sought for an imaginative maximum that transcends such categories as "real," "realistic," and "fantastic" and bring home to us, in a way both farcical and poignant, all the modes of being that surround us and are part of us. He worked biochemistry against the complacencies of fiction and fictionalized both the dubieties and the certainties of astronomers. Sporting with Nature, he ingeniously reacquainted us with the fact that trees don't laugh, mud can't read, dinosaurs can't cook, and so on.

But in the last two sections of this book, he sobers up. The subject matter remains much the same: Qfwfq, as a dividing cell, undergoes agonies of lost and plural identity: as a camel in love, he feels that his individuality and initiative are as nothing as compared to the relentless programming set up in him and in his Priscilla by amino acids lined up in a certain way. There is doom, too, on a larger plane—"from the mud of the boiling swamps the first clot of undivided life cannot again emerge . . . the spell is broken, the eternals are dead." We might have expected Calvino to get to such matters sooner or later, but not, as here, in an idiom that combines the obsessive logical exhaustiveness of Beckett with the acute creative diffidence of Borges. For example: "Time passes, and I, more and more pleased with being in it and with being me, am also more and more pleased that *there is time,* and that *I am in time,* or rather that time passes and *I pass time* and time passes me, or rather I am pleased to be contained in time, to be the content of time, or the container, in short to mark by being me the passing of time." The festive ambiguities apart (my italics), what can one remark?

If Calvino was ever one thing consistently, he was bold, and impenitently so: he bounced us into going along with him. So why, I wonder, the switch to mechanically assembled patters of lucid but stultifying casuistries? Yards of them, no doubt in tribute to the copious intricateness of being; but such prose consorts oddly with what little the mind's eye is offered, such as the male camel's nostalgia for "those sunsets in the oasis, when they loosen the burden from the packsaddle and the caravan scatters and we camels feel suddenly light and you break into a run and I trot after you, overtaking you in the grove of palm trees." It's as if there's a Hemingway locked up inside a Hegel and trying to get out.

The easiest read in the whole book is "The Count of Monte Cristo," in which Edmond Dantès breaks into Alexandre Dumas's study and reads the discarded pages of the novel, thus discovering the life he *might* have had and the fact that his true confinement is in "the concentric fortress, If-Monte Cristo-Dumas's desk." That discovery is Calvino's too. In other words, *The Count of Monte Cristo* could have been a combination of words different from the one we all know it as, whereas there was and is no alternative to $E = mc^2$. I much prefer the Calvino who explores *if* to the one who confines himself in a polysyllogistic Chateau d'*If*.

Primo Levi
The Periodic Table

A FTER A SHELTERED, almost Finzi-Contini-like childhood in Piedmont, Primo Levi went on to specialize in chemistry and during World War II worked in a semi-clandestine laboratory before joining an Italian Resistance group and, ultimately, was shipped off with other Jews to Auschwitz. After the war, he worked for an Italian company that imported vanadium from Germany, and he eventually mopped up all the Italian literary prizes as his almost posthumous literary career prospered. Of the 650 people he was deported with, only 31 came back, a quotient for whom Levi has spoken again and again. The man's energy, tenacity and will give one pause, as does his publicity photograph: a bearded version of the English actor Michael Wilding, with an expression of debonair sagacity. Levi looks 20 years younger than the mid-sixties he is in, and he has a young, powerful, holistic mind.

Best known for his two books on Auschwitz, *If This Is a Man* and *The Truce,* Levi published *The Periodic Table* ten years ago: an extraordinary, nimble, fluent book from an extraordinary life, part autobiography, part fiction, but essentially something like a memoir of elemental matter (21 elements from the periodic table, from Argon to Carbon). Here are the rites of passage—young man hunting a career in science, falling in love, winning the highest academic honors, doing vital and also trivial experiments, mountaineering, getting sucked into the rapids of power politics—intimately related to the ineluctable matrix of all life. Huck Finn of Piedmont grows into a Faust who never loses his sense of awe at what those powders, liquids, sludges and ores can really do to one another, and to us.

Scores of lively figures bring the chemistry to dramatic life—"hydrochloric acid . . . is one of those frank enemies that come at you shouting from a distance"—but Levi's main aim is to get across what almost any sentient mind ought to find in its context, savoring the intricate and invisible and quirky material relationships that surround us. Like Dreiser, he sees the human as a chemism, but goes far beyond, humanizing his chosen chemicals into performers in an erudite drama whose rules framed themselves in the first few seconds of the Big Bang.

It is an amazing, delightful conception, linking Levi to such writers as Sir Thomas Browne and Francis Ponge; he doesn't stick as closely to the periodic table as I'd hoped (he ignores atomic weight, as well as 82 of the elements), doesn't always give the titular element full play in the chapter named for it, and doesn't seem to want to exploit the table as a structure-conferring device.

Yet such carping is the measure of the man's originality. This is one of the most intelligent books to come along in years, not only because it reveals a fine mind having sport with things it knows backwards, but also because, with articulate and near-mystical infatuation, it exposes the riddles of material being. Look, says Levi, chemistry is like architecture. Look: to support himself, the chemist fornicates with matter. Certain none too sociable Levi ancestors resemble inert grasses. Fritters made with sanitary cotton have "a vague taste of burnt sugar." And, if you are tempted to try selling stannous chloride to the makers of mirrors, remember, "It is aggressive but also delicate, like certain unpleasant sports opponents who whine when they lose." This particular comparison goes on for another eight lines: copious and cogent, yet not half so telling as cosmetics made from excrement (the comic mode of alchemy) or the analogy drawn between chemistry and genocide (the tragic mode of it): "The trade of chemist (fortified, in my case, by the experience of Auschwitz) teaches you to overcome, indeed to ignore, certain revulsions that are neither necessary nor congenital: matter is matter, neither noble nor vile, infinitely transformable, and its proximate origin is of no importance whatever." That is surely one way of coping with Nazism, but as bogus as the vindication of human violence by the violence in stellar evolution. Levi makes you think, and, then, after you have thought, makes you want to think more.

The most brilliant chapter is the one about carbon (carbon "says everything to everyone"), one atom of which we observe transmigrating from limestone to a falcon's lung, thence to wine, a drinker's liver, an insect's eye, a glass of milk, and finally the brain of an author called Primo Levi. The chapter is a classic and should be anthologized all over the world. Like the carbon chapter, the entire book is what Levi calls "a micro-history" of such humans as have tied their fates, "indelibly, to bromine or propylene." Whatever your fancy—argon, potassium, mercury, tin, silver—this book will give you not only chapter and verse, but also an imaginative flight of high caliber. "The number of atoms is so great," Levi writes, "that one could always be found whose story coincides with any capriciously invented story." Some of the stories in this book are more capricious than others, but behind them all there is always the history of the element, its etymology even, its reputation and its honors, its shortcomings and its future. Processes, too, attract his eye, all of them inexhaustible objects of contemplation ("distilling is beautiful. First of all, because it is a slow, philosophic, and silent occupation . . ."). And there is a lovely opening chapter on the culture of Jewish Piedmont.

Essentially this is a book of changes, epitomized perhaps by students' making silver nitrate from 5-lire coins and chloride of nickel from "the 20-cent pieces with the flying naked lady." The same loving eye for curiosa retrieves the Yiddish word for the vomit of infants; the "inexplicable imprecation . . . May he have an accident shaped like an umbrella"; and the infinitive *laetari* ("to rejoice") in the Latin word, *laetamen,* for manure. Nothing is alien to Levi (who must not be confused with another Italian author, Carlo Levi, the "illustrious namesake" mentioned in this book).

Witold Gombrowicz
Ferdydurke and *Pornografia*

V ICISSITUDE IS A WEAK WORD for the long day's journey into light of Witold Gombrowicz, but it is vicissitude along with bitterness and frustration that made his books what they are. In 1939 he went to Argentina to lecture, active but unknown, and he did not reappear until 1963. He has been variously dubbed a Rabelais, a combination of Ionesco, S.J. Perelman and Ilf and Petrov, another Sterne, "the Polish Till Eulenspiegel" and, by *L'Express* of Paris, "the greatest unknown writer of our time." A man so various that he seems to be not Gombrowicz but all mankind's epitome—especially if we are to judge him by *Ferdydurke,* a madcap and acid extravaganza in which a malign professor sets about reducing a thirty-year-old man to boobydom, and *Pornografia,* a less self-indulgent, less fizzing, altogether more austere and baneful work that shows two aging bachelors intent on corrupting two adolescents.

The theme in common—the clever's perversion of the more or less innocent, the old's inimical and envious manipulation of the young—stems from Gombrowicz's announced resolve (a threat) to celebrate the sexuality in very savant, the feckless juvenile in every man over thirty. His hates are intellect pretending to independence of the flesh, maturity setting up as omniscience, man wanting to be a god, and even books that have nothing to offer but "meaning." I hear his plaint as an ironic hymnody for the seven ages of the flesh of man, as a plea for fusing hedonism with hilarity. Not spiritual love, not wisdom even, not fatalism, but a boisterous leer at the mind's passion to find something it can be happy about. Down—to lovingly elaborate execution in both novels—go the mores, codes, cults and nostrums of society on both sides of the Iron Curtain: education is a sorcerer's prank; liberalism is a timid vacuousness; integrity is a lie maintained in the teeth of an all-devouring body-chemistry; piety is nothing but the last vestige of man's enervated imagination. The world is bad; only the flesh is reliable. Or so it seems.

Both *Ferdydurke* and *Pornografia* imply (as all satire has to imply) a more sensible way of living than the one denounced. The Gombrowicz way seems to be an opportunistic sensualism translating Montaigne's skepticism into an 1890-ish yen to burn with a hard, gem-like flame (I mean laser), cutting the cuttable because it is cuttable, improvising evil out of sheer creative malignity, writing nihilistic books because—even among subtle intellectuals—there is a rumor that nihilistic books don't count: the nihilism kills the book; the book invalidates the nihilism.

In fact Gombrowicz mocks even satire itself for belonging to what he calls "a higher world of culture" predicated on sense, logic, decorum and sanity: all that old high camp we got from the Greeks. What he writes is really pseudo-satire, inviting us to giggle, to drown thought in the lubricious anarchy of the flesh, and then—when the flesh begins to turn to grass—to set the mind working at a lubricious anarchy of its own. The main thing is to hinder any sense of shame or of self-dividedness—never to have to cry, as Yeats once did at an Oxford stage breakfast in the Mitre Hotel quite early in the century, "Gentlemen, the perpetual tragedy of sexual intercourse is the perpetual virginity of the

soul!" Gombrowicz thinks the mind can deflower itself; not only can
but ought to. So, from him, we get no simple hipster-swyving but the
most phantom fornication of all, which—by means of voyeurism,
sadistic criminality, and all manner of perverse vicariousness—
conducts us from merely temporary conclusions of the mind (or of the
mind's rationality) to a debauching and defiling of any human faculty
capable of creating ideals that enslave and thus "infantilize" us. Our
"high" culture, based on absolutes and maxima, demands too much of
us, he says: the hero of *Ferdydurke* is "a gentleman who becomes a
child because other people treat him like one. *Ferdydurke* is intended to
reveal the Great Immaturity of humanity." Man's nature is too much
for his aspirations, and so we create for ourselves "a sort of 'subculture':
a world made out of the refuse of a higher world . . . a domain of trash,
immature myths, inadmissible passions . . . a secondary domain of
compensation."

So, Gombrowicz seems to say, the more knowledge we stack up,
the more alert and demanding our minds become—the faster we read
and travel and recover and the more efficiently we withhold the ovum
or kill sperm—the more mediocre we want to be. We want a less
intricate, less hectic, less exacting way of preserving our identities: we
reject adulthood for Yahoohood, people for pin-ups, hand-made for
mass-produced, art for *Kitsch,* love for romance, "composed of" for the
incorrect and unnecessary "comprised of," Faulkner for Irving Wallace, Gombrowicz for Ian Fleming. . . . I wonder. Most intellectuals
remain intellectuals to the end; most cultivated people remain cultivated; most grammatical people stick to their guns impenitently; the
Faulkner enthusiast doesn't defect downhill to Irving Wallace. . . . No,
the elite holds tight, no matter how harassing or comfortable its life
becomes.

What, then, does Gombrowicz mean? Who are his mediocrity-
lovers? *Hoi polloi?* Hardly, because these people stay at the same
cultural level all their lives, unclimbing and unable to fall, enslaved over
here by advertising, by propaganda over there. If Gombrowicz the
exiled Pole were protesting on their behalf he would have a better case:
the power-wielders, capitalist or communist, certainly *don't* want these
people to grow up. But Gombrowicz's heroes aren't ordinary people at
all: *Ferdydurke* is about a writer and his professor-captor; *Pornografia*
is about two twisted egg-heads. So is it the intelligentsia that

Gombrowicz is submitting to his own special brand of derision? Is he another Julien Benda, indicating in another *Trahison des clercs* the self-betrayal of the best minds? I trust not; it wouldn't be true of the best minds in the English-speaking countries, and I don't think it's true of the best minds in Russia. The real target, it seems to me, is the paranoiac second-rate mind that sells out to any totalitarian regime willing to make him important: a Goebbels, a Zhdanov. Why, then, does Gombrowicz indict mind *per se* rather than the paranoiacs of the intellectual sub-establishment? Let him by all means denounce the commissars (he has excellent reason to), but let him not denounce mind because commissars pretend to it, and let him not preach infantilism (as he does) because totalitarianism is fundamentally as infantile as Cops and Robbers. His metaphor, it seems to me, is expressionist rather than definitive, local and private rather than general and public. In other words, his own sufferings and privations have somewhat distorted his view of the world as a whole, and we have to read him (especially *Pornografia*) not so much for what he says directly as for what he reveals, in his own performance, of a man trying to say something directly but finding his own past pain in the way. What is interesting is not so much Gombrowicz's fictional specimens as Gombrowicz himself as a specimen of a certain frame of mind.

In the preface to *Pornografia* he taunts the reader: "it could be claimed," he says, "that in *Ferdydurke* I am struggling proudly against immaturity. And yet you can already perceive an ambiguous note which could imply that this opponent of immaturity is mortally in love with immaturity." Doesn't this show how despair with the antics of modern man ("rape, slavery, and boyish squabbles") can send even a Gombrowicz to the brink of near-hysterical surrender? We watch him fighting the temptation to embrace a perverse absolute of evil, of silliness, of trash. Anything, so long as it is definite, complete; anything other than middling virtue in a century of horrors. This, surely, is the kind of pornography he has in mind: a harlotry of the conscience, envisioning "An attempt to revive Polish eroticism" (i.e. Polish human-ness), but desiring mainly "a descent to the dark limits of the conscience and the body." The point of these two books which coerce and dare and blackmail us then becomes something like this: By all means touch pitch, but don't make love to it. Don't (as I, Gombrowicz do) pretend to do so, coyly winking while I undertake a feat worthy of Himmler: I mean menticide, the slaughter of mind.

I may have entirely misunderstood Gombrowicz's ironic postures: his view *would* be funny if it didn't seem so tragic in its implications, and vice versa. The mediocre grin that masks a broken heart isn't perverse at all. What is perverse (and, I think, is meant to seem emetically so) is this man's erotics of disaster—a kind of Middle-European, vengeful iconoclasm which, having rejected humanity because of the Treblinkas, sees nothing but Treblinkas and therefore wants the abolition of man. Overplaying it, as Gombrowicz does, must be his way of inviting us in: he makes deliberate mistakes to attract us to himself, there in the books, the most complex and sophistical character of all. After all, the narrator of *Pornografia* is called Witold too. His victim? The author. The fact that Witold and his Nietzschean friend, Frederick, go to visit the country estate of a friend during the German occupation, and there resolve on erotic mischief that finally entails a double murder, isn't the point; no, this plot is a piece of apparatus given to readers so that we can make the point for ourselves. We have to address the dummy before we can meet the ventriloquist.

Pornografia is both caustic and hypnotic, both overt and inscrutable, one of the most complex spare-written novels I know. Such light as it sheds is elegiac: "After the age of thirty," says Witold the narrator, "men lapse into monstrosity. *In their youth the whole beauty of the world was on their side.*" The italics are his, his creator's. No wonder, then, the novel ends with that ritualistic, muddled double murder, the fruit of monstrosity's tampering with beauty until beauty—those two adolescents already interested in each other without showing the fact to anyone else—betrays itself by taking sides out of sheer malice. Such is Gombrowicz's version of the ironical confusions we surround ourselves with. He writes as a clown who is also a scapegoat, pawning his heart and mind in order to make fables whose final point is that man is a creature still able to choose between acting badly and acting slightly less badly. The pornographic pantaloon called Gombrowicz does not even own his own flesh.

Ludvik Vaculík
1: *The Guinea Pigs*

A LL THE IMPLICATIONS of this fable's title bloom in the narrative itself, supplying knowns that generate a mysterious algebra— part political, part ritualistic, and in part a defensive enigma. Readers may wonder what they're reading, whether allegory, riddle, or cathartic imagining, but they will certainly know they are being exposed to something jauntily horrific.

First things first, however. A guinea pig is any of various South American burrowing rodents of the genus *Cavia,* having variously colored hair and no visible tail, widely domesticated as pets and often used as experimental animals. A guinea pig is also a person used for experimentation. And, although "guinea" is probably Guiana confused with the Guinea coast of Africa, it can also evoke an obsolete British gold coin worth slightly more than a pound.

In Ludvik Vaculík's novel all these significances come together and interact teasingly: Vasek, the bank-clerk narrator, a fussily affectionate domestic tyrant who keeps guinea pigs at home, is himself a guinea pig (timid and often inert pawn of the state). In vain he bullies his wife and two sons, but when he begins experimenting with his guinea pigs his world turns upside down and the humans of Prague turn into guinea pigs, and vice versa.

All this while the currency system, localized in the bank Vasek works for but implicitly nationwide, begins to collapse: Every bank employee tries to smuggle money out, is affably relieved of it by guards, but goes home wondering why the sum confiscated is always greater than the sum restored to the bank.

It's upon such cumulative incongruities that Vaculík plays in this, his third novel, combining meaning with nonsense, subjecting the reader to opposite pressures: Sometimes the fable seems only a bit more allegorical than it doesn't, sometimes the other way around. We know what we have witnessed, but must guess at its point. Things that resemble each other correspond only in their absurdity and can't be matched up as, say, theme and echo, micro- and macrocosm, worm's-eye and bird's-eye views.

From the outset we know we are dealing with a sly, unobliging narrator. "There are more than a million people living in the city of

Prague" he begins, "whom I'd just as soon not name here." Just so, otherwise the roll call would preclude the novel, and one has throughout the sense that these words, these animals, these clerks, are here only to keep other words, animals, clerks, out. It's a fiction of excluded equivalents, coined from a world in which all things have the same value, are equally worthless, in which Vaculík lives disgraced, an underground man in contemporary Prague, forbidden to publish.

Any image or emblem is as useful as another: Where the explicit is banned, any obliquity will vent the frustration and the rage. Reading between the lines, one comes to read also the blank in the margins, the space around the images, the silences in the conversations, even the silence in what is said. *The Guinea Pigs* is an enigma extruded from an intensely emotional state; we should not mind its inexplicitness any more than a Chinese minds the abstractness of his ideograms.

Supine, with a guinea pig on his stomach or nuzzling in his armpit, or violining one to sleep with an extended G-D fifth chord, or disciplining one with a pencil, or half-drowning it, or feeding it alcohol, or revolving it on the phonograph turntable at 45 rpm, Vasek is both doodling (exercizing power of life and death with compensatory impunity) and preparing himself for the moment when scale changes and "I'm so little that I barely reach up to his claw, I'm as big as a grain of wheat" a congruous effigy for Vaculík, author of the 1968 "Prague Manifesto of 2,000 Words" that got him banned.

No wonder one of the novel's constant images is Poe's maelstrom, sucking first the currency, then all else, into the nether regions. No wonder there's a character *called* Maelstrom or that Vasek suddenly begins to narrate his doings in the third person singular "I started to write this book in my own person. . . . What should I do now? All I can do is to switch over to the third person, and when I get the time, someday, I'll rewrite the beginning." He never does, but in the end manages to report his own disappearance, his son's asking for him, without explanation: A brilliant trick, showing how an "I" becomes an unperson although still a voice in his own head, in ours as well.

The novel's conclusion is obscure, apocalyptic and bloody, and one comes away from the reading convinced that something that was nothing has taken place, like a negative spell distilled from scorn and sparely crafted into a logo of impersonal defiance. Anything less socialist-realist would be hard to imagine.

2: *The Axe*

A S VACULÍK SAID in a recent interview, "For us, the main thing, the most valuable thing, is to be able to make one's existence known, to show that one has not disappeared behind bars or quit writing." With utterly comprehensible indignation, he objects to being regarded as fodder for anti-Communist propaganda, relegated from man of imagination to simplistic ideological emblem. Instead, he says, "What I ask most fervently for myself is that I be able to concentrate on creating something beautiful, something inspiring and something of lasting value, something that won't even remind the reader of the regime. I want to write as if current conditions did not exist, or as if I felt at ease with them."

It sounds preposterous, but it's valid for him and has to be valid for us. After all, just because a Nabokov regularly hands totalitarianism its lumps, we don't homogenize him into a propaganda artist. So too, with "Abram Tertz" (Andrei Sinyavsky), author of *The Trial Begins;* whatever his protestations (either about being a loyal Communist or Russia's needing a phantasmagorical art), one sees in him a sensibility naturally expressionistic, which would have been the same had he hailed from Des Moines.

Yet, having gone this far, one cannot ignore Vaculík's abiding concern with thought-control, socialist uniformity, vacuous and drab sloganeering. Vasek, the bank-clerk narrator of *The Guinea Pigs,* suddenly switches from first to third person, thus reporting his own disappearance; the eminent journalist who narrates *The Axe* returns to his native village in rural Moravia and realizes how the political system twisted and stunted his father's basically expansive, colorful personality and transformed him into a civic pawn. The reader's problem, then, becomes one of appreciating art without allegorizing it and this entails responding, almost *in vacuo,* to the loving delineation of a carpenter who spent years on end in Persia, where wages were higher (a kind of Slav Klondike); the shock of recognition when the son finds how callous he's filially been; and, above all, the holy infatuation with the Moravian landscape, its dreariness and its bellflowers, its therapeutic greens and golds.

Where *The Guinea Pigs* has a dry, almost diagrammatic quality, with lyrical excursions concerning actual guinea pigs only, *The Axe* is a brooding, undulating tone poem; the one bothers the brain, the other the heart, and in fact this novel compresses into a small portion of itself the polemical absurdities that shape the other one. Which is just as well, for the petty weights-and-measures bureaucratic to-and-fro of the communal farm which the father runs is a less than beguiling theme. On the other hand, his letters from Persia, which the son keeps dipping into, mix lush vignettes with awkward solicitude, malaria and diarrhea with yearnings for the apples and damsons of home. Rooted in this epistolary compost, the father grows into a mythic figure who, even after his return from Persia, wanders away into the hills to ski, and yet, paradoxically, prunes other men's trees on the quiet. As well as kicking over the traces now and then, he's a paragon of ecumenical care. Nazis, party officials, come and go; the narrator gets his editor sacked by over-investigating a suicide case; but the land, and the son's memory of his father's atavistic intimacy with it, stay put like eidola.

At its most ambitious, *The Axe* moves into eschatological ruminations on the atoms within the life cycle, but such isn't Vaculík's natural idiom (more's the pity). At its best, it competes with D.H. Lawrence at his least tedious, in poignant snapshots of family life; dumplings and poppyseed, parboiled potatoes, Wenceslas pears, games of halma, Number 10 nails. At its least appealing, it shows what happens when a regime bans geese from the village green and decrees it a square. The narrator and his good-citizen bus-driver brother steal wood together and manage to dodge the car which pursues them; but that engaging image of revolt dims beside the one of the father healing his son's cuts and bruises with his own saliva. Minor, mild, unostentatious and restricted as he is, Vaculík is the kind of novelist who can't tell us he's holding his breath; but the beating of his pulse comes through, like a drum roll for toy soldiers.

George Konrád
The Case Worker

ALL THE CULTURAL and linguistic way from Hungary comes this virtuoso feat of complex prose: The kind of fiction hardly anyone writes in English, or at any rate gets into print. But *The Case Worker* comes also from a much more exotic region than Hungary, from a monstrous yet ecumenically sane country of the mind in which one man, a state welfare worker, becomes for a short time the custodian of an imbecilic boy whose parents have just done away with themselves. He does this out of conscience and duty, but also because he is interested in extremes of human mutation and therefore can bear to look hard at nature's mistakes. In no time at all he is empathizing almost as if he had created the boy himself: related to him, fond of him, and responsible for him as well—as, in a pragmatic way, a case worker can be said to be; as, in a metaphysical way, a God unquestionably is.

"Behind the bars," one paragraph begins, "midget heads, distended bodies, misshapen heads, stunted bodies; pointed skulls, receding skulls, dropsically arched, hollow-sunken, lopsided, deeply cleft skulls; frilled harelips, lipless mouths open to the jaw, dribbling, black, drooping tongues, cleft palates; a fatty growth from the cheekbone to the forehead where the eye hollows should be, and on it a minute eyebrow..."

On it pours, a heartfelt catalogue of chance deformities, an elegy for grossly disqualified babies, of whom some will grow into adult surds. Against these institutionalized specters, the first-person narrator sees his charge, Feri Bandula, in sublime proportion: a child whose skull has no rhomboid fontanel, making idiocy inevitable. Deserting his own family to move in with the boy, in the home of the dead parents, he picks up where parenthood left off: "From morning to night, from meal to bowel movement, the father revolved in a closed circle with his son, confining his effort to a few precise, simple, and useless movements."

It is a sealed universe of ordure, wordlessness, and living death, exempt from the charge of sensationalism by the narrator's unshrinking total view, which includes, like some terminal moraine of disasters, what is on the shelves of the institution's morgue; the maimed brains of the defunct "like goose livers in a tub or pallid jellyfish in an aquarium."

The point is exemplary: "We have much to learn from idiots, the blood relatives of inanimate objects." Anyone who has had dealings with, as the Greek word implies, these "private persons," will see the truth of that. Even more tellingly, this novelist is a former superintendent of Budapest child-welfare organization: Not only does he know what he is talking about but in making high literary art out of biological catastrophe—not merely lament, or pleas for reform, or shadow-boxing with passive euthanasia—he reveals the idiocy in each of us, whatever our intellectual pretensions. Docile in front of Feri Bandula, the case worker becomes a Columbus of compassion, a Copernicus of ineluctable fact.

Written in the drabbest prose (which it isn't) this would have been a powerful tale. As it is, spiraling away from us, and then noosing us on the recoil, in cumulative sentences sometimes a page long, it dramatizes an outraged sense of wonder at the glut the universe contains. At so much that is unnecessary. Beating Feri on the kneecap with a wooden spoon, or brushing a sugar cube against his lips, the case worker must be pored over—like the boy, an inexhaustible object of thought: a mind addressing minds about a dysgenic non-mind. What you find here is a Camusian *juge-pénitent,* who goes light-years beyond sanctimonious obsession, a Beckettian Watt who inches into the idiot's *vita minima* as if it's red-hot lead, an expressionist novel which, like some of the poems of Gottfried Benn, seize on nature's blunders for emblems of human indignation.

Vladimir Nabokov
1: *King, Queen, Knave*

MOST ETERNAL TRIANGLES look alike and are alike, their principle—as Nabokov reveals with icy panache in this, his second, novel—being the uses to which the participants put or do not put their God-given sexuality. Eternal triangularity is as bald, as banal, as that, notwithstanding the hint in "eternal" of a sublime venality to which all triangulators, as programmed cards being shuffled in God's pack, are entitled. Ownership of the beloved's body counts for more, it seems, than access to his or her soul. Adultery is flesh and hydro-dynamics only.

Implying all this in frissons of sardonic gaiety, *King, Queen, Knave*—first published in Berlin in Russian in 1928 and itself set in Berlin—can be read as a sermon. Or as a long sneer. Ostensibly the story of Franz, who comes from the provinces to work in his uncle's emporium but soon begins to cuckold him as well, it is also, even predominantly, an exercise in articulate superciliousness. Not that Nabokov morally censures either the fumbling nephew or the expertly lascivious Frau Dreyer; for they, like the mechanical walking dolls that Herr Dreyer (say it aloud) plans for his shop and dotes upon, are puppets only: queen and knave. But he can, and does, judge them on aesthetic grounds. While lust, boredom and suburban romanticism go to work on the two lovers, conducting them to the cliché terminus of plotting a murder they cannot accomplish, Nabokov ridicules them in several ways.

Simply, he views the erotics with a mechanic's aplomb: "her rapid cries expressed fierce satisfaction." Complexly, he observes the *mise en scène* with fanatical care, as if to say: how, planted amid the lush vulgarity of the Dreyer house (all the furnishings chosen by herself), can Martha not feel herself to be part of the physical amenities? And that is how Dreyer treats and regards her. Or how, amid the shabby clutter of Franz's apartment, can they bear their lovemaking to come to an end?

Pawns rather than degenerates—he wears his pen in his pajama pocket; she, after a miscarriage, has an almost hygienic fear of pregnancy—they become "our lovers," with which proprietorially indulgent but disowning phrase Nabokov annuls them as people, only to incorporate them as Punch-and-Judy-couchant into a glittering heraldic design that includes dummies of all kinds: dolls bourgeois or battery-driven, as well as Franz's landlord ("the whole world was but a trick of his") whose "wife," of whom Franz gets only the merest glimpse, is just a wig on a stick in a shawl, forever and ever in the same chair.

These and sundry rich idiots, concupiscent stenographers, tennis athletes, chess crouchers, a whole concert of dehumanized yawns and yahoo yodels, not to mention the Nabokovs themselves ("Sometimes the man carried a butterfly net... her fiancé or husband, slender,

elegantly balding, contemptuous of everything on earth but her")—
these are the targets of his uncompassionate intelligence. The novel
develops, in fact, into a virtuoso piece in which Nabokov the sardonic
captor of specimens records his gratitude to the world of phenomena
for its just being there—a cosmic favor done him because even God
wouldn't like those verbal nets of his to rot unused.

Manifestly a young man's book, coruscating with self-conscious
but original cleverness and a-twitch with ebullient jubilation, *King,
Queen, Knave* is exactly what Nabokov himself calls it in a sly
foreword: "this bright brute. . . . Of all my novels . . . the gayest." The
only person it is about is, of course, himself; but then, he knows himself
better than many novelists know their characters. And, in an extra
sense, he is here his own specimen, introduced by a "reviser," twice
older than twenty-eight, who points up the young Nabokov's "amiable
little imitations of *Madame Bovary*," warns of "cruel traps" set for
Freudians, and remarks on "the lack of any emotional involvement and
the fairy-tale freedom inherent in an unknown milieu. . . . I might have
staged KQKn in Rumania or Holland."

Just a pack of cards, then, as Nabokov said, having even so early
the sterile sheen, the scalpeled, gloating precision that make his
detractors envious at times and send his admirers into an aristocratic
trance.

2: *A Russian Beauty*

CONSPICUOUS AMONG AUTHORIAL WAYS of having cake and
eating it as well is Samuel Beckett's doing his *Murphy* into
French and then, in full creative spate after switching languages, doing
his French novels into English (often without assistance): a burly
symbiosis within one career. In contrast, Vladimir Nabokov fetched
works from his fairly distant past (the earliest story in the present
volume of 13 was written in 1924, the latest in 1940) and usually helped
his son to translate them, thus engineering not so much a transposition
as a self-renaissance, opsimathically perfecting his youth through the
time machine of language.

Elegantly hard-boiled, the title story tells of an exile who marries
"a well-off athletic widower, author of books on hunting" and dies in

childbirth the following summer; but then, after all, her mother had died of typhus, her brother had been shot. What she lost in fulfillment the family gained in constancy of waste. There follows, in "The Leonardo," the knifing-to-death of an eccentric who might have been played by Edmund Gwenn: thought a poet, he was in fact a counterfeiter, and might well have been credited with the visual audacity of the youth who, in the next story, looks through his lashes and achieves "an illusionary perspective . . . a remote mirage enchanting in its graphic transparency and isolation."

Meatier, and more upsetting, are the stories about people trying in vain to tell a deaf old widow of her son's death (she hospitably and uninterruptably talks them down) and a passionate anti-sightseer who ends up in a museum oneirically fulfilling a request to examine a certain painting (he gets lost in exhibit after exhibit until, trapped in an indoor panorama of Russia, the land he'd left, he's arrested). Acerbically told, but lovingly tooled, these two stories belong together; the pain of not getting through matches that of getting beyond oneself; the pain of isolation matches that of trespass, both at root states of mind. As well, Nabokov includes a duel story almost Maughamian; a sly one about doomed explorers (one of whom has a butterfly net); a funny one about a *viveur* picking up a woman on a train; and a weakish long one ("not my favorite piece," Nabokov says) about a dwarf. As always in this man's work, the crass fail; the ungifted dither; the best groom their intensity into *savoir-feral*. Sharing his character's expatriation, but having transcended it, Nabokov writes them up to write them off, an arbiter of *virtu,* William Tell at the turkey shoot.

One of these pieces, however, is extraordinary: the first act of an epistemological opera, a comic rune. In the spring of 1940, Nabokov left Paris for America, gave up writing in Russian and took to English. Before he left, he destroyed all but the first two chapters (and some notes) of an unfinished novel, and these he reprints as "Ultima Thule" and "Solus Rex." Having lost his wife, the narrator distracts himself with an imaginary country that soon becomes an obsession, but his initial—and initiating—experience is with his former tutor, Falter, who accidentally solves "the riddle of the universe," screams in a hotel room for 15 minutes and shares the solution with a psychiatrist (who promptly dies of astonishment). Granted that this first chapter (30 pages) has all the spectatorial suavity we expect from Nabokov, it also evokes Beckett and Borges. For obvious reasons, the book couldn't be finished: how sustain it by procrastinating an outcome not available? The second chapter is less brilliant, less probing, less riddling, but it offers the irony of the narrator's wife being resuscitated (only, a note informs us, to be killed by a bomb in the nonexistent chapter three). According to Nabokov, "what really makes me regret its non-completion is that it promised to differ radically by the quality of its coloration, by the amplitude of its style, by something undefinable about its powerful underflow, from all my other works in Russian."

One shares that regret, but is grateful for what is left of that lost stylishness. Such a book is clearly best left open-ended, although Nabokov might have taken a hint from his character who says "everything beyond death is, at best, fictitious." This novel would have been Nabokov's *Watt,* the last novel Beckett wrote in English (*Watt*'s theme, in part, the enigmatic nature of Mr. Knott, in whose house Watt works for a period). As it is, Nabokov's remnant is just as conclusive in its dubiety as Beckett's completed work, a lovely triumph of agnostic tact. And of style. Part of it goes as follows:

> Apparently, then, if I admitted that, in moments of happiness, of rapture, when my soul is laid bare, I suddenly feel that there is no extinction beyond the grave; that in an adjacent locked room, from under whose door comes a frosty draft, there is being prepared a peacock-eyed radiance, a pyramid of delights akin to the Christmas tree of my childhood; that everything—life, patria, April, the sound of a spring or that of a dear voice—is but a muddled preface, and that the main text still lies ahead—if I can feel that way, Falter, is it not possible to live, to live—tell me it's possible, and I'll not ask you anything more.

Thus the hero, Sineusov, addresses Falter, while the skeptical reader conjectures that the main text, on the contrary, has already been written, in 25 books; and how glad of them we are. It's as if the concluding story, "The Circle," opening with the phrase "In the second place" and ending with a sentence that starts "In the first place," were an index to Nabokov's whole oeuvre: second things first, which means art before ultimate solutions. Longing for a lost Russia—"dazzling green mornings when the coppice deafened you with its golden orioles"—the émigrés of this book generalize themselves into exiles from heaven. "Utterly unlike any of the Nabokovs" they may be, as the author points out, they are pretty much like everyone else, whereas Nabokov's English is not.

William H. Gass
1: *Omensetter's Luck*

IN THE FIRST PART (very brief), during an auction long after the Omensetters have gone, someone mutters, "Omensetter, now—he was—." No one ever knows quite what to say about this almost legendary man who seemed preternaturally endowed with vigor, hunches and healing power. Dark as pot-roast gravy, he loomed up one day with pregnant wife, daughters and dog. Sundays he strolled by the river and then, sprawled on the gravel with his feet trailing in the water, heard the Reverend Mr. Jethro Furber preach. Like the sun indulging a half-moon. Dionysian he was, but the Ohio locals construed his superhumanity as mere luck, minimizing him the whole way. All the same, he cured Henry Pimber of lockjaw.

So it goes, with Gass himself entering into the garrulous, half-catechistic evocation of this masterful figure. Pimber admires, tries to emulate. Furber, whose bitter, lubricious maunderings occupy most of the novel, timidly casts Omensetter as an agent of the devil. Gass is like Joyce hymning the rivers, and one would have to be criminally tone-deaf and almost snow-blind not to register the sonic and visual brilliance of the language. It has a pregnant, swaying physicality, with an undertow of festive and smutty limericks: a delight to say aloud and a continuing sound in the mind. In short, a style.

But the broken music of Jethro Furber's interior fire-sermon grows into an excess: not so much verbose as obese. The self-inflicted talk peels away from events like (to borrow from Gass) "skin that's bubbled from the bone as paper does sometimes from the plaster." The problem is the novel's density, which Gass relieves only by changes in rhythm—convulsive shudders of an epileptic having an attack in deep mud.

The main thing, however (and it would be grossly ungrateful not to say it), is that William Gass is a writer of muscular prowess. Getting Ohio people into language such as this is an almost campanological feat: there they are, all talking at once in the belfry of Gass's head, blotting out the presence and the memory of Omensetter as if fending off God Almighty. There's a mythical side to this gifted first novel, usually embedded, like a root, in the incessant, hitherandthithering yap-yap of the onlookers: "Mrs. Valient Hatstat, rings spotted on her fingers, a small white scar like an unwiped white of egg lying in the corner of her mouth . . . Doctor Truston Orcutt of the rotting teeth and juice stained beard, who looked like a house with a rusting eave. . . . Israbestis Tott, together beggar, hurdy-gurdy, cup, chain, monkey . . . and all those others . . . making sounds to celebrate the death of tea-weak Henry Pimber."

2: *Willie Masters' Lonesome Wife*

A LOT OF WHAT is visually verbal in our society isn't paginal at all, but bombards the eye in various ways through neon or through posters, labels, buttons, postmark legends, and so on. The eye wearies, but it nonetheless absorbs information from what might be thought of as being beyond the traditional visual field, the page (or the TV screen). In other words, our reading habits in the largest sense are more elastic, more three-dimensional, than they used to be, so it's inevitable that we should approach the format of the printed page with an acute sense of its limitations—of its top-to-bottomness, its left-to-rightness, its essentially chronological mode. We miss, perhaps, the random grouping of the non-paginal, and what it has in common with the randomness of what is non-verbal.

Not surprisingly, writers have acknowledged these changes in our ways of looking at print. Stultifying to read in bulk, concrete poetry nonetheless delivers and emphasizes something morphological in individual letters, and a goodly number of novelists have resorted to visual devices that recall Sterne and Lewis Carroll, not so much supplanting word with icon as augmenting the one with the other. No doubt of it, the writer in the third third of this century is in the interesting position of, as a communicator, having at his disposal not only all the orthodox deployments of typography but also what, by now, are the orthodoxies of advertising (giant lettering and lettering in color; fast-registering logo's and subliminal residues), not to mention those of the comic strip (words in balloons) and the movie (the subdivided screen). It's only reasonable that the writer should add to his arsenal in this way, winning for himself some of the still-surviving visual impact there is in Japanese or Chinese, and fortifying semiology with something graphic or even sculptural.

All very well, many readers and some writers might say, but visual gimmicks are a feeble supplement to printed texts and run contrary to the principle of reading, which is to chart your way painstakingly from line to line, registering the connected argument as you go, all startling effects having to be made in the same material and not imported from an alien medium. Well, I for one don't buy that: There are no rules about mixing media, not even about which mixtures work and which don't. And here comes an established and respected novelist, with a performative text that's something between collage and recitative, a text that regales the eye with combinations of italics and bold face, footnotes and headnotes, asterisks and treble clefs, placards that tend to dominate the page and parabolical tails of words that go wagging off it, lines that curve up and down as if seen through a distorting lens or arrange themselves into the shape of a Christmas tree, a page faced by its mirror-image, pages ringed brown-maroon by coffee cups, and interleaved shots of nudes that sometimes have the text itself elbowed into a corner as if in parody of Life's ousting Art. All in all, it's a defiant, ingeniously staged typographical concerto for eye and berserk compositor, in the course of which Gass keeps the mind at full stretch as he feeds it information from all quarters of the page and sustains as many as three parallel streams of narrative all competing for simultaneous attention.

Ostensibly this is a lament uttered by Babs Masters on the occasion of her recognizing what the onset of aging can do to any woman, and a lonely one in particular. Ranging as far and wide as she mentally can, she plucks the joys and monotonies of her life together into an erotic, uncouth, and sleazy synopsis which is as centrifugal as the typography. On one hand, this is a case history volunteered by the case herself; on the other, it's an essay on the mind-body nexus. You would expect the first from the author of *Omensetter's Luck,* in which

Gass's reverence for unmetropolitan eccentricity develops into an eloquent general summation, and you would expect the second from the professional philosopher which Gass happens to be. What's new, at least from him, is the liberties taken for the sake of making a prose monologue seem, on the page, less rehearsed, less glib, and less groomed than usual. Let's face it: The lonely Mrs. Masters has an untidy head whose quality could not, I think, have been gotten convincingly across in conventional prose conventionally set out. It's no accident that the sixty-odd pages are unnumbered and that all but the last eight (which are glossy white and where Gass more or less speaks in his own person) are a matte gray; the telling is as much tactile as verbal, and as much visual as it is either.

I mentioned Gass's beginning to speak in his own person, and he makes it clear that Mrs. Masters, once again (but this time verbally rather than sexually), is being used: "I," she is made to say towards the end, "am that lady language chose to make her playhouse of." And what we have, after finishing the book, is a retrospective sense of having witnessed—assisted at—a ventriloquial showpiece of literary style in which Gass, by juxtaposing the humdrum with the histrionic, has worked compassion into a just rhetoric that runs the gamut of human commotion from spit to spirit. Mrs. Masters tells you to "expectorate into a glass... Drink... Analyze your reluctance. And wonder why they call saliva the sweet wine of love," a bit of perception from which, although in a footnote, we soar into an anthem on the notion of whiteness:

> marbles, japonicas, and pearls, as in a joyful day, the innocence of brides, benignity of age, superiority of race, the robes of the redeemed, the bear of the poles, albino seas, their sharks and squalls, their whales; and thus univer-sals ...

Predictably, the peroration to all this is earthy and urbane:

> It's not the languid pissing prose we've got, we need; but poetry, the human muse, full up, erect and on the charge, impetuous and hot and loud and wild like Messalina going to the stews, or those damn rockets streaming headstrong into stars.

To my mind, Gass here proves that straight, rectilinear prose is no longer sufficient for the writer who wants to discuss the spirit of the age with the people most aware of it. How right and fitting it is that one of the evoked ghosts in *Willie Masters' Lonesome Wife* is "Sam" (not Johnson or Beckett, but Samuel Taylor Coleridge, high priest of imagination, the "esemplastic" or unifying power). For Gass here raises that power to its highest and, in so doing sets an alternative standard for American narrative prose. It's no longer useful to try to imagine imagination in the act of imagining, for this is just what Gass makes happen here, low-level through the sluttish Babs, high-level when she tries to think—like a performing flea in Emma Bovary's navel—what it might be like to have a high-caliber litr'y gent talking on your behalf while feeling you up.

3: *The World within the Word*

W HERE GASS STANDS—and like some genie sways to the beat of his own heavy breathing—is clear. His brow is high, his taste learned and eclectic; his responses to books and their authors are both delicate and earthy, and sometimes orchestrated in their own right as complex fugues of unapologetic, wry inventiveness.

"Loud impatient honks and heartfelt belches... pass these days for books," he says in a keen, parabolical essay on Proust. "Cowards and nincompoops abound" as well as "dunderheads reading Balzac the way they would skim *Business Week*." He twice in this book quotes George Eliot's unworldly dictum about living faithfully a hidden life and then reposing in an unvisited tomb. He dotes on Sterne's out-of-time sentence, "A cow broke in tomorrow morning to my Uncle Toby's fortifications" and admiringly dubs Faulkner "Maestro Crescendo."

Who then is Gass? And what? The Phantom of the Opus? The Satrap of Succulence? He is the poetic essayist doubling as critic, but also, through some agile feats of mnemonic possession, being Proust, Valéry, Colette, Malcolm Lowry and Gertrude Stein (as all of whom he is superb), and Freud, Sartre, Henry Miller and Faulkner (as all of whom he is very good). As if hypnotized. As if ravished. As if, thanks to a book review editor who gives him lots of space, driven to disgorge an ectoplasm that, while being superprose, is also one form of interference with the soul, the belly, the very chemicals that transmit thought. Uncanny stuff, his essays are a series of autos-dâ-fé staged in the central nervous systems of the writers he likes. He tells how it feels to be Proust, and the others, and how it feels to be them in the act of being creative. If a tag be needed, this is biotic criticism.

If that seems to type Gass as a highfalutin or ethereal ventriloquist, it shouldn't; he's not. Every essay he writes has a tonic undertow of backsides and blatant vulgarities, not to titillate or be raw but to evince the All—the flux, the heterogeneous plenty—in which, for Gass and others like him, all elements are equal, grist for the stylist's mill. As in this bristling collage from a lecture-essay, "The Ontology of the Sentence, or How to Make a World of Words," in which Gass the professional philosopher and analyst of language gets Gass the verbal Daedalus to do his stuff.

"Every nullity has parents, husky sometimes too, and normal as napkins, even when the warp is square and the weft is round; and the absence of money in an empty purse, the annoying nothing of the nebbish, the missing numbers in an otherwise winning lottery ticket, a fellmonger who sells pans, the unavailable elevator's vertiginous shaft, the apparently adequate parking space, an inexplicable hiatus in some notorious continuum (puzzling as an armistice in peacetime), not to mention, as I nevertheless shall, those peculiar anomalies, the lady novelist, the vaginal orgasm, and the raisinless strawberry; or at bedtime that familiar dry wave dashing against the soft line of some snickering pillow: every one of these catacritical errors is as otherwise to the other as ostrich and angular are, prune and juice too, box and cox, *sic et non,* dear Mom and dearer Dad, and each erupts out of its own emptiness and with its own emptiness into its own emptiness like a cartoon volcano."

See? He reaches a point of voluptuous crisis, at which there is nothing that doesn't belong in the next sentence. No categories prevail except that of what gets into his words and what does not. And this isn't "mere" panache, impasto, purple patch, it's *vision,* fleshed out with jackdaws, snowmen, cascara ("a purge with a name like a river"), his own mother's "miscolored toes," and such a recognition as "There is no o'clock in a cantina." His world is words, his way of being. No wonder he likes images of hurdlers, waterskiers, and that of Cyrano led by the nose. Gass sings the flux, under this or that commercial pretext, and in the end renders what he calls "the interplay of genres...skids of tone and decorum" into cantatas of appreciative excess. A rare gift that yields startling art.

Yet, for most readers, in the end, I suspect, not half so startling as the aphorisms with which he undercuts and counterpoints his flow. Of Proust: "one wonders first if the book will ever end, and then in despair, if it will ever begin." Valéry "kept his notebooks the way some people keep cows—perhaps there would be a little milk." Sartre "lies to look over the edge of an idea like a tourist at a canyon." Paradoxically the effect of these—as of certain cameos (Bertrand Russell as "a unicorn hitched to a beer wagon")—is that of a soothing blink among too many photons. But open your eyes and there again are the waves of Gass's vision rolling in to dazzle and absorb.

Walter Abish
How German Is It

L IKE SNOW, this novel accumulates delicately, lulling the mind with an inaudible dream. At the same time, it keeps the reader busy since it permits, indeed requires, at least three kinds of attention, one of which is to keep straight what happens to Ulrich Hargenau, a novelist formerly implicated in a terrorist plot, after he returns to Germany from Paris, where he's been cooling his heels and his prose. The second kind is to watch how the novel drifts and swells into becoming a metaphor for postwar Germany, and in so doing to figure out (if you can) how accurate the metaphor is. The third, implied perhaps in the book's splintery format (words, lines, short paragraphs isolated by deliberate spacing that suggests continual omissions), is to guess at what isn't there, as if you were flying low over a bombed-out landscape. To do all three at once is best, however, because then you're tuning in to the story line while getting its metaphor in full.

The title itself seems a warning. Neither question nor assertion, it re-forms itself in the mind's ear as "How German It Is," which seems a clever way of getting you (again, as if in a dream) to presuppose a conclusion the book never reaches. And can't, because what the book's about is the arbitrariness of labels contrasted with the teeming individualities lumped together in something called, for convenience's sake, a nation.

Take Ulrich Hargenau, or his conniving brother Helmuth, a famous architect. They're both German, in a very special way, in that their father was executed by firing squad "early one August morning in 1944" for being one of the Stauffenberg group. Now that's a vintage German fate, having a father to whom that's supposed to have happened; I say "supposed" because I don't believe it—after the instant reprisals of July 20, the day of the attempt on Hitler, no one was executed, but all were interrogated, and when executions resumed, early in August, the method was hanging. Between the attempt and early August, the only conspirators shot were those who shot themselves.

So, in one sense, Ulrich's father's fate is mythical, and I think Abish makes it deliberately so, even though the facts are easily found in history books. In other words, the entire tale may not be "true," at least not on the level of the first kind of attention I mentioned above. So the book shifts, almost at once, into metaphor and splinter, tempting you to keep saying, "How German it all is," as if echoing Helmuth's funeral oration on Brumhold, the famous philosopher after whom the local town was named. Invoking "the German passion for exactitude and abstractions," Helmuth conjures up an image of Brumhold (a thinly disguised Heidegger), "sitting at his worn oak desk in his cabin in the Black Forest...the German forest in which dwells our spirit, our ideals, our cultural past, our poetry, our truth." And so on. Per se, all this may not be true, but successive generations of Germans, all saying it, have made it true; and so, in that sense, both Ulrich and Helmuth, harping on what's German as distinct from what's French or international, are doing the same. Nothing is more German than the discussion of whether a thing (Brumhold's and Heidegger's *Ding*) is German or not.

Hence, I think, the ambivalence of the book's title. All the dreams about truth become truth, and the clincher comes at the very end when Ulrich, speaking under hypnosis(!), reveals the book's main fact; he isn't his father's son at all. "I had been born too long after my father's imprisonment and execution for me to be his son. I pretended that it wasn't true.... am a bastard." The whole novel turns inside out at that point, and you realize it's not really about a martyred father's son who turned to terrorism to be somehow heroic like his father, but about a bastard son who failed himself (turning state's evidence to save his skin) because his ostensible father "was not cut out to be a conspirator" either. The effect of this reversal is to make two novels out of one, and to send you back along the course of all its fine cumulative shadings to reinterpret everything Ulrich has said and done and everyone he has known, from his jettisoned French mistress to his new American girl friend, from his estranged wife to his mother, whom he never sees.

Nothing stays put or intact, and the clincher to the clincher comes when Ulrich, emerging from hypnosis without knowing what he's said, at the doctor's command raises his right hand "in a stiff salute." Both the doctor and Abish's narrator have the advantage of him, retrospectively anyway, in this extraordinary kaleidoscope in which labels, slogans, titles of books and people, reputations and reflexes, flutter about incessantly and mutate in the twinkling of an eye. "Is it possible," the book concludes, "for anyone in Germany, nowadays, to raise his right hand, for whatever the reason, and not be flooded by the memory of a dream to end all dreams?" In a word, this fastidious, honed optical illusion of a book is yet another example of its own theme: individual and national trauma. The net effect is moving, not least because the protagonist, unable to face the truth of his existence, invents for himself a fake identity that's less individual than national. And all that comes his way—the matchstick replica, made by an old Hargenau family retainer, of the nearby death-camp; the mass grave uncovered in the main street of Brumholdstein; almost being knocked down twice in the street by passing vehicles, and being shot in the arm—sharpens the poignancy and makes his fake identity an expendable piece of trash, a figment, a cross.

Abish writes here with some of the meticulous, almost philatelic obsessiveness of what used to be called the French New Novel, but in his hands the technique is never boring or flat, mainly because every shred of the evidence he records has a vast emotional hinterland. Everything is ponderable here because it's mysterious, and the mysteriousness comes in part from the "fact" with which an interviewer confronts Ulrich: "One reads your books, always feeling as if some vital piece of information is being withheld." The missing piece is Freudian, it seems; but the best measure of Abish's skill is the way in which, while giving the reader that same feeling of being denied something, he supplies all you need. Read him once for story, then again for the personification of Germany, and then a third time to fill up the lacunae. The uncanny thing is that, once you know the truth that Ulrich knows about himself, the novel—far from being defused—takes off again, like an erupting guidebook. Note "the magnificent landscapes, *die Land-schaft*" and "the blue sky, *der Blaue Himmel*," ladies and gentlemen. These things keep the tourist sane and drive the German mad. Abish's masterly novel does a bit of both, and much, much more.

Guy Davenport
Tatlin!

TIME CANNOT STOP, but there do come times when writers look back to get a sense of what has been done already, as Borges did, for example, with ostentatious diffidence concluding it wasn't worth writing *Don Quixote* all over again—but a footnote to it, yes.

This is not to say that the straightforward yarn, beloved of middlebrow reader and conservative critic alike, won't keep on getting cranked out. But art has moved on, to a silver age in which embarrassment, a sense of second-handedness and a tendency to essay come together to produce fiction that evinces the mind of its inventor more than it repeats the old tropes of storytelling. Examples abound: one need only allude to Beckett's *Molloy,* Nabokov's *Pale Fire,* certain very different works by Sarraute, Blanchot, Cortázar, Calvino, Queneau and Gombrowicz. This is the age of suspiciousness, of the psychological backward glance, of the writer who figures in his own fiction as an implicated character or a puppeteer protagonist, not so much through some access of honesty as through an increased awareness of what imagination entails.

Into this development, the fictions of Guy Davenport congruously fit. Davenport has a sophisticated, erudite mind which he isn't ashamed to show, even to show off. These six stories, better dubbed assemblies or constructions or narrative editorials, range far and wide into literature and culture, raising the ghosts of an interesting team: Herakleitos; the Dutch philosopher Adriaan van Hovendaal; Franz Kafka and Max Brod; the Abbé Breuil, the discoverer of Lascaux; Samuel Butler of *Erewhon;* and Tatlin, the Soviet engineer-sculptor.

The point is that not only these few, but, say, Descartes, Edmund Spenser, Isaac Newton, Clive of India, De Lesseps of the Suez Canal, are all worth invading and impersonating. The corollary point is that the fiction writer need no longer restrict himself to "pure" invention. A fiction has arrived that can address itself to anything known and rearrange it into fresh and startling configurations that have little to do with What Happened Next.

Davenport's long title-story confronts us with a full-size glider which Tatlin designed after Leonardo's ornithopter, an airplane with flapping wings—lovingly described as "a bird's ossature with syndactyl wings." What is fascinating, in this cinematic synopsis of a life lived to the full in spite of an ideological strait-jacket, is the way Tatlin's mind is made to reveal itself both as a denuded power and through its things, its concrete output, while Soviet history rumbles its bloody way (embodied in black-and-white full-page portraits of Lenin and Stalin larded into the text).

Embedded in this imaginary feat is something else, an excursion into the even more engrossing life of Tsiolkovsky, the deaf and ignored rocket pioneer, functioning in "Tatlin!" as an almost choric figure, especially when the moon crater named for him shows up at the end of the story.

Another story, "The Aeroplanes at Brescia," evokes an article Kafka wrote about his visit in 1909 to an Italian airshow, where he sees Blériot and an agitated-looking chap who turns out to be Ludwig Wittgenstein. This just-about-perfect piece is as rich in ambience as exact in focus, and more immediately captivating than the reconstruction of how a French dog named Robot helped the Abbé Breuil discover a paleolithic cave full of astonishing drawings.

The Herakleitos piece opens out like a fan, inviting the pensive reader to halt, move back, revisit the instances after getting the point, revise the point after refeeling the instances. The way forward is one of the ways back.

The other two pieces are just as finely balanced, just as replete with

mind-tingling moments, from the vibrations of a year called 1830 to
André Chenier introducing himself ("I was guillotined thirty-six years
ago . . . I am a ghost"); to the dawn in Butler's Erewhon, when the wind
from Sarawak blows as the starlight fades in the arc of Sagittarius; the
Conowingo hydroelectric station conjures up the Pons Aelius; and, as
the linear mosaic unfolds, the Royal Dutch Marines, Sir Philip Sidney,
Bosch's Saint Anthony and the fish of Lascaux come together,
complementing a trio of indefatigable sensualists who, taking turns,
also keep coming together under the Baltic sun of a vene-real utopia.

As one's impressions of this brilliant book settle down, it seems
that nothing relevant has gone unimplied, nothing irrelevant hasn't
been suavely shut out. *Tatlin!* closes with the very thought on dreaming
and rain that Beckett adapted from Wittgenstein in *Molloy,* and with
Neil Armstrong's left foot in the dust of our moon. Davenport's
majestic fabrications multiply one's sense of the confusion that has
been fattening since the big bang, and it will be a churlish reader indeed
who won't register thanks for incredulity increased on the level of
educated, allusive talk.

Evan S. Connell
Points for a Compass Rose

COMPASS ROSE SOUNDS like a flower, emblem of the polymath,
that Leonardo da Vinci might have come up with. As it is, and by
its other name—"compass card"—almost as suggestive, this free-
pivoting circular disc carrying the magnetic needles of a compass and
marked with 32 points becomes for Evan S. Connell a combination of
mandala and mosaic. Everything belongs and, in theory at least, could
be fitted in. But the book that's to accommodate the total mess ends up
epitomizing it with so jaundiced an awe that I reckon most readers
couldn't stomach, even if they could have it, the complete cosmic
catalogue in which man, the brainy fleck, looms narcissistically big.

No plot, no consistent retinue of characters, no delimited venue,
but actually a semidramatized commonplace book in which mind-

boggling saliences from every field of knowledge swirl around as if in some epistemological spiral galaxy, and all the rest—rumors, guesses, ruminations, asides, riddles, cries, jokes, recipes, prayers, chess moves and map coordinates—is gas clouds, the shapelessness of things to come. Let the following contingency sample provide, as best it can, the feel and scope of Connell's happenstance microcosm.

Four thousand autumnal crocuses are necessary to make an ounce of saffron. Asked to name his reward, Sissa the Brahman asked only for some grains of corn on a chessboard, one on the first square, two on the second, four on the third, and so on: in fact, enough corn to cover the earth's surface to a depth of nine inches. Gismunda ate her lover's heart. On Feb. 16, 1568, every inhabitant of the Netherlands was condemned to death for heresy. Scriabin delivered a sermon to the waves from a boat on Lake Geneva. Deaths attributed to leukemia are more frequent at Hiroshima, where uranium was used, than at Nagasaki, where it was plutonium. Maidanek: 1,380,000. A magnet rubbed with leek loses strength. N-Q 2. P-QB 4.

The U.S. antipersonnel mine hops up to genital height when detonated. Hercules's golden apples may have been strawberries. Columbus wrote a full account of his voyage, wrapped it in waterproof cloth and put it in a barrel on Feb. 14, 1493. When told Danish soldiers were near, nuns in the Coldingham convent sliced off their noses and lips. A single cubic inch of Procyon B weighs 200 tons. The Kaffir have 26 terms to differentiate the various color markings of cattle. André Pujom, realizing that his name was an anagram of Pendu à Riom, committed there a capital crime for which he was hanged. Chelmno: 600,000. German soldiers in World War I carried bats' wings as a protection against bullets. Roc eggs are 13 inches long.

Such is the miscellaneous ground against which the nebulous host of this copybook figures. The ground is many things: something to hold to, something to shed; a sparkling panorama, a glut of what Darwin called *panmixis;* a centrifugal encyclopedia peddled by an Autolycus gone mad with stargazing as an alternative to pondering the news from Vietnam. The persona keeps on interrupting the flow of data, and the effect is uncanny. Set in *versets* of varying length, the text looks like poetry, not prose, and you brace yourself for significant autonomy of line, make your eye-span more flexible, become a little tenser perhaps. But the text isn't poetic (exalted, distilled) at all, and it isn't one persona interrupting; it's a crowd, a compound ghost, with each component phantom protesting its self in the same voice.

I think Connell intended a ventriloquial roll call during a drum roll, or some such effect; an American Express Tiresias who's both magus and Ancient Mariner, both mouthpiece and voices off, a Mister Everybody forever striking out in front of a mirror. As it is, his protagonist's patently a man of conscience, a disciple too of Paracelsus, Sir Thomas Browne, and Borges, an admirer of the cosmos who'd rather be a liker of humans (as distinct from their artifacts). But, as we go, we have to reconcile successive informations. The narrator is Pope Gregory VII, but also Dom Helder Camara (Archbishop of Recife), Lully, Kepler, Newton, a plowman of Bohemia, and many others. Formerly in the army, he has his portrait in the Louvre, has had two sons, has never had any children or been married, is married to Margaret, has an awkward hippo of a daughter, is neither Goya nor Henry the Navigator, though he resembles both. It's like waiting for the human race to jell back into Adam, the Many into the One.

On the one hand, I welcome this summary, synoptic, anachronistic mode of fiction, which more ambitiously resumes the method of Connell's novel of 10 years ago, *Notes From a Bottle Found on the Beach at Carmel.* The anthropological novel (what Cortázar calls the anthropophanic) is overdue, and it's good to find someone promenading *homo sapiens,* with grade C branded on that creature's brow, through the House of Knowledge. On the other hand, I think Connell has missed exploiting some opportunities of his own making: over the book's length the data mode might have shrunk while the synthesized hero swelled (a matter of proportional plasticity); and, instead of being delivered undifferentiated, the verse paragraphs might have reached crescendo or whimper (a matter of transforming thematic materials, of not leaving them intact).

The book works, and I'd rather read it than "straight" fiction, but I'd like to have seen it moving a good deal farther from the diffident-personalized scrapbook, or the cloth sampler allowed to ripple in the *Zeitgeist's* draught. Comes a point at which the hero with 1,000 faces seems to have 1,000 backsides as well, gets our nominal recognition but ill-conveys whoever's multiplying by 1,000. If science is We, and art is I, there's too much We in this book, a colony where a Connell should be, all his first-person pronouns notwithstanding.

Ivy Compton-Burnett
The Last and the First

FEW FICTIONAL WORLDS are more consistent, unmistakable, and stylistically of a piece than that of the late Ivy Compton-Burnett. A country house, we might imagine her saying in lethal parody of Jane Austen, is the very thing to work upon. Set it in late Victorian times—a world that Lytton Strachey characterized in terms of gas lamps, enormous bedpans, and terrible disasters in bed—and expose the brutality of the well-to-do. Her creatures hold forth interminably and are crazily articulate. The matriarchs puff and rear; the patriarchs huff and bristle; the small go through all the levels of nursery hell; the young capitulate or stalk away; the butlers and other servants in the retinue fawn, snoop, and leer. Though we never see their faces, her characters' utterances plague us; the screen is blank, but the sound is always on. Words fill the debating chambers that their homes are; everyone talks as if raised to his highest power; and the cumulative result over twenty novels, of which this is the last, is a mordant, elegant synopsis of domestic tribal warfare, in which the people do not fare any better for being so verbal.

The force of her vision is indisputable—Ivy Compton-Burnett graduated early in People, *summa cum laude*—but its catalyst is that unchanging prose style in which the characters seem communally in the grip of some supervernacular St. Vitus's dance. Insulated from one another and the outside world, they embody a mode of writing so stylized that one's own imagination leaps into almost competitive mimicry. For example: "Self-praise is no recommendation, Mater," says one daughter in *The Last and the First*. "I think it is a great one," says another. "Who would dare to indulge in it without conspicuous cause?" Our pleasure at the lapidary completeness of that—not so much an exchange as the execution of the first speaker with a weapon she unwittingly provides—vies with a desire to cap it with one's own retort: "I think it is neither. Those who resort to it are our scapegoats; those who don't are our blackmailers." Or some similar put-down. We become tensely involved in these games of thrust and counterthrust, of equilibrium and topple, so much so that the word play takes on a life of its own regardless of plot. This is the intoxication, the infection, of

Compton-Burnett's novels: the reader ends up as an admiring voyeur or an invasive accomplice. Either way, the experience is exciting; seldom do we take leave of a writer with such an exhilarated sense of having been mentally tuned up, challenged and dominated, made, to eavesdrop upon humiliating proxies of ourselves.

The Last and the First, put together (the English edition tells us) from "twelve shabby little exercise books" found under a cushion in the author's flat, amounts to the *coup de grâce* in the IC-B mode. Scalpel-sharp, yet suffused with an almost ritual urbanity, it has little plot, but that doesn't much matter. The plot's flimsiness—an imminently tyrannical young woman overthrowing her despotic stepmother—is that of an epitomistic abstract from Compton-Burnett's other books, and its sketchiness evinces the sure-minded allusiveness of someone with a finely developed sense of her own thought's edifice.

The strategies and conventions are largely like those in the previous novels: we begin with breakfast, less a meal than a parliament of rhetorical vultures, in a house in a village which, for once, is named—Egdon, in Somerset County. The really new factor is that Compton-Burnett condemns Eliza Heriot, the domineering mother ("The First"), and contrasts her didactically with Hermia ("The Last") who, coming into money left her by a suitor whom she rejected, divides it between her family and his, thereby retaining power in each.

The book can be read as the final lesson in Compton-Burnett's long course in intransigent charity, but is just as well taken as an instructive fanfare of histrionic expertise, making verbally a great deal out of a next-to-nothing that evokes Mallarmé's zero—as when, in the last chapter, ten different speakers are manipulated into saying something distinctive about why they need or do not need an extra sheet of paper for a word game they intend to play.

At one point a character remarks, "I wish I had not the power of thought," only to be told, "I wish you had not. You are being too prodigal with it." Ivy Compton-Burnett was always prodigal with it. To our inestimable gain, she was one of the most austerely thinking novelists in what is generally an unthinking English tradition. She emerges from this novel, and the materials that accompany it, as both worldly and unpretentious, a woman whose angular intelligence promoted high society into low comedy and that, in turn, into a high, almost mandarin, art.

Michael Ayrton
Fabrications

T HE ENGLISH PAINTER, sculptor, and film-maker Michael Ayrton is a writer of unusual caliber, as I discovered on reading his novel *The Maze Maker,* an opportunistic, vivid, and rippling "autobiography" of Daedalus the Greek protocraftsman. It was clear that Ayrton's prose is no mere avocation but a belated delivery by a complete man whose creative output is all of a distinguished piece.

Fabrications is a collection of 27 short pieces having to do with the labyrinth, not of one man's life, as in *The Maze Maker,* but of history reconceived, their pretext being a comment of H.R. Trevor-Roper's: "In history there are no reserved areas in which the ordinary laws of evidence may be suspended, no documents which are exempt from the ordinary rules of source criticism. If there were such privileged areas, or documents, how would we define them?" Ayrton's answer is "as fabrications."

Opportunistic again, he exploits his brainwave for all it's worth and succeeds, after Borges and Cortázar and Calvino, in fabricating extraordinary mutations of, and exceptions to, what supposedly happened. With the ordinary laws and ordinary rules suspended, he creates a "reserved area" of his own: a noetic reservation with no horizon, in which scores of incalculable fugitives can be found at play (in retreat from myth, theology, musicology, biography, rumor, slander, eye-witness—you name it). His manner is ascetic, sometimes mandarin, but its dry suavity fits his matter well; after all, Ayrton is teasing us here, insinuating that things were not thus but otherwise, and his circumspection is the foil to his essentially deviant view of history.

For instance, Racine, working in the royal library of James II during James's exile at the court of Louis XIV, happens upon a second folio of Shakespeare, huffily stuffs it back between Vergil's *Eclogues* and the Gospels, and goes about his business; but the folio keeps coming back to his hand whenever he uses the library. Just as unverifiably, at the siege of Jotapata in AD 67, Flavius Josephus, the most learned Jew of his generation, evolves a way for the last survivors to die without recourse to suicide (B kills A, then C kills B, and so on) and then finds himself alone with one other, whom he talks into living.

This man, however, has a telepathic ear which reads minds, the result being that his head is such an interesting Babel he doesn't think twice about Josephus's copping-out and certainly won't inform on him. During a performance of "Saint Joan," the actor playing Gilles de Rais electrifies the audience by ad libbing a passionate vindication of the character (who died absolved, whereas Joan died a heretic). In a cupboard, Kierkegaard finds "a bulging rectangle of light" in which Abraham and his son are talking folksy American English. A medieval bronze head tells an abacus-maker he lacks the symbols for zero and infinity. We meet an imaginary beast named the Minocorn (bull's body, horse's head, human torso) who depends for refreshment on the London Metropolitan Drinking Fountain and Cattle Trough Association. Credit these things or not, there's no disputing the constructive elegance with which they're offered.

Wry saliences and preposterous incidentals enliven the fabricating no end. An art connoisseur falls from a scaffold he's mounted in order to inspect a canvas by a painter who also fell from a scaffold. Sousa came into being as a Yorkshireman, Sam Ogden, whose baggage was stenciled "SO" plus "USA." Attending a summer stock production of the *Bacchae* at a small campus in New York State, Dionysus hears a hippy asking him, "Man, are you high?" Ayrton also plays some clever, confounding games with mirrors and identical twins, with unicursal mazes and painterly perspective. His grandparents get into the act, as does an alter ego called "Lameich Torjan," and an Ayrtonized death mask of the architect Brunelleschi mysteriously becomes one of J. L. Borges. My favorite piece of all, "Threat," is spoken by the moon, complaining that men no longer personify it: "You have set down a pellet in my navel, daring to call this costive canister after my brother Apollo." And, should the meticulous, riddling text occasionally send the eye afield, there are graphics (a maze, a big revolver) and photographs as well.

Some readers will find this tricksy cerebrality too demanding and too allusive; it isn't addressed to them, anyway, but to Borgesians who relish a mind game in its own right and can see how the artist's lies conduct us to *some* kind of truth, the kind in this instance being stranger, and, in texture, much more orthodox, than fiction itself. One of the stories mentions a person who "knows everything, but nothing else," the implication being that to fabricate is to enlarge an All we can't envision. Ayrton's plus we take on trust, or we lapse back into a traditional factuality which, of course, fits Sir Robert Walpole's remark, "Anything but history, for history must be false."

G. V. Desani
All About H. Hatterr

T HE INDIAN WRITER and professor of philosophy, G. V. Desani, seems to have got nowhere at all in spite of impressive tributes to his work. When *All About H. Hatterr* first appeared, in 1948, T. S. Eliot called it "a remarkable book" and added, "In all my experience, I have not met with anything quite like it. It is amazing that anyone should be able to sustain a piece of work in this style and tempo at such length." And E. M. Forster described Desani's prose poem *Hali* as work "genuine, personal, and passionate." But, such is the nature of the book business, Eliot might have served better if he'd just left it at "amazing" and Forster if he'd said nothing at all. The one thing unlikely to lodge an author securely in the public's brainpan is a reasoned, literate specification of his virtues; huzzahs and mind-blown superlatives win the day.

Frisky, eccentric, and farcically ebullient, *All About H. Hatterr* is hard to classify, as Anthony Burgess points out in his brief introduction. Essentially a novel about the education of the son of a European erchant seaman and a lady from Penang (H. Hatterr gropes into the world while the world grows into him like a rainbow fungus), it is also a running mockery of what British English can become in the hands of a self-taught oriental equipped with an English dictionary and a French and a Latin primer. "Is it Right?" asks H. Hatterr, "Hell, I won't controversy. Why the chick first or is it the egg-ovum? Does a feller wear braces to keep his trousers *up,* or is to stop 'em slipping *down?* Did he say, Kiss me, Hardy! or *Kismet,* Hardy!? Is Hanchow pronounced &cow, &CO., or what the hell?"

H. Hatterr, in fact, is an innocent mentally abroad in an oral No-Man's Land cluttered with homonyms that confound, argot that defeats, and information that fails to inform. The sound of words infatuates him, but it's the fact that they stand for something else—or are meant to—that sobers him up. The entire book is a tug of war between bedlam and learning, between English as a Ganges riff-competition played against himself by a pun-mad Indian, who is both a Mad Hatter and a Mercutio, and English as the vehicle of a responsibly undertaken course of seven autodidactic bouts which all have Hatterr appealing for guidance to seven sages (each from a different oriental city). Receiving The Sage's Message (which he then seeks to pass on, preferably in capital letters), and then rapping with his chum Banerrji about the learning experience as it proceeds. So the book has a plan, but its plan matters little; the real fun here is the collision of cultures via the collision of words, as if some propagandistic UNO firework display has gone hopelessly wrong. The result is razzle-dazzle, festive anti-climactic vaudeville, and a sustained adventure into what H. Hatterr calls "rigmarole English, staining your goodly godly tongue." Linguistic fur, indeed, symptom of the global malaise called endless talk.

Underlying all, in fact, there is the pathos and the exasperation of the outsider who, yearning to understand and to conform and to be accepted, finds himself coining an idiom that wraps flagrant solecisms in oblique servility: the underdog, unleashed from the British Raj, learns to bark. Hatterr's head fills with sounds that, instead of equipping him to enter genteel society, ensure for him its derision: the x in algebra is also the sign for kiss; Einstein is Eisenstein is Rubenstein; and D. Litt. means "the Light of the World" (with D. standing, one presumes, for Deity or Desani). The farther Hatterr goes, the more his head swims; it cannot refuse or discern; and what is already within it interacts and multiplies, compounding the problems of understanding until he seems quite alone, not merely in the wasteland of educated British English but also in some intergalactic Gehenna where all the tongues of man cancel one another out while the brain slows to a stop. Language out of control is Hatterr's Medusa and yet also his joy, since where no one can understand anything he is like anyone else.

In the last analysis (and H. Hatterr has such a thing in mind all along), this book is frightening in the same way as *Finnegans Wake*, or Flann O'Brien's *At Swim-Two-Birds*, or Lewis Carroll's *Jabberwocky*, for it evokes the mind out of control, the medium become mucilage, and reveals how words pour into a void they cannot describe or account for. The rocket of ages (to lapse into Hatterrian for a moment) founders like a cleft palate on the sperm of the moment, a mere stichomythia in the Nike of time.

"Words fail me," we sometimes say; but words fail us very rarely in point of fact, and it is no small feat on Desani's part that he sets his reader mouthing and raving along with H. Hatterr who, down-at-the-mouth and yet Promethean, lingers in the mind long after the book ends.